The author, Philip Vic... author of Das Reich – D... As a result of his survey of ... ...w France he was invited to present a ...regular warfare at a CIA Conference Intellige... and National Security in Peace, Crisis and War in Washington, DC. For this book he had access to private Thoroton family archives.

By the same author

Das Reich, 2nd SS Panzer Division, Drive to Normandy June 1944
Leo Cooper Pen & Sword Books, 2000, 2003
USA Edition, Combined Publishing PA, 2000
French Edition, Lucien Souny, 2003-2012

FINDING THOROTON

The Royal Marine who ran British Naval Intelligence
in the Western Mediterranean in World War One

By

Philip Vickers

Series Editor
Colonel Brian Carter OBE

ROYAL MARINES HISTORICAL SOCIETY
SPECIAL PUBLICATION NO 40

First published 2013 by the
ROYAL MARINES HISTORICAL SOCIETY
Royal Marines Museum
Eastney
Southsea
Hants PO4 9PX
United Kingdom

Cover, design and layout
Tim Mitchell
www.tim-mitchell.co.uk

Printed and bound in Great Britain by
CPI Antony Rowe Ltd, Chippenham and Eastbourne

Dedication

To Charles the Bold's grand-daughter Katharine Myfanwy Thoroton Vickers and for his great great grandchildren, Georgina, Victoria, Archibald, Perdita, Eleonore, Katharine, Theodore, Charles, Horatio, Celia, Bartholomew, Alexandra, Miranda and Richard.

Contents

The Theme

'Our Intelligence Service has won and deserved world-wide fame. More than perhaps any other Power, we were successful in the war in penetrating the intentions of the enemy. Again and again the forecasts of the military and naval Intelligence Staffs were vindicated to the wonder of friends and the chagrin of foes. The three successive chiefs of the Naval Intelligence Division, Captain Thomas Jackson, Rear-Admiral Oliver, and lastly, Captain Reginald Hall, were all men of mark in the service, and continually built and extended an efficient and profound organisation. There were others – a brilliant confederacy – whose names even now are better wrapt in mystery. Our information about German naval movements was principally obtained (1) from the reports of secret agents in neutral and enemy countries and particularly in Germany, (2) from the reports of our submarines, which lay far up in Heligoland Bight in perilous vigilance, and (3) from a special study we had made of the German wireless'.

(Winston S Churchill, The World Crisis 1911-1914, Chapter XX. Copyright, The Estate of Sir Winston S Churchill.)

"If I had a big proposition to handle and could have my pick of helpers I'd plumb for the Intelligence Department of the British Admiralty",
(Blenkiron in *Greenmantle* by John Buchan following Buchan's experience of Sir Reginald Hall.)

Abbreviations

BEF	British Expeditionary Force	MFH	Master of Fox Hounds
BI	British Intelligence	MI	Military Intelligence
BNI	British Naval Intelligence	ML1c	Military Intelligence, predecessor of MI6
BSC	British Security Coordination	MO5/MI5/MI6	British Secret Intelligence Departments
C	Originally Captain Mansfield Cumming, later signifies DNI	NA	National Archives
CB	Companion Order of the Bath	NID	Naval Intelligence Division
CEO	Chief Executive Officer	ONI	Office of Naval Intelligence
CFR	Council on Foreign Relations	OSS	Office of Strategic Services
CIA	Central Intelligence Agency	PRO	Public Records Office, now NA
CID	Criminal Investigation Department	RFC	Royal Flying Corps
CMG	Commander Order of St Michael & St George	RM	Royal Marines
COS	Chief of Staff	RMLI	Royal Marine Light Infantry
DID	Director of Intelligence Division	RMHS	Royal Marines Historical Society
DNE	Director of Naval Education	RN	Royal Navy
DNI	Director of Naval Intelligence	RNR	Royal Naval Reserve
DTD	Director of Trade Division	RNVR	Royal Naval Volunteer Reserve
FO	Foreign Office	SHM	Centre Historique des Archives, Vincennes
GC&CS	Government Code & Cipher School	SIGINT	Signals Intelligence
HMG	His Majesty's Government	SIO	Senior Intelligence Officer
HMS	His Majesty's Ship	SIS	Secret Intelligence Service
IDC	Imperial Defence Committee	SNO	Senior Naval Officer
INI	Italian Naval Intelligence	SOE	Special Operations Executive
KCB	Knight Commander of the Order of the Bath	TFA	Thoroton Family Archives
KCMG	Knight Commander of the Order of St Michael & St George	USMCR	United States Marine Corps Reserve
KGB	Soviet Intelligence & Security Service	WO	War Office
MA	Master of Arts	W/T	Wireless Telegraphy

Preface

This book arose through our inheriting a glass cabinet of awards and decorations of my wife's grandfather Charles Julian Thoroton (1875-1939). We knew him to have been a Colonel in the Royal Marines Light Infantry, but, beyond that, virtually nothing was known about him in the family. This started our research, firstly amongst family memorabilia[1]; then through such offices as the Central Chancery of the Orders of Knighthood; the Royal Marines; and even the then Minister of Defence Christopher Soames. Our research widened to cover inquiries in the National Archives at Kew and in such countries as Spain, Morocco, Italy, France, Germany and the USA.

Early on we found him to have been an Intelligence Officer, a member of 'Blinker' Hall's Room 40 team, responsible (1913-1919) for British Naval Intelligence in the Mediterranean throughout WW I. It immediately became evident that his activities were well concealed and that he was one of the men who, in Winston Churchill's words, were "wrapt in mystery"[2], not only then but even up to the present day.

Here, I am inclined to quote from Sir John Fortesque[3] in his introduction to another book[4] where he writes of the vicissitudes of historical research "…we know nothing about our fellow men and each other. Moreover these histories, unless shown to be false, tend to be accepted as true; though he would be a bold historian indeed who would claim to have penetrated to the inner truth of any historical transaction. For always there remains the insurmountable fact that we are and must continue profoundly ignorant concerning even those who are nearest to us".

In the only "official" family history, *The Thorotons* by Myles Thoroton Hildyard (published privately in 1990 at Flintham, Nottinghamshire) – a work full of interest and detail along with the inevitable omissions, it begins only in the 17th century – Charles Julian Thoroton is described merely thus:

> **Charles, Colonel R.M., Legion of Honour, Order of the Crown of Italy, and of Ouisam Alaonte of Morocco.**

That was the sum of the then family knowledge. The reasons for the award of the various decorations were unknown and there was no mention at all of the most important of all the decorations he received, the Order of St Michael and St George.

In the labyrinthine paths of the secret services, few facts are crystal clear. Certain individuals have much to hide. In the leading histories of the secret services, due to

---

1. *TFA.*
2. *The World Crisis 1911-1914.*
3. *Author of The History of wthe British Army and Librarian at Windsor Castle.*
4. *Henry Williamson, Tarka the Otter.*

the paucity of information available, Thoroton gets only the most passing of references, usually accompanied by expressions of regret, and comments such as how surprising it is that his work is still regarded as something to be covered up. More than this are the inaccuracies recorded in several histories which this book corrects.

The first article devoted exclusively to him was this author's in *The Globe & Laurel* (the Royal Marines own journal) of Jan/Feb 1998. The single most detailed account of Thoroton's activities in Spain appears in Patrick Beesley's *Room 40 — British Naval Intelligence 1914-18*, in the story of the brigantine *Erri Berro*, the whole of which appears in this book thanks to the most generous permission granted by Mrs Judith Evans, Patrick Beesley's daughter.

This book is more than a research amongst authorised historians of the intelligence scene, in official and private archives, and on the ground investigation. It is also a search for an understanding and appreciation of the character of the central figure, known as Charles the Bold, as he was called when a Royal Marine[5].

While this is centrally the biography of one man, Colonel Thoroton, the subject is also the Thoroton Network, that complex of agents and activities for which he was responsible in the Mediterranean in World War I. It continued to function after his retirement and throughout World War II. Predominant amongst those personalities who played a major role in the work of the Network are 'Blinker' Hall, Juan March and Marshal Lyautey. Of these three men, Juan March is the most enigmatic and virtually unknown in British circles. Thoroton's winning over of March, in what was virtually a personal duel between him and German Intelligence, ensured the supremacy of British Intelligence in the Med. Without the wholehearted support of Hall, the co-operation of March and Thoroton's liaison with Lyautey, the Network could not have been so effective. Had Thoroton failed to secure March the entire history of Mediterannean operations would have gone awry with fatal consequences. 'No man is an island' and no single intelligence agent nor spy functions on his or her own. The team is crucial to performance and it is up to the leader to weld them together, in this instance into the Thoroton Network.

In "Sources and Acknowledgments" we give full credit to all who have contributed to our understanding of the Thoroton Network. Here it should be emphasised that in telling the story of a Royal Marine Intelligence chief we are bringing to light a little known aspect of the Royal Marines' wide and complex role in history. That much remains to be discovered will also be evident.

Original documents, the most important of the information sources we can have, have proven to be extremely rare. This is not surprising as very rarely do secret agents or spies leave behind any written accounts of their activities. We know that Thoroton retained very few and these were only papers which he considered necessary should he find the need to defend himself on some of his more nefarious activities. The few papers that remained at the time of his death were, to the best of our knowledge, finally destroyed by his brother Frank, just as Ralph Straus' papers on the life of 'Blinker' Hall were destroyed at the time of his death[6].

---

5.   See Patrick Beesley, Room 40, p 190.
6.   Timothy Stubbs' letter to the author, 2 August 2007. For this reason the draft of Chapter 2 in Annex C is all the more important.

Charles Julian Thoroton commissioned 2nd Lieutenant, 1893.

Happily, there is a brighter side. Again, paraphrasing Fortesque's perceptive comment, as well as the "musty papers and printed books" which are the historian's stock-in-trade there are "old buildings, old roads and old tracks". The Royal Marine barracks still stand, the Rock of Gibraltar has not budged, the dusty roads around Tangier and Cueta remain dusty, and Malaga still exerts its Andalusian appeal. We have been to all these places and this book takes the reader there.

Chapter 1
Lineage and early years

T his is the story of a Royal Marine officer, Lieutenant Colonel Charles Julian Thoroton CMG RMLI, who was chief of British Naval Intelligence (BNI) for the Mediterranean in World War I. He was born on 9 August 1875 in Coberley, Cheltenham, Gloucestershire, the youngest son of Edward Thoroton, Barrister at Law, MA Oxon, and Catharine, one of the two daughters of the distinguished theologian Canon Charles Atmore Ogilvie, Canon of Christ Church, Oxford and Fellow of Balliol. He was one of a family of six children, four boys and two girls. Charles attended Allhallows School in Honiton and later Rossall School in Fylde, Lancashire. He joined the Royal Marines in 1893.

His origins go back to the first recorded Thoroton, namely Roger de Thurveton in 1216. Their even earlier origins were of Viking descent, probably a member of Ingva's "great army of Danes" who landed in East Anglia in 866[1].

Charles Julian Thoroton (CJT) aged two, Cheltenham, Gloucestershire.

But this is more than one man's biography. It is also a story of British Naval Intelligence in the Mediterranean against the build-up to war in 1914, the war itself, particularly in the Western Mediterranean, and also makes reference to the subsequent influence of the Network he had created, up to the Second World War.

From 1893 to 1894 he was at the Royal Naval College. He was commissioned as a Second Lieutenant in 1893 and promoted Lieutenant RMLI in 1894. In 1895 he completed a course in Wireless Telegraphy (a skill which has a bearing on his subsequent career) and qualified in Military Law. He was promoted Captain in 1900 at age twenty five. This was the same year as his marriage to Eleanor Theodora Mayor, daughter of Thomas Orlando Mayor of Clifton. This was an unusually young age at which to marry in his circumstances but it parallels his future chief's equally youthful marriage, 'Blinker' Hall (the future chief of Room 40, BNI) marrying as

---

1. *Anglo-Saxon Chronicle. Thoroton was Torvertune in 1066, derived from the Danish, Thorfrothr.*

a Lieutenant at the age of twenty four a girl to whom he had become engaged at nineteen. Neither of these men were to let the grass grow under their feet. None of his brothers and sisters ever married and Charles' line is the only Thoroton line to exist to this day, now four generations down and it is to his fourteen great, great grandchildren and his grand-daughter Katharine Thoroton Vickers to whom this book is dedicated.

His reports always read well: "A personable young Officer and likely to do well" and "Very Good" from 1901.

He first went to sea in 1895 aboard HMS *Empress of India* in the Home Fleet for a one year's cruise and then on the *Minatour* Training Ship in 1897. After a spell in Chatham Division in 1899 he served in HMS *Duke of Wellington*, then at Portsmouth Division followed by HMS *Monarch* in the South Atlantic Ocean. He was noted as a zealous, good officer and 'Recommended'. A second entry also comments on his fluency in French and he later became qualified as a French language translator.

In July 1903 their son Thomas was baptised in the parish of St Mary's, Georgetown, Ascension Island. The island had been under the charge of the Royal Marines since 1823, having been occupied by a small British garrison in 1815 to deny it to the French while Napoleon was interned on nearby St Helena.

On board HMS Empress of India, 1895.

Left: Royal Marines on the beach, Ascension Island

Middle: Raising the flag salute, St Mary's Church, Georgetown, Ascension Island.

Bottom: Ascension Island barracks and cantonement, 1903.

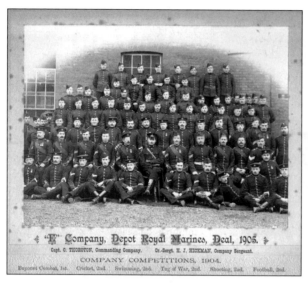

"F" Company, Depot Royal Marines, Deal, 1905.
Capt. C. THOROTON, Commanding Company.   Cr.-Sergt. H. J. HICKMAN, Company Sergeant.
COMPANY COMPETITIONS, 1904.
Bayonet Combat, 1st.   Cricket, 2nd.   Swimming, 2nd.   Tug of War, 2nd.   Shooting, 2nd.   Football, 2nd.

CJT (centre), OC F Company RM, Deal, 1904.

In 1904 he joined the Royal Marines Depot in Deal for eighteen months. In March 1906 he embarked in HMS *Black Prince*, returning to Portsmouth Division until February 1909. His daughter, Katharine Phoebe Grace, had been born in 1906 while he was at sea in the Black Prince. He subsequently transferred to HMS *Prince George*, before joining HMS *Cressy*.

In 1909 he received the Order of the Sword of Sweden (Knight 1st Class). This Order is awarded for "long or meritorious service in or for the Armed Services". We then discovered that a special section of the Court, called *Kunglig Majestats Orden*, handled all royal orders with an Archivist in charge and the King as Chairman of Chapters. Finally we learnt the reason for the Order. It was due to the state visit of King Gustaf V in 1908 when, on his arrival at Portsmouth, the King inspected two guards of honour, Thoroton being the commander of the Royal Marines.

HMS Black Prince (1910). 2nd Cruiser Squadron, on which CJT embarked in 1906 and 1908, his 6th Sea Cruise. Later involved in the Pursuit of the Goeben.

HMS Black Prince crew, 1906

HMS Hogue (1909). CJT's 10th Sea Cruise, December 1910 – May 1911 under Commander Wrotesley. Postcard datemarked 1 November 1911.

On 9 May 1910 it was noted that he had "indifferent health, defective eyesight, both of which cramp much of his sphere of usefulness in a ship's Captain's command". He had short periods in HMS *Grafton* and HMS *Hogue* until May 1911. Two of the ships in which he had served, the armoured cruisers *Cressy* and *Hogue*, were both to be sunk in 1914 by a single U-Boat shortly after the outbreak of war – an early reminder of the changing nature of naval warfare. More than 1,800 men were lost. A long spell at Chatham, as Staff Officer, from May 1911 until September 1913 saw him promoted Major in September 1911 aged thirty six. In 1913 he was appointed Senior Naval Intelligence Officer for Gibraltar and sailed for the Rock on 12 September of that year.

CJT, his wife and son Tom with staff on Ascension Island.

MÁLAGA
LA CATEDRAL

Malaga in 1906, the cathedral as CJT knew it. (From one of his postcards.)

HMS Monarch (1896) in Portsmouth Harbour. CJT
sailed to Ascension Island on 16 March 1901.

To add to this very brief summary of his Military Record[2] Thoroton Family Archives (TFA) provide some more personal insights. First, his correspondence with his wife while on his various cruises gives a picture of his ports of call and how they looked at the outset of the 20th century. A postcard of March 1906 shows Kandy, Ceylon and others from Shanghai in May of that year and from Nagasaki, Japan, which features Mt Fujiyama, provide evidence of shore leave. In August he was in Yokohama, having visited Daibutsu, Kamakura. Here he signs himself F.S.G. which may have some family code significance. From Malaga a postcard dated 3 November 1906 reports he will be "posting tomorrow after the King's visit to the Club". On 10 March 1907 he writes from Penang.

---

2. See his Military Record in the National Archives, Kew.

Second, his reading shows a distinct interest in the African continent. He inscribed a book he gave to his future wife in 1900, *African Incidents* (by Brevet Major Thruston of the Oxford Light Infantry and an Intelligence Staff Officer) with the following significant words:

> E.T.M. from C.J.T. 30.8.00
>
> Soldier and dreamer; he has found his grave
> His heart had longed for through the years of strife
> And this, his work, I send to her who gave
> To me an object and an aim in life.
> The lesson that he taught, God grant us learn
> That all the world is empty without love
> Glory may come but still the heart may yearn
> For that one perfect gift, all gifts above.

Other books share an African slant: *The Ban of the Bori Demons and Demon Dancing in West and North Africa* and *Mahdism and the Egyptian Sudan*, the latter by Major Wingate DSO RA, who was head of Intelligence for the Egyptian Army. CJT read this at age nineteen while he was at the Royal Naval College. He would also have read John Buchan whose *The African Colony* appeared in 1903 and, no doubt, *The Thirty-Nine Steps* (1915) and *Greenmantle* later in 1916, as had almost all the reading public in Britain. Given Buchan's work with 'Blinker' Hall there was a natural link. Another book from his library is A E W Mason's *Ensign Knightley* which is set in Tangier. Mason was ten years Thoroton's senior and it is curious that, long before they were to work together in the Royal Marines, he was reading Mason's work and that it touched on Morocco.

To return to May 1910, his medical downgrading may seem, as was the case with Hall, to have led to his appointment to Intelligence, but given the high priority put on Intelligence by Churchill downwards it is unlikely to be the main reason, albeit the opportunity. When Captain Hall's ill health forced him to resign his command of the battle cruiser *Queen Mary* following the Battle of Heligoland Bight, he was immediately offered by the Admiralty the appointment of Director of the Intelligence Division. Admiral Beatty saw this as a "far more important office" than the one Hall had held under him. The two men were to meet up in 1914 when Hall took up the appointment as DNI in November of that year, some fifteen months after Thoroton's arrival in Gibraltar.

HMS Cressy (1910) off the White Cliffs of Dover. CJT sailed in her April 1909 – May 1910.

Chapter 2
The World Crisis, 1905-1914

In Winston Churchill's book *The World Crisis, 1911-1914*, Churchill traces the origins of the war back to 1905 when the French annexed Morocco, thereby breaking their obligations under the Treaty of Madrid. The Sultan of Morocco appealed to Germany, asking whether France had been given authority for this action in the name of Europe. Dramatically Germany responded with an emphatic negative and the Emperor, now the self-styled 'Admiral of the Atlantic', himself went to Tangier. There, in an inopportune speech, he threw down the gauntlet to France and Britain, demanding a conference of the signatories of the Treaty of Madrid. The French case was of course flawed and the country was entirely unprepared for war. The French agreed to the conference (held at Algeciras) and the Foreign Minister, Monsieur Delcassé, resigned. Britain, uncomfortably brought in by German insistence, found itself committed to arguing the French case because, in the event of war, Britain felt obliged to support France. Russia, Spain and other countries joined Britain. Austria tactfully supported Germany which could therefore withdraw without further commitment. But, allegiances had been formed, the military threat was recognised and the arms race was put in hand. As Churchill wrote: "Algerciras was a milestone on the road to Armagedon"[1].

In 1908 the Naval Prize Bill was introduced which was to become significant in terms of contraband control. It provided for three types of contraband; 'absolute contraband'; 'conditional contraband' which concerned food for military or naval use and barbed wire; and 'absolute non-contraband' in neutral ships. This had concrete results in 1915, causing irritation in neutral countries but also influencing Germany's response of unrestricted submarine warfare.

As President of the Board of Trade, Churchill reports on the Agadir crisis of 1911, caused by the French occupation of Fez. This precipitates us into the ultimately significant world of the Atlantic seaboard of North Africa, specifically of Morocco. The German Emperor's despatch of the gunboat *Panther* to protect German interests in Agadir, raised alarm bells in Paris and London.

Following this crisis, Churchill was called to the Admiralty (as First Lord of the Admiralty) by the Prime Minister Asquith where he remained until 1915. Asquith had been in receipt of Rear-Admiral Slade's report in 1909 that he, Slade, had been "disconcerted to find that the Naval Secret Service was not organised in any way" in 1907.

---

1. *The World Crisis* began publication in 1923. Room 40 was kept completely secret even in the official history of the war on which work began in 1920. Only a passing reference was made to it in the official history.

Winston Churchill, First Lord of the Admiralty, 1915

In his 1907 War Plans, Slade had advocated the organisation of Secret Service agents and "the necessity of training both officers and agents to a certain extent"[2].

As the world crisis mounted, Churchill drew up his *"17 Points"* "to focus them in my mind". Significantly as high as *Point 3* was 'Mediterranean movements', only preceded by *Points 1* and *2*, both of which related to major issues concerning the First, Second and Third Fleets. Churchill "ticked them off one by one as they were settled", leaving only three unticked, one of which was Point 14 'K - espionage'.

Britain declared war on Germany on 4 August and the first British Expeditionary Force troops landed in France on 7 August. Churchill had on 2 August alerted all the Royal Navy of the need to mobilise.

The Royal Navy in 1914 was Britain's most prized possession. At the 1914 Spithead Review, King George V had inspected forty miles of British warships. It was vital: vital to guaranteeing the importation of two thirds of Britain's food; to prevent any invasion of the British Isles; to escort the BEF to France; to bring troops home from India; to safeguard British seaborne commerce over all the oceans of the world. British merchant ships represented 43% of all the world's total merchant tonnage and carried more than half the world's sea borne trade. British naval nerves were at stretching point with the fear of a major clash with Germany in which the RN would be at risk in just one corner of the globe, the North Sea, whereas it had Suez, Persia, India, the Far East, the Cape, Africa, the USA and Canada, the Caribbean, the West Indies, the South Atlantic, the South Pacific, South America and Australia to defend. Admiral 'Jackie' Fisher First Sea Lord feared that a clash with the Kaiser's fleet, second only to the Royal Navy in power, might result in a Tsushima, a repeat of the Japanese destruction of the entire Russian fleet. Germany could risk such a battle, Britain could not. The *Goeben* and the *Breslau* were in the Med; the *Dresden* and *Karslruhe* in the Atlantic; the *Scharnhorst*, *Gneisnau* and *Emden* in the Pacific, but the High Seas Fleet was in Heligoland. Composed of sixteen Dreadnoughts, twelve older battleships, three battle cruisers, seventeen other cruisers, one hundred and forty destroyers, it also numbered twenty seven submarines. It was the submarines which were to pose the greatest of all threats once the German High Seas Fleet was confined to harbour following the battle of Heligoland Bight on 28 August 1914 when four German ships were destroyed and sunk, a further three badly damaged and over a thousand men killed and more than two hundred taken prisoner. The RN lost no ships and incurred only seventy five casualties. On the orders of the Kaiser, German naval policy dived under the waves and the U-boats went to work.

The complex situation in the Mediterranean is covered in detail in *The World Crisis* and only a few aspects are relevant to this story. As soon as he describes the mobilization of the Navy he addresses the Mediterranean: "…in the Mediterranean a drama of intense interest and as it ultimately proved of fatal consequence, was being enacted". The matter concerned the urgent transfer of French colonial troops to Europe under the threatening guns of the German ship *Goeben* which could blast the entire convoy out of the water. The only defence of the French were three British battle-cruisers. Churchill ordered in a fourth battle-cruiser but the crisis was averted by the French postponing the convoy, of which they unfortunately failed to inform the Admiralty.

At this crucial moment Italy declared its neutrality, later to enter the war on the Allied side thanks in great part to the diplomacy of Sir Edward Grey. At this time the closest collaboration was formed between the British and the French in the Mediterranean. An historic telegram was sent: "You can enter into the closest co-operation with the French Officers on your Station". Major Charles Julian Thoroton RMLI would have received this order.

In no time at all German warships were calling at Sicily for re-fuelling while RN ships were re-fuelling at Bizerta and Malta. As German battleships swung eastwards, four of Rear Admiral Troubridge's ships (including the *Black Prince*, in which Thoroton had served in 1904) were sent in pursuit. Later, Churchill picks up the history of the cruisers *Hogue* (in which Thoroton had served in 1910) and *Cressy*. These were 'on watch' south of the 54th parallel. Sunk by a single German submarine[3], along with the *Aboukir*; more than 1,400 sailors perished. Thus, on 21 September 1914, two of the ships Thoroton had sailed in disappeared below the waves.

On Naval Intelligence it is worth repeating here that Churchill writes: " Our Intelligence service has won and deserved world-wide fame. More than perhaps any other Power we were successful in the war in penetrating the intentions of the enemy. Again and again the forecasts both of the military and of the naval Intelligence Staffs were vindicated to the wonder of friends and the chagrin of foes.

---

3. The sub was the U-9 which, during the attack, became the first submarine to reload while submerged.

The three successive chiefs of the Naval Intelligence Division, Captain Thomas Jackson, Rear-Admiral Oliver, and lastly, Captain Reginald Hall, were all men of mark in the service, and continuously built and extended an efficient and profound organization". This ultimately became known as 'Room 40', taking its name from the room it occupied in the Admiralty building. It is worth repeating what Churchill wrote concerning the significance of the SIS and NID: '**There were others – a brilliant confederacy – whose names even now are better wrapt in mystery**'[4]. Amongst those 'whose names even now are better wrapt in mystery' was Major Charles Julian Thoroton.

He continues: "Our information about German naval movements were principally obtained (1) from the reports of secret agents in neutral and enemy countries and particularly in Germany, (2) from reports of our submarines, and (3) from a special study we had made of the German wireless".

The reference by Churchill to the need for secrecy "even now" was written in 1923. With regard to the emphasised statement not much has changed over the last eighty or more years.

In this Chapter XX text of his *World Crisis*, Churchill laid out the essential elements behind the work of this "brilliant confederacy" and thereby behind Major Thoroton's work: the placing of his Network of spies and intelligence agents in neutral countries; his links with submarine traffic; and his expertise in wireless telegraphy. However, before we can come to meet the Major, known generally as Charles the Bold, the world he lived in, that of British Naval Intelligence, needs to be described.

Building the Thoroton Network

What is called the Thoroton Network was constructed and directed by Thoroton from his arrival in Gibraltar in 1913, later under the control of Captain (later Admiral Sir Reginald) 'Blinker' Hall. Hall was Director of the Intelligence Division of the Naval Staff (later renamed Director of Naval Intelligence Division, or DNI) who was in charge of Room 40 (also known as 40 OB) which was the headquarters of Naval Intelligence, housed in the Old Building of the Admiralty in London.

In this story the personal history of

Admiral Sir Reginald 'Blinker' Hall of Room 40, here shown as Captain of HMS Queen Mary in 1914.

---

4. *The World Crisis 1911-1914, Winston S Churchill.*

Thoroton is pertinent as it explains, to some extent, why it was that the Thoroton Network was of such importance and was so successful in the secret war. Equally significant are the reasons for the need of the Network, set against the run-up to war in 1914 in what Churchill called The World Crisis.

The hero of the story is not one man but the Network itself. Just as Thoroton came to find himself in a virtually personal duel with German agents on the Iberian peninsula, so too did other significant figures play crucial roles in the secret war in the Med: British and German agents, French men and women allies, Spanish supporters and opponents of the Allied cause, Moroccans, Italians and Greeks.

Other historians deal with these events in some detail and make reference to the Mediterranean theatre, to Thoroton himself and to the other significant figures in this scenario. But, up to now, no full length account has concentrated on the Network, passing references only appearing in the leading histories of the secret services. Reasons for this will become apparent in the course of this book.

The run-up to war and the initial Naval operations in the Med are therefore the logical starting point for this history, together with a summary of the history of British Naval Intelligence. In this we will see how it was that a Royal Marines Light Infantry Major was selected for the part of Senior Naval Intelligence Officer, HMS *Cormorant*, Gibraltar responsible for the Mediterranean Theatre, Ascension Island and Contraband Control. The man fits the frame. The framework is The World Crisis and everything which flowed from that into his field of responsibility.

History of British Naval Intelligence

In the earliest period of Naval Intelligence, that of 1882, it was Admiral Sir George Tryon who took the first tentative steps. These had been forced on the Admiralty by none other than General Gordon (of Khartoum fame) who had highlighted the Royal Navy's lack of appreciation and usage of secret intelligence in a communication to Lord Northbrook, the First Lord of the Admiralty. The first Director of Naval Intelligence (NI) was Captain William Henry Hall who began to get some wheels turning. Then in 1887 the Naval Intelligence Division (NID) proper was set up under Admiral Tryon. Predecessors in cryptography included Edgar Allan Poe (1809-1849) and Lieutenant R P Cator[5] in the USA and in England Admiral Sir Francis Beaufort (1774-1857). Although Poe and Cator were not associated with Room 40 their pioneering work was of great influence and was developed by Sir Francis Beaufort at Naval Intelligence under Admiral Sir George Tryon's Foreign Intelligence Committee. Then came Commander Richard James Morrison who combined intelligence with astrology. In spite of his seeming crankiness he was regarded as something of a genius by Commandant Bazeries of the French Army Cryptographical Department who was one of the world's greatest authorities on ciphers.

---

5. Cator was one who responded to Poe's cipher challenge in Alexander's Weekly Messenger in 1840, not under his own name but through an intermediary. For the full story see Richard Deacon's History.

From 1895 Admiral Beaumont was able to expand the NID so that when Rear-Admiral Sir Reginald Custance took over as DNI in 1899 "he inherited what was then the best intelligence service of all Britain's armed forces"[6]. One of his first actions was to organise a section devoted to trade intelligence, a field in which Thoroton was to perform particularly well. At the same time German Naval Intelligence had created a sub-section devoted to North Africa as Germany had long seen this area as a cockpit of Britain, France and Germany. Morocco was the centre point and from this was to flow the Agadir crisis of 1911.

1898 had seen the defeat of the Spanish overseas empire by American armed forces, Cuba, Puerto Rico and the Philippines falling into American hands, while Hawaii was annexed in 1898 by the United States following the death of its King, David Kalakaua, in 1891. This placed the USA on the world scene as a major power for the first time. Almost as a consequence Britain, in complete secrecy, established the Secret Service Bureau for espionage and counter-espionage. In 1903-05 Admiral Prince Louis of Battenberg was DNI, later to be grossly maligned as a friend of Germany.

By now the power and influence of the armament manufacturers was such that vital national decisions were increasingly being made by them rather than by national governments. They were the richest men in Europe: take-over bids, amalgamations, mergers and cartels had placed them virtually beyond the reach of control by their governments. Some were behind both sides in every conflict. Krupp, Vickers and Scheider-Creusot were now the leading companies along with Nordenfelt-Maxim, perhaps directing better industrial intelligence systems of their own than those of national governments, at least in the opinion of the US Office of Naval Intelligence.

Battenberg was succeeded in 1905 by Ottley and then King-Hall. Then came Slade in October 1907 and Bethell in 1909. Bethell was charged with setting up a Secret Service Bureau by the Committee of Imperial Defence for which he recruited Commander Mansfield Cumming as Head of the Foreign Section. Cumming began first with Germany but initially only on published information. During Bethell's occupancy close liaison was established with France resulting in the production of an Anglo-French code-book.

Jackson (1912) and Oliver (1913) followed, thus bringing us up to the Thoroton era. However, during this period the Trade Division had been abolished and the section concerned with war preparations was disbanded. By 1913 the NID had been reduced to half its strength. In spite of this its original brief still stood:

"to collect, classify and record, with a complete index, all information which bears a naval character, or which may be of value during naval operations, to keep up our knowledge of progress made by foreign countries in naval matters and to preserve the information in a form readily available for reference".

6. *Robert Mullins, Sharpening the Trident.*

CJT represented the Royal Marines at the 1911 Delhi Durbar attended by over half a million Indians and over 26,800 British.

Oliver established a special section of the NID to intercept German naval signals and decipher them under the direction of Sir Alfred Ewing, Director of Naval Education, who brought in Alexander Guthrie Denniston who had been educated in Bonn and at the Sorbonne in Paris and who became the Royal Navy's cipher mastermind.

In effect the overall NID priorities in the run-up to war in 1914 might be summarised as concentrating on four heads: cryptology, particularly in respect of enemy naval signals; trade intelligence, in spite of the abolishment of this section; and, particularly, the German High Seas Fleet movements; and, finally, North Africa with special reference to Spain and Morocco.

With regard to the setting up of Room 40 in November 1914, a 'War Diary & Log Book' (filed under ADM 223/767) describes in handwritten form the personnel and work of Naval Intelligence at the Admiralty. This War Diary is not very long lived and only a few pages are written up[7].

The first, undated, entry gives MO5 at the Admiralty as consisting of eight men: Ewing (DNI), Denniston, Herschell, Parish (NI), Curtis (NI), Henderson, Norton and Lister. No mention of Hall as yet. It describes the administrative methods to be employed and detailed staff instructions with particular reference to German Naval communications. It says that anagrams are being used in German 'double-codes'. It provides a long list of code-names to be employed: SPOONFUL, ESSTOFFEL for submarine; PROFESSOR, PEPER and PAPIERS for the Mediterranean Fleet being examples.

---

7.   The setting-up of Room 40 followed from the Russian gift of the German code book from the Magdeburg, wrecked 25 August 1914.

This very early War Diary was soon set aside but it provides the original starting point for BNI establishments around the world.

Captain Hall when appointed had just one civilian clerk to assist him and virtually neither staff nor funds. He concentrated on the detailed assessment of foreign armaments production so that they could be reviewed against Britain's.

This was essential information as at that time the great armaments race, engineered by the armaments manufacturers, was mushrooming all over the world: Skoda in Austria; Hiram Maxim, Torsten Nordenfelt and Krupp in Germany; Putiloff in Russia; Vickers in England. Basil Zaharoff[8] was as yet unknown to the American secret service, his identity only being uncovered by Lieutenant W S Sims (later Admiral) of the US Navy who had been posted to Paris as Intelligence Officer. He discovered the name of Zaharoff from Russian sources where he was operating as salesman for Maxim-Nordenfelt. Zaharoff, Sims reported, was not only close to the Russian Imperial Court but in high social circles in Madrid as well. Later he discovered, in US Treasury files, that Zaharoff had been

Captain Mansfield Smith Cumming. Founder of the modern SIS.

involved in the Bolivian-Paraguay Chaco War. Then Zaharoff married the Duchess of Villafranca (of the Spanish Court) and had acquired £30 million worth of orders in Spain only two months after his meeting with the Duchess. To step up arms sales to Spain, Zaharoff helped precipitate the war which resulted in the total destruction of the Spanish Fleet in Manila Bay and the surrender of Puerto Rico and Guam to the USA.

To turn for a moment to on-the-ground *humint* (Human Intelligence Work), a well known technique of British Intelligence which the Thoroton Network employed, was the shadowing of suspects. This could last sometimes for as long as a year or more, regular reports being sent back to HQ where they were collated, interpreted and forwarded to the appropriate authority. One such example is that of two ostensibly archaeological researchers who may have been seen examining telegraph poles, noting the distances between them, sketching around the walls of the city and so on. The diligent building up of such reports could lead to an official letter being sent by a British Ambassador to the Foreign Ministry of the country to whom such nationals belonged.

---

8. For detail on Zaharoff, his associates and the arms cartels see *The Merchant of Death* by John T Flynn, Ludwig von Mises Institute, www.mises.org.

CJT promoted Major, 1910. Note the monocle, "defective eyesight".

The selection of secret agents

It was in March 1913 that the first serious efforts were made to recruit secret agents and this move came principally from Winston Churchill.

There is no record available on how, precisely, Thoroton was selected. A Royal Marine recommendation must surely have been involved. This could have been from the Deputy Adjutant General of the Royal Marines who, from 1911 to 1916, was Major General W C Nicholls, and from the senior RMLI officer, General Sir William Campbell, KCB (1911-1913), or General Sir William Thompson, KCB (1913).

While we do not know who was involved, Captain Mansfield Cumming RN of ML1c[9], as the founder of the modern Secret Intelligence Service (who "looked for what he called as 'the cut of the gib' of an alert agent") is certainly a reasonable contender. Cumming's priority at this time was naval rather than military[10].

In 1909 Cumming had been appointed Chief of the Secret Service for the Navy and he developed a programme demanding "full scope to make inquiries, sound every personality to be of use" and "be able to offer substantial retaining fees and rewards for valuable information". At that time he considered "most important work of all" to be concerned with ship movements, transports and supply systems and "the agents selected must be of reliable character and position"[11]. Andrew (op cit) writes that "early in the war" Cumming left control of secret services (in Spain) to the NID.

Here it should be noted that Cumming's SIS was reported, after the war, as having been reorganised in 1917 by the WO which shows it to be the paymaster for the four Secret Service organisations, Admiralty, Air, Political and Economics Intelligence. By the summer of 1915 Cumming had a London HO staff of over thirty. Jeffrey in his *MI6* quotes "during the whole of the war the Admiralty conducted secret service

9.   Cumming was known by the initial "C".
10. Andrew, Secret Service.
11. Jeffrey, MI6.

work in Spain and Portugal". When the WO began to make arrangements for an army officer in Gibraltar to carry out some form of secret service in Spain, Hall was reported to be very angry. Indeed, Cumming called himself one of Hall's "lieutenants" in an October 1917 letter to Hall.

Conventional wisdom makes it clear that intelligence agents were 'found' and recruited, never were they accepted as 'volunteers' seeking such a role on their own behalf. (This is sadly no longer the case.) Amongst such men were Sir William Wiseman ("one of the keenest, most analytical minds in the espionage game") and Sidney Reilly, born Sigmund Georgievich Rosenblum in 1874 and who was reputedly shot dead in 1925 by the OGPU (predecessors of the KGB). Reilly is described as the "ace of spies" by Bruce Lockhart (in his book *Ace of Spies*) and Christopher Andrew, who is not given to excessive praise, goes a long way to confirm this in his *Secret Service*. Reilly had a strong ally in Sir Henry Montague Hozier, the father of Churchill's bride-to-be at the time. Hozier was also in the Secret Service having been one of the first officers in the Military Intelligence Division (MID) some time in the early 1870s. Later he too was known as C.

It was only much later, in 1939, that a subsection of the War Office was created, MI1x, in an attempt to bring some order into the recruitment of intelligence officers. This employed a card index of those thought to be suitable for such work. The original list included 400 possible recruits, most of whom were found to be dead, abroad or otherwise unavailable. This rather belated attempt to bring some sort of administrative order into the search for suitable men was in no way comparable with the flair; 'old boy network' involving bankers, lawyers, classicists and service officers; and that element of sheer chance and inspiration on the part of such people as Oliver and Hall. Nor does it mesh with the German analysis of the success of the British Secret Service[12].

International banks, which employed their own undercover agents, were a fertile source of intelligence agents. Rothschilds, Hambro, Schroeder and others all contributed to Room 40, including Lionel Fraser and Frank Tiarks. Claud Serocold (a stockbroker from Cazenoves) is another example. In Spain it was the March Bank. Later, it was to be Barings and the Bank of England.

In his May 1914 'Memorandum...on Naval Staff Training & Development' Churchill reveals his thoughts on Intelligence which, while it required "little change", was to be divided into three sections: hostile countries; friendly countries; and neutral countries. The DID reported through the Chief of Staff to the First Sea Lord. Churchill writes: "These new duties open to the Intelligence Division a large creative and imaginative sphere, and offer opportunities for the highest tactical and strategic ability". For Fleet Flagship Staff, the Intelligence Group (one of three groups, the others being Operations and Communications) was composed of one Staff Officer in peacetime, two in wartime.

---

12. See Annex E.

Royal Marines group photo Chatham. Dated 1913, the time of CJT's posting to Gibraltar. CJT second from the right, seated.

Sailing to Gibraltar 1913

And now a new vista opens up. The photograph taken at Chatham in 1913 shows him with the rank of Major, as he was just before he sailed for Gibraltar. He had served on the Chatham Division staff from 16 May 1911 to 11 September 1913 and in 1911 he was present at the Delhi Durbar following the coronation of King George V. On 12 September 1913 he joins HMS *Cormorant* as a General Staff Officer and Intelligence Officer, Gibraltar with special responsibility for Contraband Control. He was to remain there until 31 March 1919. World War I broke out on 4 August 1914, just under a year after his appointment to Gibraltar. He was to leave this position four months after the Armistice.

Thus, he was well positioned in 1913 to begin his intelligence work in Gibraltar, work which was to spread into Spain, Portugal, the Canaries, France, Morocco, the Balearic Islands, Italy and as far east as Greece.

From 1909 onwards, as President of the Board of Trade, Churchill was in close collaboration with British Intelligence. The initial 'K' in his 1914 'Espionage' checklist referred to Vernon Kell, a cosmopolitan, complex character, and a Captain in the South Staffordshire Regiment who had been Intelligence Officer in Tientsin during the Boxer Rebellion. He had been given the job of organising MO5 which became MI5 under his direction. In 1911, as First Lord at the Admiralty, Churchill was active with Kell in combating the activities of German agents targeting the Royal Navy and RN establishments in Great Britain.

Churchill's role as First Lord was "partly to compel the Admiralty to set up an efficient Naval Staff". But in the *World Crisis,* Volume I, 1911-1914, Churchill makes no mention of Vernon Kell, nor of Captain Mansfield Cumming[13]. He picks up with Captain Thomas Jackson, Rear-Admiral Oliver and Captain Hall in Chapter XX dated 13 December 1914.

In 1912 the Committee for Imperial Defence decided on cutting all German-owned transatlantic cables in the event of war. Oliver was made DID in August 1913 and one month later Thoroton was appointed Head of Naval Intelligence for the Mediterranean. Hall was appointed DNI in November 1914, that is fourteen months after Thoroton's appointment. Hall's appointment would not have been instantaneous but the result of due consultations. He was Captain of the battle-cruiser HMS *Queen Mary* under Beatty at the time when a telegram arrived from the Admiralty offering him the post of Director of Naval Intelligence. Thus in some way Thoroton's appointment corresponds with Oliver's and was, most probably, confirmed by him.

In 1913 Churchill was at the Admiralty. Knowing his penchant for on-the-ground details[14] and his deep involvement with the secret services at this time, as well as the outstanding importance of Gibraltar and the Mediterranean (which Churchill had noted in his checklist), he may well have had some interest in the selection of a Chief of Naval Intelligence for Gibraltar in 1913. He would not of course have been involved in any way in such an appointment.

Gibraltar, Rock from North Front Camp.

Thoroton postcard dated 16 May 1915.

13. *Cumming was the first chief of Secret Intelligence Service (SIS, later MI6), 1909-1923, but from 1898 head of Foreign Section of Naval Intelligence.*

14. *For examples see pages 646 and 690, Randolph Churchill's Young Statesman 1901-1914.*

Chapter 3
War in the Mediterranean

As early as 1898 the Mediterranean was home to thirty-eight RN capital ships, the highest number for any of the nine worldwide Naval Stations, the second being the China Station with twenty-seven capital ships.

The Mediterranean theatre was much to the fore in 1912, the subject of debate by the politicians and by the press[1]. Churchill had made an all-embracing analysis of German sea power plans in July at the 118th meeting of the Imperial Defence Committee. It left no doubt as to the seriousness of the German threat nor of the dire consequences for Britain should a High Seas Fleet battle arise throwing the entire country into ruin. The debate was long, complicated and, occasionally, acrimonious and it involved all the leading members of the government and the Admiralty. In May Churchill had visited Naples, Malta and Gibraltar on board the Admiralty ship *Enchantress*. At the previous 117th meeting in July the IDC had agreed to the need for a battle fleet to be deployed in the Mediterranean, based on Malta, and when Anglo-French naval discussions finally took place, with an agreement signed on 10 February 1913, co-operation was established on naval matters not only for the Mediterranean but also for the Straits of Dover, the Western Channel and the Far East.

Naval Operations in the Mediterranean

In 1914 the Western Mediterranean sea lanes were primarily the responsibility of the French Navy[2]. In terms of Intelligence, that same year Room 40 felt, misguidedly, that it was in a good position to locate German U-boats in various naval theatres. But this did not apply in the Mediterranean to which many U-boats had been transferred in 1915 due to American pressure on Germany to call off unrestricted sinkings. RMS *Lusitania* had been sunk in 1915 by German submarine U-20, with the loss of 1,198 lives. In fact it was only by the autumn of 1916 that submarine warfare became the top priority for Room 40 and only by December 1917 that it began to be truly effective in the Med, Adriatic and Aegean Seas. It was a long and perilous state of war.

---

1. *For a review of Churchill's 1912-1914 naval policies (in particular with regard to Anglo-French co-operation and the Mediterranean) see Volume II of Randolph Churchill's biography of his father, Young Statesman 1901-1914. In 1912 the 4th Battle Squadron was based on Gibraltar and the Submarine and Destroyer flotillas at Malta with a lesser submarine flotilla at Alexandria.*

2. *At the 1915 Paris Naval Conference the Med was divided into three zones, British, French and Italian. The French zone began along a line drawn south from Cartagena and east to the Levant. Britain and Italy shared the other two zones. It was a bad arrangement and France rejected any unified command until later in the war. For detail on naval engagements in the Med see the website www.naval-history.net, Med 1914-1918.*

German sea-plane from Friedrichshavn (Lake Constance) with despatches for a U-Boat in the Mediterranean.

The French liner Sontay torpedoed and sinking in the Mediterranean, 16 April 1917.

Naval operations in the Mediterranean began with the French fleet, a large but elderly force, deployed on escort duty to convoys against the smaller but more up-to-date Austrian fleet and as cover against a possible Italian entry into the war on Germany's side. Royal Navy ships were also sent in as reinforcements to the British Mediterranean Fleet. When Germany's battlecruiser *Goeben* and light cruiser *Breslau* failed to find the French convoys they bombarded the then French cities of Bizerte and Bon, Tunisia, until they were pursued to Turkey by the superior French and British forces. With Italy's entry into the war on the Allied side in 1915 the main strategy was to blockade the Adriatic and to combat submarine attacks. Later, Constantinople and the Dardanelles, with the battle of Gallipoli, became the Mediterranean focus, followed by the sinking of two Austrian Dreadnoughts in 1918. Allied fleets were also occupied by events in Greece, Palestine, Macedonia and the Suez Canal, finally ending up supporting the White Armies in southern Russia.

The Western Theatre

Concentrating on the western end of the Mediterranean, *The Naval Records Society* Volume 126 for the years 1915-1918 gives a strategic map listing five places: Cartagena and Capo de Gata in Spain; the Spanish island Alborán; Gibraltar; and Oran in Algeria. While these five places were pre-eminent centres of interest for the Royal Navy, Naval Intelligence Division in Gibraltar had a wider remit.

Germany was in fact the first country to employ submarines as commerce raiders even though she only possessed 38 submarines at the start of World War I[3].

---

3. *German U-Boats communicated with the control centers in Germany on the 400 metre waveband.*

The peak strength of U-Boats was 140 in October 1917 and Germany never had more than 60 at sea at any one time. The U-9 sank the *Aboukir, Hogue* and *Cressy* on 22 September 1914 with the loss of 1,400 British sailors. In February 1917 Germany instituted unrestricted U-Boat warfare against merchant ships and by April of that year 430 Allied ships, representing 852,000 tons, had been sunk, a small percentage being unarmed sailing ships. During 1914 to 1918, over 10,000,000 tons of Allied shipping had been sent to the bottom of the oceans and seas. Ludendorf himself wrote that the role of the German submarine fleet was of absolute crucial importance to the German war effort[4].

The effect on the British Home Front of these massive shipping losses is exemplified by the 1917 food rationing system. Just one example: Evelyn Waugh, at school at Lancing, received 4 ounces of meat per day, cocoa without milk and jam not more than three times a week, resulting in persistent hunger. This situation was to deteriorate.

1915 had seen a renewed effort by German submarines in the Med, one of which was U-35. Fifty four Allied ships were sunk in three weeks. Another submarine, U-21, spent three weeks in the Med on its way to Turkey. On 9 January 1917 the Imperial German Chancellor, Dr von Bethmann-Hollweig, said, "The U-Boat was the last card". Central Powers' submarines in the Med sunk about 35% of the whole Allied tonnage in World War I. Of the 199 total German submarine losses, 175 were destroyed by the Royal Navy, 13 by the French, 2 by the USA and 2 by Russia. 17 could not be accounted for.

The reports contained in the *Naval Records Society* Volume 126 emphasise the extreme difficulty, indeed near impossibility, of preventing German submarines from entering the Mediterranean through the Straits of Gibraltar. Rear Admiral Cecil Thursey, in 1915, reports on "the inadequate force in the Straits" and on French complaints that Gibraltar was not blocking German submarines more effectively. He expresses sympathy with the French view but also points out that the various efforts to prevent U-Boats from entering the Mediterranean had proved ineffective and that there was a general misunderstanding concerning the impossibility of blockading submarines passing at considerable depths. However, by 11 September 1918, Admiral Godfrey is able to report on the success of anti-submarine warfare as conducted by Gibraltar.

Reporting from Malta, on 4 September 1918, Admiral Sir Somerset Calthorpe (C in C, Mediterranean, 1912-1919) communicated to Sir Eric Cambell Geddes (First Lord of the Admiralty, 1917-1918) that the Gibraltar Intelligence officers were concerned about German intrigues in Morocco and along the Rif coast.

---

4. Andrew Marr's 2009 *The Making of Modern Britain* (McMillan) asserts "The greatest danger to Britain from U-Boats came in 1917". Admiral Henning von Holzendorff, head of the German Imperial Navy, said to Hindenburg in 1916, it was only because of "the energy and force of England" that France and Italy were still fighting. Unrestricted submarine warfare was undertaken, turning the intended destruction of Britain's sea lifelines into "a very close run thing".

Arms and money were being smuggled into Morocco but no U-Boat bases had been established there. He goes on to report on his visit to Gibraltar where he was "very impressed" by Rear Admiral Grant and his staff. A Spanish coal strike was in force at the time and the Naval and Intelligence staff had managed to circumvent it and restore supplies. He wrote, "A great deal depends on Gibraltar...not only...but for our own Balloon and Flying Bases, etc".

U-35, Submarine used to collect Wilhelm Canaris from Cartagena and later to land agents and a consignement of anthrax and glanders infected sugar cubes.

King Alfonso XIII to whom Lord Hershell showed the germ infected sugar cubes collected by CJT's agents off the U-35 shipment.

In his admittedly incomplete book *U-Boats Destroyed* (Putnam, 1964) Robert M Grant reports on only one U-Boat in the Mediterranean, U-35, although twenty seven were known to be operating there in July 1918. U-35 was one of the fastest, travelling at 16.5 knots surfaced and at 9.5 knots submerged. She weighed 680 tons and had a crew of four officers and thirty five men. She was never sunk.

U-35 had sailed from Heligoland on 29 April 1916, travelling at some 12.5 knots. She reached Cartagena in June 1916 carrying a personal letter from the Kaiser to the King of Spain. Four months later she was back again to collect Lieutenant Wilhem Canaris who had been attempting to establish U-Boat fuelling points in Spain. By 14 February 1918, when she landed two agents off Cartegena, she was carrying anthrax and glanders germs. The head of the Cartagena police, who was pro-British, was alerted to this by Room 40 and the consignment was seized. Subsequently Hall sent Lord Herschell to the King of Spain to show him some of the sugar cubes containing the poisons. In spite of full Intelligence information, and the despatch of HMS *Newcastle* to intercept another batch of germs, the French mistress of the German Naval Attaché was able to reach South America on the Spanish liner *Reine Victoria Eugenia* and hundreds of mules destined for the Western Front were injected and died[5].

The importance of the mules, which had been targeted by the Germans, needs to be emphasised. They were, along with horses, the vital pack animal of the Great War. On the Western Front, in Belgium and France, they were the essential means for moving supplies up to the front line trenches: ammunition, barbed wire, duck boards, food and medical supplies. Without mules it was impossible to maintain essential supplies. They were also used to bring back casualties from the front line. By Christmas 1914, the first year of the war, Britain had run out of its domestic mule supply and it turned to the Americas for reinforcements. During the course of the war more than a million mules died in service to the British Army alone. Many were lost at sea due to U-Boat attacks (the White Star liner *Armenia* was sunk off the Cornish coast with 1,400 mules on board - none of their muleteers would

Mule train on the Somme, 1916.

5. Germ warfare is hinted at in Buchan's *Mr Standfast (1918)*, perhaps he learned of this from Hall.

abandon them and went down with them) but poisoning was seen, by the Germans, as the more certain, targeted method.

Canaris himself had arrived in Spain under the name of Deed-Rosas on a forged Chilean passport in order to wage an almost one-man war against the British. He was operational in Spain from 30 November 1915 to 20 October 1916. He is credited with the destruction of nine British ships in Spanish ports and waters and some success in fomenting trouble amongst the tribes in Morocco. He survived an assassination attempt by Stewart Menzies (the future 'C') who had been sent to Spain by MI6 to this end, Canaris being No.1 on their list of enemies.

In his 1987 book *The Naval War in the Mediterranean 1914-1918*, Paul G Halpern reports on Hall's transfer of British cryptographers to Taranto and to Rome in the late spring of 1917. On his map Cueta, the Spanish port in Morocco, is added to the Naval Records Society's map. However he gives no account of any naval operations concerning Morocco and we can accept there were virtually none.

In *U-Boat Intelligence 1914-1918* by Robert Grant, we are able to see several photographs of interned German submarines which had been taken by Allied agents. U-39 is shown in dry-dock, possibly photographed by A E W Mason. (This photo is now in the possession of the US Navy). UC-48 is shown in four photos: its propeller shafts and rudders being dismantled; in dry-dock; under tow; and moored alongside the *Tallers de Corch Hijos* building in Ferrol in March 1917. UC-56 is shown interned in Santander in May 1917. Regarding the attacks on Spanish shipping by German submarines, U-157 is pictured in Edwyn Gray's *The Killing Time – The German U-Boats 1914-1918*, holding up the Spanish liner *Infanta Isabel de Bourbon* on 28 March 1918. In George Hills' *Rock of Contention - A History of Gibraltar* reference is made to U-Boat activity, noting "Individual Spaniards may possibly have secretly helped the Germans...not all the fuel and provisioning carried by German submarines in the Med were taken aboard at the German bases in the Adriatic". As well as Spanish shore-based provisioning we know of maritime provisioning by Spanish ships and of cross-U-Boat supplies provided by German sea-planes in the Med. This subject will be returned to later.

As to U-Boat activity in the Med it was, in 1916, the theatre in which almost all of Germany's submarine warfare was conducted even though, as the *Mittelmeer Division* of the German Navy, it only ranked third in order. In 1917 U-Boats based on Pola and Cattaro in the Adriatic joined in and conducted operations throughout the Med from Port Said to Gibraltar. Of the 435 U-Boats commissioned during World War I, 203 were lost to all causes, 170 of these to enemy action. Eighteen U-Boats have been identified as having been sunk in the Med: four U-type boats; eight UB-types; and six UCs. UB-68, sunk near Malta on 4 October 1918, was captained by Oberleutnant zur See Karl Dönitz, the future Commander-in-Chief of the German Navy in 1943 and the last head of the Nazi government in 1945. He had been rescued from the waters by HMS *Snapdragon* which picked up the entire crew except for four men.

UB-80. 3rd generation U-Boat, UB-80 was similar to UB-71, sunk on 21 April 1918 by depth charge in the Straits of Gibraltar.

Interestingly, Dönitz "a cool and realistic calculator" according to Goebbels, remarked to Hitler in 1943: "The enemy knows all our secrets and we know none of his".

For our purposes the most interesting fact to emerge from a study of German U-Boat losses in the Med is the identification of those ports in Spain into which damaged and disabled submarines were steered. Cartagena, Corruna, Santander, Vivero, Cadiz and El Ferrol are specifically mentioned and in every case we know the Spanish government ordered their internment. UC-52, damaged by RN torpedoes, took refuge in Cadiz in June 1917 having sunk 18,213 tons of Allied shipping. U-293 entered the Arsenal de San Fernando in September 1917 evoking considerable concern and diplomatic difficulties. It's departure was photographed and appeared in *La Esfera*[6]. We reproduce in a later chapter a photograph of four submarines in Cartagena harbour, although we have been unable to identify their nationality they are of World War I vintage. UC-49 had escaped from internment at Cadiz but was later sunk by depth charges in the English Channel on 8 August 1918. That all five ports were secured against German U-Boats is convincing evidence that the denial of port facilities to the Germans by the Spanish government was effective and that any pro-German activity by, for example, Juan March (a Majorcan smuggler who was to become Thoroton's N° 1 agent) was not particularly successful.

6.   *Carolina Garcia Sanz, La Primera Guerra Mundial en el Estrecho de Gibraltar, p 278 & 281.*

Into the Eastern Mediterranean

The Mediterranean had long been pin-pointed by the Admiralty as the crucial theatre for naval operations. In 1912, Admiral Sir Archibald Berkeley Milne had been appointed Commander in Chief Mediterranean, seen perhaps not as the premier post in the RN but certainly the most fashionable one. This appointment, by Winston Churchill, provoked a characteristically hysterical outburst from Fisher who saw in it the appointment of a future Commander in Chief of the Navy, a post he wanted reserved for Jellicoe. In the event Churchill reassured him that Milne was not in line for the senior post and Fisher subsided.

In 1912 the German battle cruiser *Goeben* had been launched and had been despatched to cruise the Med in company with the light cruiser *Breslau*. "No other single exploit of the war" wrote Barbara Tuchman, "cast so long a shadow upon the world as the voyage accomplished by their commanders during the next seven days". As such, the history of the *Goeben* and the *Breslau* is an essential element in the story of BNI in the Med.

Admiral Souchon, appointed by Admiral Tirpitz, had hoisted his flag on the *Goeben* in 1913, the same year that Charles the Bold arrived in Gibraltar.

He steamed the Med familiarising himself with all the places and personalities he might have to deal with in the event of war: Italians, Greeks, Turks, Austrians and French but never with the British who would not permit German ships to anchor in ports at the same time as the RN. Germany had the second largest fleet in the world but only two warships in the Med. The *Goeben* displaced 23,000 tons and was the equivalent of a Dreadnought. She had a speed of 27.8 knots, equal to that of the British Inflexibles, and was their equal in firepower. The Breslau (4,500 tons) was on a par with the British light cruisers. The *Goeben* was capable of "brushing aside or outstripping (the French) cruisers, breaking in upon the transports and sinking one after another crammed with soldiers", in the words of Lord Fisher.

The French had the largest fleet in the Med: sixteen battleships, six cruisers and twenty four destroyers, employed in protecting the troop transports of colonial troops from Morocco and Algeria. The British Mediterranean fleet, based on Malta, consisted of three battle cruisers, *Inflexible*, *Indomitable* and *Indefatigable*, each of 18,000 tons. Armed with eight 12" guns and with a speed of 27 to 28 knots they were deployed in order to overtake and destroy anything that floated except a ship of the dreadnought class. In addition the Mediterranean fleet included four cruisers of 14,000 tons, four light cruisers and fourteen destroyers. Italy was neutral and the Austrian fleet based on Pola had a total of some fifteen ships including eight capital ships but it was, in fact, unprepared for action and played a very minor role.

Churchill took a close interest in the movements of U-Boats as reported to Room 40. In respect of the Eastern Med he was concerned with U-35; U-21, which had entered the Med and had reached Kotor in May; U-40; and U-27. It was U-21 that torpedoed the battleship HMS *Triumph* off Gallipoli on 25 May towards the end of the Dardanelles operation.

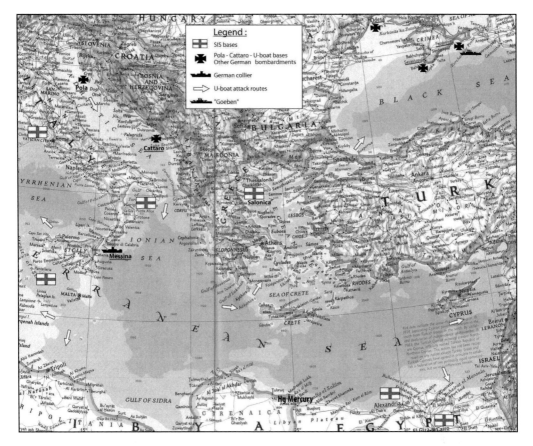

Eastern Meditterranean

Transporting 80,000 colonial troops from North Africa to the Western Front, the equivalent of an entire army corps, was crucial to the French battle plan, as was the timing of their shipment. Both the French and the British fleets were dedicated to protecting their safe passage.

However, on 3 August 1914, the German Admiralty was suddenly alerted to the essential need of persuading Turkey to come into the war on the side of Germany. When the British ultimatum to Germany had run out, and the commitment to the defence of Belgium in the event of it being invaded had been confirmed, rioting mobs attacked the British Embassy in Berlin hurling their worst slogan 'Rassen-Verrat!' – race treason! "Our country is not much loved anywhere and frequently hated" William the Crown Prince noted while on his travels. We have "no friend but Austria" remarked a Deputy. Germany scratched its head and came up with "the Turks and the Japanese". But on 15 August Japan declared for the Allies: Turkey became their sole remaining hope.

Accordingly Admiral Tirpitz ordered the *Goeben* and the *Breslau* to turn round while on their way towards the North African coast where they intended to bombard Philippeville and Bone, and "to proceed at once to Constantinople".

There followed a series of German countermanding orders and the hot pursuit of the German warships: "*Indomitable* and *Indefatigable* shadowing the *Goeben* and the *Breslau*, 37.44 N, 7.56E" read Admiral Milne's wireless message to the Admiralty. Prior to this the British fleet had lost their two German targets even though they were instructed by Churchill on 1 August to put to sea from Malta; on 2 August Churchill ordered "*Goeben* must be shadowed by two battle cruisers" and the Adriatic "watched". The light cruiser *Chatham* failed to find Admiral Souchon. It was here that the Thoroton Network provided one clue which, although the report was correct, was misconstrued as to intent. This report concerned a German collier which was waiting at Majorca. Milne, believing (as did everyone else) that the *Goeben* was heading westwards to attack the French transports, concluded that, after refuelling at Majorca, she would make for Gibraltar and the open seas. He despatched *Indomitable* and *Indefatigable* from the Adriatic to hunt for the *Goeben*.

Churchill's third order included the direction "…shadow her wherever she goes and be ready to act upon declaration of war which appears probable and imminent". The search was on. The French fleet was then steering southwards for Oran and Algiers, the same destination as that of the two German warships. August 3, 6:00pm, Admiral Souchon, receiving the news that war was declared on France, put on speed, outdistancing the French ships. Running up the Russian flag he opened fire "sowing death and panic" along the North African coast. Then he turned for Messina for re-coaling. Just after this Milne sent his "shadowing" message but the two German ships out-ran the British ships and disappeared in fog and a gathering storm. Throughout this period the Admiralty's and the Navy's conviction was that Souchon would run westwards and escape the Med via Gibraltar. Instead, the *Goeben* was to head for Greece, the Dardanelles and Constantinople in order "to force the Turks, even against their will, to spread the war to the Black Sea against their ancient enemy Russia".

Before this happened however the light cruiser *Gloucester*, patrolling the exit to the Eastern Med, spotted the German vessels in the Straight of Messina, which she trailed, incapable of attacking as the *Goeben* would certainly destroy her before she got the *Goeben* within range. *Gloucester's* signals (which Souchon attempted unsuccessfully to jam) indicated the *Goeben's* change of course away from the Adriatic and Milne ordered the *Defence, Black Prince, Warrior* and *Duke of Edinburgh*, armed cruisers of 14,000 tons each, to intercept even though they only carried 9.2" guns compared with the *Goeben's* 11" guns. Further confusion ensued as no one on the British side could ever have conceived that the German ships would head for Turkey. The Germans put enormous pressure on Enver Pasha, the War Minister, and on the Grand Vizier, the *Goeben's* mighty guns being trained on Constantinople. When finally the Turks agreed to the two ships entering the Dardanelles, they were "sold" to the Turkish government, but still commanded and crewed by the Germans, and renamed the *Janus* and *Midilli*. As such they were reviewed by the Sultan amidst the wild enthusiasm of the people. Later, on 28 October, the former *Goeben* and *Breslau*, flying the Turkish flag and the German sailors wearing Turkish fezzes, entered the Black Sea in company with several Turkish torpedo boats, and shelled Odessa, Sevastapol and Feodosia, sinking a Russian gunboat and killing a number of civilians. An act of war had been committed in the name of Turkey: Russia declared war on Turkey on 4 November and Britain and France followed on 5 November. The consequences were monumental.

Greece

Thoroton's spy Network was largely land-based and it would seem that, at this stage, it was not particularly strong in Italy (the German re-fuelling in Messina went unreported) nor in the Greek archipelago, where Compton Mackenzie was operating.

Room 40 had had some success in a similar naval situation concerning the *Dresden* which had escaped the Falklands Island battle. The ship having disappeared for a time, Hall then received a telegraphic report from an agent in Chile which revealed where she was to meet up with a collier in one of the San Fenandez islands and where she was subsequently sunk by the *Kent* and the *Glasgow*. This incident was followed immediately by the Turkish episode. It was following the entry of Turkey into the war that Hall took steps to establish contacts in this area. He started with Mr Griffin Eady, head of Sir John Jackson Ltd, important contractors. He knew the Near East well and, for Turkey, put forward the name of Mr Gerald Fitzmaurice who was attached to the British Embassy in Constantinople. "Nothing happens in that city of intrigue without his knowing every detail". Thus Hall was able to organise a network of agents in the Eastern Mediterranean and German and Turkish wireless signals began to be intercepted, telegraphed to Room 40, deciphered and passed to the First Sea Lord, Lord Fisher.

In May 1915 Hall wrote to Commander Keyes, Chief of Naval Staff, warning him of German submarine dangers and the fact that his Eastern Network should "be able to give you due notice of any base supplies". At the same time he wrote: "I find it easier to get news and reliable information from the East than it is from Spain. But I am endeavouring to improve our organisation there to compete with the Huns"[7]. As early as 1913, only "modest results" had been obtained in Spain. At this stage, Thoroton was primarily engaged with Morocco and Hall's concentration on Spain itself must be dated from May 1915. That the build up was both rapid and effective is fully evident, even though only three more 'Special Services' officers were added in Gibraltar in 1915. Others, not entered in the Navy Lists, were also there.

Greece, as the farthest outreach of the Thoroton Network, remains something of an enigma. For a long time the country had suffered from insurrections and foreign interference and domination culminating in its various Germanic kings from the Wittenbach and Oldenbourg families. King George I was assassinated in 1913 and

---

7. *Cumming had originally recruited only Captain Boyle, Naval Attaché in Rome, to cover Austria, Turkey and Greece in 1909. Later he redeployed Sir William Wiseman from New York to the Eastern Med on counter-intelligence work when Hall decided Wiseman was no longer needed in the USA in 1915, thus further strengthening Hall's Eastern network.*

succeeded by his son, Constantin I. Naturally supporting the Central Powers, he dismissed his pro-Ally Prime Minister Eleotherios Venizelos. From 1914 even up to the start of World War II Greece was in a state of perpetual turmoil.

Compton Mackenzie's role there was as a Royal Marine on intelligence duty but there is no evidence of any line control between Thoroton and Mackenzie, rather the contrary. John Coleby, in his *A Marine or Anything, (Royal Marine Spies of the World War One Era),* mentions two Royal Marines, Captain Farmer RMLI and Major Lampen RMLI, with whom Compton Mackenzie had "a useful working relationship" and these are said to be the first personal contacts between Mackenzie and the Royal Marines on record. They would seem to have met up in Malta. Previous to this he had been in Athens "for the good of (his) health", on the orders of his Commander-in-Chief Sir Ian Hamilton. Then Mackenzie went to the Cyclades under Sir Francis Elliot where his plan was to win control of the key islands and persuade the inhabitants to support the Provisional Government. He sailed on the SS *Thessalia* "with one hundred and eight members of our mission, their wives, children and friends", eight French cabaret girls as his "agents" and a further one hundred and fifty Venizeulist refugees favourable to the Allied cause. The whole Ruritanian adventure can be read in Coleby's account but enough has been said here to clearly convince us that this was not part of the Thoroton Network.

In 1932 Compton Mackenzie published his *Aegean Memories* (and also his *Greek Memories*) which led to a monumental kerfuffle ending in his Old Bailey trial. Mackenzie went on to make capital out of it by writing his satirical book *Water on the Brain* which ridiculed the secret service, but not the NID.

Circulating in Greece during the war was Sir Basil Zaharoff (the ex-brothel tout of Constantinople and now international arms dealer) on an unofficial British secret mission organised by Lloyd George himself. His intrigues played a role in the departure of Constantine I and the return of Venizelos. Alkin E Johnson wrote, in the French journal *La Lumière*, that while Zaharoff was used "as a kind of super-spy in high society and influential circles…we had him watched by two or three of our best agents". It is perhaps only here that we may find traces of the Network in Greece, but we do not know their names. If this is the case it would further underline Zaharoff's intense dislike of Hall, a sentiment shared equally between them.

Apart from this, Greece gets very little if any reference in the major intelligence literature and we conclude that it was of less importance than other areas in the Mediterranean theatre.

Chapter 4
The Royal Marines and Naval Intelligence

What kind of an organisation was Major Thoroton RMLI, aged thirty eight, sailing to at HMS *Cormorant* on 12 September 1913?

The background to the Naval Intelligence Division (NID) can be summarised briefly but, before doing so, the strategic, political and military situation must be sketched in. Although it is beyond the scope of such a biography as this to delineate the overall war concerns of Britain in the Mediterranean theatre of operations, concerns which were enmeshed with those of France, Germany, Austria, Italy and Turkey in particular, it does require some consideration of government and Admiralty problems in the run up to war.

This is put into sharp perspective by Admiral Sir John Fisher's 23 March 1899 statement: "I don't like the Mediterranean! However, there's no mistake about it, the Mediterranean is the tip-top appointment of the scene..." The Kaiser's visit to Tangier in 1905, the "Dreadnaught scare" of 1909 and German plans for a base at Agadir were all contributory to British worries.

RM Pageant 1911, Chatham.

In 1905 the DNI had proposed sharing Naval intelligence with France but Fisher was opposed to this even though the French fleet had been concentrating on the Mediterranean largely as a result of Fisher's initiatives. The First Balkan War broke out in 1912 and this had shifted attention to the Eastern Mediterranean. By April 1913 Churchill was moving Royal Navy ships to the Mediterranean, including the old *Black Prince* on which Thoroton had serverd in 1906 and 1908. With Gibraltar holding the key to the Mediterranean, Thoroton's appointment to Naval Intelligence for an area from Gib to Greece can well be seen as a "tip-top appointment".

In the event British NI was to concern itself very largely with the submarine menace which developed into the major naval engagements in the Med in the Great War; along with smuggling and sabotage; code intercepts; port activities; counter-intelligence; propaganda and countering agitation plots; the safeguarding of Allied shipping and the tracking of enemy vessels. Morocco was to be the scene of very important developments. The internal strife in Spain was also to be a major concern of Thoroton on whose intelligence services the Spanish government came more and more to rely. Many of his reports (but by no means all) on these activities, and particularly on smuggling, were to be seen on the original pasteboard cards held at the Public Records Office (PRO) at Kew in 2003 but subsequent visits failed to trace them. They covered the period 1915-1917 and ended 1919. The NA staff could not find them in 2008, and could not account for this themselves[1].

The Naval Intelligence Division

Turning now to the Naval Intelligence Division, this was the Intelligence arm of the British Admiralty, established in 1882 as the Foreign Intelligence Committee and renamed Naval Intelligence Department in 1887. Its first head was Captain William Henry Hall. William Reginald 'Blinker' Hall, who was Director of Naval Intelligence (DNI) during World War I, was his son. In 1897 what has been called 'The Great Naval Race' was launched by the appointment of Alfred von Tirpitz as Secretary of State for German Naval Affairs. This was just ten years after the re-invigoration of the NID in London but in 1892 the NID had established its first overseas station in the Mediterranean, five years before Germany launched the 'Race'.

The NID staff were originally responsible for fleet mobilization and war plans as well as foreign intelligence collection; thus in the beginning there were originally two divisions: (1) Intelligence (Foreign) and (2) Mobilization. In 1900 another division, War, was added to deal with issues of strategy and defence, and in 1902 a fourth division, Trade, was created for matters related to the protection of merchant shipping. A coastal defence division was added in 1905 which took over duties related to intelligence on port and coastal defences of foreign powers. The Trade Division was abolished in 1909 in the wake of the Committee of Imperial Defence inquiry into the feud between the First Sea Lord, Admiral Sir John Fisher and former

---

1.   *See Annex B for an analysis of this affair.*

Eastney Barracks, 1907. This shows a visit by officers of the Japanese Imperial Navy.

Commander-in-Chief Channel Fleet, Admiral Lord Charles Beresford, when it was discovered that the captain heading the Trade Division had been supplying the latter with confidential information during the inquiry.

In 1910, the NID was shorn of its responsibility for war planning and strategy when the outgoing Fisher created the so-called Navy War Council as a stop-gap remedy to criticisms emanating from the Beresford Inquiry that the Navy needed a naval staff, a role the NID had in fact been fulfilling since at least 1900, if not earlier. After this reorganisation, war planning and strategic matters were transferred to the newly created Naval Mobilisation Department and the NID reverted back to the position it had held prior to 1887, an intelligence collection and collation organisation.

The importance of the NID early on was recognised to a degree that by 1902, under Rear Admiral Prince Louis of Battenberg, no issue within the Royal Navy was decided, no matter how trivial, without the NID having its say on the matter. It was in 1902 that Lord Selbourne, the First Lord of the Admiralty, commented, "If the German fleet became superior to ours, the German Army can conquer this country". During World War I the NID was responsible for the Royal Navy's highly successful cryptographic efforts.

It was in August of 1913 that Rear Admiral Henry Oliver (COS) was appointed Director of the Intelligence Division (DID) at the age of forty nine.

This was the senior division of the Naval Staff. Clever, able and a 'workaholic' he was to die at age one hundred, an Admiral of the Fleet. Oliver, one of the First Sea Lord Jacky Fisher's men, was the creator of Room 40, named after the number of the room in the Old Admiralty Building which was used by the Admiralty code-breakers. Room 40 has gone down in history not only for its incredible achievements in World War I but for its follow-ups, Bletchley Park Station X in World War II and for the Government Code & Cipher School (GC&CS). But this is in the future.

As Christopher Andrew has pointed out in his *Secret Service* book, there were certain failings in Oliver's performance, failings due to overwork, partly due to a reluctance to delegate. He quotes Stephen Roskill, the naval historian, on his book on *Admiral of the Fleet Earl Beatty* (1980) that Oliver, alerted by Hall, took steps against an Austrian wireless engineer, named A S, who was passing German code books to British Naval Intelligence[2]. Hall's fear was that the Germans might be alerted to the insecurity of their codes which would have been disastrous for Room 40. Towards the end of his long life Oliver several times told Roskill "I paid £1,000 to have that man shot". I quote this rather grim example to emphasise that it was not only signals intelligence (Sigint) and decrypts which concerned the NID. The lives of agents were sometimes perilous and while no evidence of such affairs exists in the case of Spain it is as well to be remembered that the world of the secret service has its darker aspects.

Oliver (known as 'Dummy' because of his taciturnity and, reputably, as being the worst dressed officer in the Navy), the creator of Room 40, had as his Deputy Captain Thomas Jackson (known as 'Old Art' or 'Tug') who had retired in 1912, aged seventy, but returned in 1914 on an unofficial and unpaid basis. Oliver then brought in Sir Alfred Ewing, the Director of Naval Education and a fellow member of the United Services Club. Ewing had a 'hobby' interest in ciphers and had developed what he called "a rather futile ciphering mechanism". Ewing was fifty nine, a brilliant engineer whose career included Edinburgh, Tokyo, Dundee and Cambridge Universities. His work on Magnetic Induction was rewarded with the Gold Medal of the Royal Society. He is known as the Father of Room 40.

He admitted to being woefully inadequate for the job. In the first few days of his appointment he prowled through "Lloyds, the GPO and the British Museum to see their collections of code books..." From these he "was able to glean...certain general notions..." He immediately saw this could not be a single-handed task and he picked out a thirty three year old Scot, Alastair Denniston, educated at the Sorbonne and Bonn Universities, who was a great athlete and had represented Scotland in hockey at the Olympic Games in 1908. In no time at all, Denniston was second in command and was, later, to lay the foundation of Bletchley Park where he was its chief until 1942. Two men then joined in: R D Norton, ex-Foreign Office, and Lord Herschell, aged thirty eight, Eton and Magdalen, Oxford who had a string of Royal Household appointments including Lord in Waiting to King George V, and

2. *See Chapter 8, The Szek Affair.*

an intimate knowledge of the less travelled parts of Persia. He was partly appointed for his linguistic abilities. After them came Charles Godfrey, the Headmaster of Osborne Naval College. The total staff at that time could be counted on the fingers of two hands and included Professor Anderson of Greenwich Naval College and Parish and Curtis, Naval Instructors, giving him a cryptographer team of six.

The operational structure under Oliver might be over-simply stated as Ewing, Denniston, Herschell, Godfrey and now Hall comes on the scene. He was made Director of Naval Intelligence in 1914 and was a walking genius, "the one genius the war has developed. Neither in fiction nor in fact can you find any such man to match him" wrote the American Ambassador to London, Dr Page, in a letter of March 1918 to President Wilson. Dr Page's extraordinary letter is quoted in full in Admiral Sir William James' *The Eyes of the Navy* and it is only by reading that account, *A Biographical Study of Admiral Sir Reginald Hall*, that a real appreciation of the man can be obtained[3]. Mention of his involvement with von Rintelen (*The Dark Invader*), Mata-Hari, the Zimmermann Telegram, Sir Roger Casement and the Battle of Jutland gives but a small indication of his scope. And it was to Hall that Thoroton was to directly report as he became responsible for Naval Intelligence in Spain and the Mediterranean from his base on Gibraltar.

William Reginald Hall was born in 1870 at Britford, Wiltshire. His father, Captain William Henry Hall RN was the first Director of the Intelligence Division at the Admiralty. He joined the *Brittania* in 1884, became a Lieutenant in 1891 and, after the Royal Naval College at Greenwich in 1892 he was at sea again in the *Australia*, rapidly becoming a senior Staff Officer at Whale Island and Commander in 1901. In 1908, at age thirty eight, he undertook his first espionage activity in an adventure reminiscent of Erskine Childers' 1903 *Riddle of the Sands*, a cruise along the German coastline to spy out the location of German forts and dockyards, their ship building capabilities and anything else of value. Indeed, their only knowledge of the Friesian coast was derived from this story, there were no up to date charts at Admiralty.

So successful was this assignment he was to instigate another, organising four of his officers on a three week walking tour to Borkum which commanded the deep-water approach to Emden with its shipbuilding (*Nordseewerke*) and the Ems-Dortmund and Ems-Jade canals, the latter giving access to the strategic Nord-Ostsee Kanal to Kiel.

Then he was back at sea, first on HMS *Natal*, then on HMS *Queen Mary* and other ships until the outbreak of war when he saw action under Beatty in the Heligoland Bight in August. Then, because of faulty health, he was found unable to command a battle cruiser and a telegram arrived appointing him DNI in November 1914. On arrival at Room 40 he found the small group of picked men under Ewing at work on intercepted German naval signals. It was not long before a string of talented and indeed brilliant individuals was

---

3. And now, David Ramsay's 'Blinker' Hall – Spymaster.

Gibraltar, The Mount. Posted 17 November 1915.

recruited by Hall. He had "a multitude of secret agents in covert operations around the globe" and Room 40 began to take off in a most spectacular way. In the end, by 1919, Room 40 would have read over 15,000 intercepted German messages.

Thoroton enters the scene

It was into this field of operations that Thoroton came to be inserted in 1913.

Here we can surmise that his fluency in French, wide reading and evidently high IQ were seen to qualify him for intelligence work. He was also steady, tactful, a hard worker, an all-rounder, someone who could be relied upon to carry out a task professionally. This was in some contrast to what Captain Compton Mackenzie RMLI himself described as 'gilded popinjays' living it up in GHQ or to such spies as Sydney Reilly who in Christopher Andrew's words suffered from an 'extraordinary range of personal fantasies'. Compton Mackenzie is described as "the complete egocentric" by John Coleby in his RMHS monograph *A Marine or Anything* where he writes that "the staff of MI1 rebelled over his appointment as C's Number 2". That all such men, such characters, had their valued contribution to make is gainsaid but they were never responsible for a huge area of operations.

Thoroton and Cumming may have met in circumstances more reminiscent of Mason's later description, in *The Summons*, of Martin Hillard's (Mason himself)[4] meeting with Commodore Graham (Admiral Sir Reginald Hall) "in the dingy house in the neighbourhood of Charing Cross after climbing many little flights of stairs (he) was

---

4. *Perhaps Mason created the name Hillard as a result of his acquaintance with Thoroton whose family was linked with the Hildyards.*

brought up outside a mean, brown-varnished door" It was here that Hillard meets "a thin man with the face of a French abbé" who says, "Bendish tells me that you know something of Spain". (Bendish is Professor Dixon). This could well have been 2, Whitehall Court[5].

The way in which the Thoroton Intelligence Network fitted in to the overall structure of the NID is, of course, the central core of this book. That his role was of crucial importance has been indicated by the quotation from Winston Churchill. Thoroton's significance, as Chief of Naval Intelligence for the whole of the Mediterranean throughout World War I, is again emphasised by Churchill's Point 3 note, already referred to, while the following chapter adds flesh to that rather bare bone. As will be seen, throughout this account, leading histories make reference to Thoroton but this book constitutes the first ever research in any depth on the man who, during his career, was known as Charles the Bold.

Given the size of the Corps only a few Marines were involved in intelligence work and given the nature of what they did not much exists in the record.

While Gib was to be his main operational base, Morocco was to be the scene of some of his earliest concerns. German infiltration of French Morocco from the Spanish zone had preceded 1913. Not only were RN communications centered on Gib, surveillance of enemy wireless traffic with Cueta and Mellila was also carried out. By 1914 German agents were everywhere, stirring up rebellions. The French had only a tiny garrison at Marrakesh and were surrounded by tribes loyal to the Lords of the Atlas, the generic title by which the House of Glaoui was known[6]. Colonel Mangin, who was Marshal Lyautey's officer commanding the troops at Safi, drew these Lords together on 2 August 1914 and persuaded them to support France. Lyautey's war in the Middle Atlas Massif and in the South was to continue throughout World War I.

With respect to the inauguration of the BNI services in Spain, Garcia Sanz has written[7] that it actually constituted the first modern intelligence system whose wide powers gave it a very special nature. There was no precedent at organisational or institutional levels and it took shape in a network of "mobile agents" along the coast and a structure of management for commercial information which clearly showed that much FO work was under the control of BNI. By January 1916, the FO's *New Rules for the Secret Services* sanctioned the autonomous status of the BNI in Spain which also resulted in the FO Information Service "being swallowed up by the NID". This was an unprecedented development in the British secret services. "Concentration of power from the Gibraltar Centre appeared unstoppable". This was quickly followed by Military Intelligence being subsumed by the NID at Gibraltar.

---

5. *"'Blinker' Hall had a genius for picking people"* (Rankin, *Churchill's Wizards*).
6. See Gavin Maxwell, *Lords of the Atlas*.
7. *Ref Thoroton.pdf 14 February 2012, Garcia Sanz to author.*

Chapter 5
The Secret War: Gibraltar, the Iberian Peninsula and the Barbary Coast

Every schoolboy knew, in those days, that much of the world's surface was coloured red in the atlases. However, the actual statistics are even more telling. There are many different assessments of the numbers involved but Niall Ferguson gives the following in his 2004 book *Empire*[1]: for 1909, he gives 350,000,000 alien people, about one quarter of the world's population, and one quarter of the world's land surface. Britain also dominated almost all the oceans and seas. The French Empire came second but the scramble for empire went on; France and such countries as Germany, the Netherlands, Spain, Portugal and Belgium all participating. The Maghreb saw French incursions starting in the 18th century in Algeria and Tunisia and in Morocco in 1902 leading to Lyautey's invasion of the country by occupying Oujda in 1907, following the murder of Dr Mauchamp in Marrakesh and the slaughter of Europeans in Casablanca[2].

Morocco was a country rich in natural resources (it held 75% of the world's supply of phosphates), its Sultans, Caids and Kings possessed untold wealth bolstered by massive French loans and gifts.

Morocco itself is part of what the Arabs of the Middle East call 'The Island of the Maghreb' which means 'Western Land', that vast expanse between Egypt and the Atlantic coast. Anthropologists have sometimes thought it is not actually a part of Africa but really an extension of Europe and its inhabitants to be of white Mediterranean stock but little affected by the invading Arabs.

The chaotic and continually horrific history of the country is beyond the scope of this account but it needs to be noted that German secret agents were behind the agitation of 1907, the chief of the German Secret Service, Herr Holtzmann in Marrakesh, being the prime culprit. German agents were at work before and after 1907. The Kaiser's visit was in 1905[3]. The Sultan, with whom Thoroton was to become closely allied, was Moulay Youssef (1882-1927) who had become Sultan in 1912. The French, under Lyautey, employed him to pacify the south: "We must do nothing to compromise the success of the Great Caids, or to be compromised by their lack of it" wrote Lyautey.

---

1. *Niall Ferguson is described by The Times as "The most brilliant historian of his generation".*
2. *QUID, 2001.*
3. *QUID, 2001.*

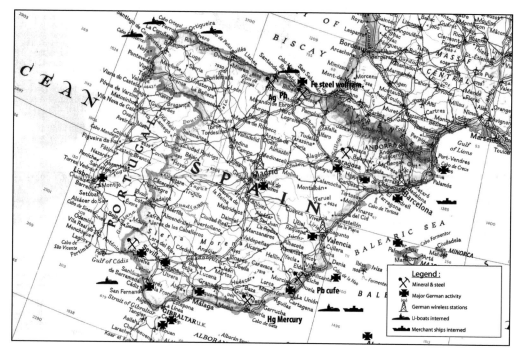

Spain & Portugal

Bitter fighting continued throughout the First World War, bolstered by modern French weaponry enabling the Caids to rule as despots. Nevertheless Lyautey's policy had genuinely been that of a Protectorate.

At that time Pétain was Vice-President of the *Conseil Supérieur de la Guerre* in Paris. He was sent to Morocco by the government to institute a policy of 'destroying' the people rather then 'winning over' the people which had been Lyautey's policy all along. When this became clear to Lyautey he had no choice but to leave as he did in 1925. He was succeeded by Théodore Steeg, former Prime Minister of France and Governor-General of Algeria, a total Colonialist who reduced the Sultan Youssef to puppet status.

Against this background Thoroton's liaison with the French in Morocco, and his French and Moroccan decorations, can be seen in clearer perspective. (See Chapter 8).

Winston Churchill never harboured any doubts on the importance of Spain in a European war. He quotes the Duke of Wellington in 1820: "There can be no country in Europe in the affairs of which foreigners can interfere with so little advantage as those of Spain. There is no country in which foreigners are so much disliked, even despised, and whose manners and habits are so little congenial with those of other countries in Europe". Churchill himself, writing of World War II, says, "Spain held the key to all British enterprises in the Mediterranean, and never in the darkest hour did she turn the lock against us". Britain then, as in the Great War, had need of trade with Spain, the denial of her ports to enemy

Camp in the Rif. Lyautey and an unidentified companion.

submarines, and especially of her iron ore from ports on the Bay of Biscay. That he could write that Spain never did "turn the lock against us" tracks back to the activities of Hillgarth, March and many others, inheritors of the Network.

The Spain of those days is hard to imagine. As readers of Laurie Lee and Gerald Brenan will know, it was a poverty-stricken, badly governed country, many of its streets filled with beggars, gypsies, even twelve year old children barefooted and naked; half-wits and amputees.

Bilbao, the scene of some significant events in the story of Naval Intelligence in Spain in World War I, was already a major iron and steel centre, its river, the Nervion, crossed by five bridges. Vessels of up to 4,000 tons could enter its harbour where, even after the war, many of the stevedores were women.

We show a photograph of a line of women carrying heavy baskets on their heads down a ramp formed of wooden planks and under the watchful eyes of armed *Guardia*. Cartegena, a city of over 100,000 at that time, exported lead, copper and iron, much of it transported from the mines by donkey cart. Asturia was, and is, the great mining centre of Spain and also the centre for its worst labour troubles. Iron, coal and copper (mined by Rio Tinto under British control) supplied some two million tons a year, about a quarter of the world's supply. Lead, zinc, manganese, cobalt and sulphur yielded fortunes during the Great War, as did Spain's famed leather industry. Railways, few and far between, were built and controlled by foreign firms and remained inadequate. Communications were difficult and life was hard. Malaga, where Thoroton was to make his home on retirement from the Marines, was famed for its wines and was beautifully located. The roads were poor and if he used the single track railway from Algeciras or Gibraltar he would have had to wander up to Bobadilla in the *Sierra de Yeguas*, some forty miles to the north.

Cartagena at the time of the Grat War. Mule carts unloading lead, copper and iron.

Bilbao, women unloading a steamer in the port, Great War period.

On 7 August 1914 Portugal proclaimed allegiance to the Allies and on 23 November 1914 wished to take action against Germany using its bases on the African continent, particularly in Mozambique. The British government requested Portugal to seize German ships in Portuguese ports and Germany declared war on Portugal on 9 March. The war was to have dire consequences for Portugal: food and fuel scarcities quickly arose; she suffered heavy casualties in Africa and on the Western Front; a great part of the officer corps became alienated from the cause; crippling debts were incurred with Britain; and very little compensation came to be paid by Germany at the war's end. Corruption, violence, bankruptcies and military insurrections followed until the Salazar regime established the *Estato Novo* in the 1920s and 1930s.

In Spain a similar situation prevailed. As a result of the war wages declined, erupting in the Great Barcelona Strike of 1919, the most spectacular in Spanish history. This was accompanied by a wave of assassinations by criminal gangsters employed and paid for by both the anarchists and by the employers who had profited greatly from the war. Towards the end the Unions were agitating for change and disillusioned junior officers were forming juntas. The Anarco-Syndicalist movement achieved great power and employed a terrorist wing to challenge the employers.

Similarly, the Balearic Islands, Morocco and the Barbary Coast remained deeply backward at this time. Majorca was also to benefit from the Great War. New industrial organisations sprang up, accompanied inevitably with strikes and labour unrest. Bankers and lawyers replaced the old landed families as the powers on the island.

And now the great rock of Gibraltar comes into view.

Britain had been installed in Gibraltar since 1713 under the Treaty of Utrecht,

GIBRALTAR — Governor's Cottage and Europa Point

Gibraltar, Governor's Cottage and Europa Point, 1915

having captured the Rock in 1704 during the War of the Spanish Succession. By 1881 it was a neutral zone, subsidised by Britain, and then a British territory becoming a centre for smuggling and contraband against the interests of Spain. (Indeed, it remains so even to today, the Spanish government protesting in the 1990s against Gibraltar as a centre for smuggling, drug trafficking and money laundering.)

In 1895 the British established a submarine base on Gib and in 1908 constructed a wall separating it from the rest of Spain. Several of Thoroton's postcards from Gib portray it as it was at that time.

Spain had been involved in violent conflicts in Morocco, starting in the 1860s and then near Melilla in the 1890s. Under the *Entente Cordiale* of 1904 between Britain and France, Spain was allocated the smaller, northern part, France the southern. Morocco was, at that time, backward, lawless and ripe for European interests which centred mainly on the iron mines of Mount Uixan and on the lead mines. By 1909 the Spanish Army was suffering serious set-backs and, with 40,000 of its soldiers in Morocco, was faced with a military position far beyond its financial capabilities. There were hostile repercussions at home: strikes in Barcelona; the *Semana Tragica*, fifty churches were burned down; criminals and prostitutes attacked nunneries, killing and disinterring bodies; some 120 died. A violent Spain lay beneath the surface of constitutional rule. The war in Morocco continued, unsuccessfully.

The Treaty of Fez was signed in 1912 by Sultan Moulay Youssef (1882-1927, Sultan from 1912) described as "an indolent Sultan" who was as critical of these arrangements as were his own people and a lot of people in Spain. Many concessions

Caravan halt, sketch by Lyautey.

passed to the "Mines from the Rif", a foreign company. Because of the mines' remoteness a railway had to be constructed to Melilla. However the Moroccan people resented the French and Spanish occupation and Youssef's reign was marked with frequent revolts, so much so that he was obliged to transfer his court from Fez to Rabat. This resentment existed in Spain also. Tangier was made an international city and port in 1912.

In Spain, José Canalejas's government of 1910-1912 had made some progress on Catalonia; taxation revisions for the poor; a compromise with the Church; and by abolishing the system whereby the rich could buy themselves out of military service. As a result he was assassinated by an anarchist in 1912.

Thus, 1912 saw a hopeless war for Spain in Morocco, a simmering class war at home and the assassination of the head of government. Religious practice was declining. Morocco was divided between France and Spain who were exploiting its mineral resources and creating tribal wars against themselves culminating in the Rif War of 1921-1927, also known as the War of Melilla.

Into this Spanish serpents' pit steps Major C J Thoroton, RMLI, charged by the Admiralty with setting up an effective British intelligence service.

English perceptions of the secret war

The so-called 'spy fever' which had erupted in England in the late 19th century certainly influenced Thoroton himself. It was in the early years of the twentieth century that the industrial and military rivalry between Germany and Britain intensified dramatically. This has been ably documented by Paul Kennedy in his 1980 book *The Rise of Anglo-German Antagonism, 1860-1914*. Global hegemony was the lodestar. Spy fever was in the air in Britain, fanned by such writers as George Chesney (1871), William Le Queux (1894), Headon Hill (1899), E Phillips Oppenheim, John Buchan and others.

Le Queux's *The Great War in England in 1897* (published in 1894) was backed by Lord Roberts, Britain's leading military authority who then collaborated with Le Queux in *The Great Invasion of 1910*, published in 1906. Oppenheim also brought in the role of the secret societies, some of which were said to serve supra-national interests, thus over-riding national patriotism, which raises the role of Freemasonry in espionage and the use of double-agents. Buchan was to echo this later in *The Power House*, published in 1920, and Buchan's Bullivant in *Greenmantle* is said to be based on his personal acquaintance with Hall. Unquestionably Thoroton would have been familiar with this literature, all of which was in popular demand in the period leading up to his appointment as Chief Naval Intelligence Officer for the Mediterranean in 1913.

And here I must declare my hand since for much of the foregoing I am indebted to David Thomas and his masterly Introduction in the Oxford World's Classic series of Erskine Childers' *The Riddle of the Sands – A Record of Secret Service*, first published in 1903. Mention has already been made of this book in the context of Captain Hall's use of the Walker & Cockerell maps and charts for his 1908 espionage mission along the German coast to Kiel. How close *The Riddle of the Sands* comes to reality, in its depiction of a planned German invasion of England from the East Friesland channels and estuaries, only became known when research, undertaken in 1980, was reported by Paul Kennedy in his article in *The Times* of 3 January 1981. This research reveals that German naval archives contained plans for the invasion of England which were first drafted in 1896.

In his Chapter 3, Spy Fever of *Churchill and Secret Service*, David Stafford makes reference to the danger to the South Wales coal fields posed by possible enemy agents. South Wales coal was essential to the Royal Navy, the mines being owned by Lord Bute (of whom more later in the context of the Spanish Civil War). This report dates from 1912.

We cannot say to what extent, if any, the actualities of potential German aggression against England were known to Thoroton. We have found no record of such in the available activities of Room 40, nor in Patrick Beesley's authoritative book of that name, but his chronicle begins in 1914. Certainly, Thoroton would have been familiar with the writings of Le Queux and others and fully aware of the climate of public opinion created by that generation of spy writers. In addition, Thoroton would certainly have been informed of the activities of people like Holtzmann in Marakesh six years earlier.

BNI staffing and individuals

In Spain the Ambassador Sir Arthur Hardinge had overall, if seemingly remote, control of the SIS. Pérez-Gruesco, in her paper[4] describes Gibraltar as of "fundamental importance" for three reasons: first, it controlled the Strait of Gibraltar; second, it exerted control over Portugese interests in Madeira, Cape Verde and the Azores and extended its reach into the Atlantic Ocean; third, it opened up on important sea passages with the USA. Her organigram gives Sir Arthur Hardinge; Sir Percy Lorraine, First Secretary; and Lord Herschell, Admiralty War Staff Intelligence. Colonel Thoroton is then listed as being charged with setting up the Gibraltar base for intelligence and espionage. As Gibraltar was outside the jurisdiction of Spain, this gave him great liberty of action. He was in secret correspondence with Percy Lorraine with whom he elaborated his "black list". She comments that the Naval Attachés of

---

4. See Dolores Pérez-Gruesco, *Los Servicios de Inteligencia Britanicos en España Durante la Primera Guerra Mundial* in Revista de Historia Militar.

A E W Mason, the prolific thriller writer who was one of CJT's most effective agents in Spain and Morocco.

other countries established contact with Thoroton rather than with Lorraine, by-passing him in this respect. The primary targets for BNI were the submarine war and surveillance of German activities along the Spanish coast.

Back in London, as we have seen, in the Admiralty we have essentially Oliver, Ewing, Denniston and Hall. In Gibraltar the SNO (Senior Naval Officer) is Vice Admiral Frederick E E Brock CB. In Spain Thoroton had working with and for him a number of agents. Included are A E W Mason, thriller writer and Royal Marine officer; Gerald Kelly (later Sir Gerald Kelly, President of the Royal Academy); Commander Maurice Mitchell RNR, in Bilbao, Spain; Lieutenant Dawson RNR, at San Sebastian, Spain; and Lieutenant Commander G H Pierce RNR at St Jean-de-Luz in France.

From Churchill's "brilliant confederacy" statement we were made aware of the existence of unidentified Network agents. Now, for the first time, research has uncovered some these hidden heroes and, honour where honour is due, we can reveal at least some names.

Navy Lists for the period 1914-1918 throw considerable light on the Gibraltar set-up. Officially designated as HMS *Cormorant* (a late sloop of 1,130 tons with 2 x 7" muzzle-loading guns and 4 x 64 pdr rifled muzzle-loading guns, which became a receiving ship at Gibraltar in 1889 and later renamed HMS *Rook* in 1946) it was commanded, in 1914, by Vice Admiral Brock who had taken charge on 20 September 1912. It had a roll call of fifty seven officers including three RNR Lieutenants on 'Special Service'.

Thoroton is ranked third after Brock, having arrived 12 September 1913. The full complement includes submarines, torpedo boats and shore gunnery. In 1914, three submarines were operating out of Gib (B6, B7 & B8) but after this no details are given, probably for security reasons.

A major RM, Richard Willis, had been appointed 1 March 1912 'for W/T Station', indicating the first Royal Marine involvement in wireless telegraphy on the Rock. Four other RMs are listed for 'services at Ascension' but none at Gibraltar. But these Navy Lists do not seem to be complete as a Memorandum of 1918-1926 in the NA gives Lt Cdr A T Blackwood as Thoroton's number two and Miss Mahony as his secretary. In 1915 there were six 'Special Service' RNR officers. In 1916 these had increased to forty one and Major Thoroton had risen to "Tempy. Lt-Col General Staff Officer 1st Grade" as in the original text. One of the RNVR officers working for Thoroton was Lieutenant Frederick Bruce. (See Mason's N° 7 Report in Chapter 8.)

1917 sees the addition of Captain R Yeo Moritz, RM on 4 April, as someone reporting directly to Thoroton. Out of a total roll call of eighty, thirty four are on 'Special Service'. Thoroton now has a RM staff of two.

In 1918, Moritz is still there and Thoroton has added Major Gerald R S Hickson, a 1st grade General Staff Officer, (later to become Lieutenant General Sir Gerald Hickson KCVO, CB, CBE, DL) and 2nd Lieutenant Charles Foster. Thus a Royal Marine staff of four is involved: Willis, Moritz, Hickson and Foster. These are all now listed under 'Administrative Branch' and 'Special Services' has become 'Special Duties'. A total roll call of one hundred and thirty pertained in 1918. Willis was the longest serving officer (1912) followed by Thoroton who had been appointed just eight days prior to Admiral Brock's arrival. We cannot tell how many of the 'Special Services' officers may have been involved in intelligence work. Might not Willis, Moritz, Hickson and Foster also qualify for inclusion in Churchill's "brilliant confederacy"? In Malta Major Lampen RM was collecting U-Boat call signs and enemy signal and cipher books[5].

Fuller details of some of the Network's agents are available from Vincennes. In Seville, Cadiz, Huelva, Malaga and Almeria we find Lt Kelly, RN, Lt Bleck (Military), R G Hempson, Lt Scaniglia, Lt Patron, Lt Weston and Lt Walsh plus Maj Hickson and Capt Douglas.

Working for Thoroton was Captain John Harvey RN. He was summoned by the Admiralty in December 1917 from Gibraltar to Madrid as Naval Attaché, arriving there in March 1918. In the Embassy he became responsible for the co-ordination of Intelligence missions in Spain, for which task he was well-prepared thanks to his experience in Gibraltar[6]. In another paper, *Les Relations Entre la Grande-Bretagne et l'Espagne pendant la Première Guerre Mondiale par le bias des Services des Renseignements*[7] Pérez-Gruesco explains in greater depth the complex role to be fulfilled by Captain Harvey.

Harvey's role, as Flag Captain, was directly concerned with ship movements. His mission was to co-ordinate the French and Italian secret services with those of Great Britain, an activity in which he was highly successful. In this he was supported by Lt Oliver Baring whose conspicuous qualities were recorded by Thoroton and by Ambassador Hardinge[8]. This co-ordination programme had become necessary as the French secret services had been rather struggling since their inception in May 1916, and the Italians since March of the same year. The French became confused by the double-game BNI was playing, especially with regard to Juan March's smuggling and co-operation with the Germans.

5. See Beesley, op cit.
6. Revista, op cit.
7. Guerres Mondiales et Conflits Contemporains, Revue d'Histoire, France, No. 226.
8. Garcia Sanz, op cit.

That March was detailing safe anchorages and caves for U-Boats in the Balearic Islands and ferrying their agents into Morocco was the basis by which BNI could identify, and so neutralise, German efforts in these fields. The French only became fully aware of March's role in 1918.

Thoroton's HQ staff was rather small in number, even if it seems to be in line with Churchill's 1 May 1914 memorandum, but his Network was very extensive, amounting to some 40,000 agents[9], almost all in the Iberian peninsula and Morocco. The restricted staff number reflects other well known examples. R V Jones, in his *Most Secret War*, writes:

> 'It has been part of our policy to keep the staff to its smallest possible limits consistent with safety, because the larger the field any one man can cover, the more chance there is of those fortunate correlations which only occur when one brain and one memory can connect two or more remotely gathered facts. Moreover, a large staff generally requires so much administration that its head has little chance of real work himself, and he cannot therefore speak with that certainty which arises only from intimate contact with the facts.'

He goes on to remark that it was "an encouraging experience to find just how much a few individuals can do, and how even a single individual can be more effective than a large organisation". Janet Adam Smith, in her biography of John Buchan, highlights how A E W Mason in his novels (based on his secret service work) often features how "one man, or a small group of men, takes on hopeless odds", a characteristic of Buchan's own novels. As well as the names so far recorded, we may add that of Mr Winch, a civilian, who also features in our archives. Cumming thought there might be "about 50 "staff and agents in the Admiralty network in Spain[10].

In Bilbao was Commander Maurice Mitchell RNR. However, it was through Lieutenant Commander Pierce, RNR, in St-Jean-de-Luz, just over the Pyrénées in France, that Thoroton and his team reported to the head of the British Naval Mission in Paris, Commander Edward Heaton-Ellis, and then to Lord Herschell as personal assistant to Hall, Herschell having been put in charge of Spanish and Spanish American affairs. Thoroton established "excellent relations" with Lord Herschell and worked with him on the development of the secret services in Spain which culminated in the creation there of "one of the most active" of such British services in WW I[11]. Paymaster Lloyd Hirst was by then Head of the NID's Latin American section. Some of these men were to become involved in the *Erri Berro* adventure. As events built up Thoroton came to be more and more in direct liaison with Hall.

9. *Admiral Sir William James, The Eyes of the Navy, p 107. A large part of these 40.000 men were employees of Juan March.*

10. *Keith Jeffrey, MI 6.*

11. *SHM, Vincennes, Garcia Sanz op cit.*

New infra-structure and methods

The exact scope and nature of Thoroton's intelligence network is elusive, much of it unrecorded or, at the very least, still under security embargo. Many records have been destroyed, many doors remain firmly closed and securely locked. Little of the available published accounts of his activities, limited as they are, give any clues as to who or where his agents were located. NA papers document Bilbao, Vigo, Barcelona, Seville, Cadiz, Malaga and the Canary Islands as primary centres for the Network in Spain. Many other cities and towns in Spain, including the Balearic Islands, are listed in various documents. To these must be added St-Jean-de-Luz in France; Fez, Tangiers and Rabat in Morocco and a number of towns along the North African coast. Lisbon in Portugal and Malta are also featured. That said, it is certain that Thoroton's spy network in Spain and his intelligence services in Morocco were his greatest achievements. The accompanying maps help to pick out the major centres of activity.

Also in 1915 Thoroton created a new infra-structure for his Network of agents involving three types of informants: "naturals", that is members of the British colony in Spain; "sympathisers", Spaniards and other nationals supportive of the Allied cause for ideological or economic reasons; "professionals" such as those whose work took them onto the quaysides and into ports.

In Hall's unpublished autobiography he outlined the methods employed in gathering intelligence. This is of direct interest to the Thoroton Network as it details the principles under which it operated. We have his literary estate's permission to reproduce this text which is available in the Churchill Archives at Churchill College, Cambridge, particularly ref Hall 2/1 *Intelligence in Wartime*. Hall's Forward to *Strange Intelligence - Memories of Naval Secret Service* by Hector Bywater and H C Ferraby, is full of enthusiasm for "...this fine...Great Game". This 1931 book is notable as it gives a good description of the *modus operandi* of the Base Intelligence Officers. These used wireless direction finding stations to decrypt enemy signals; plot the positions of U-Boats; and to track their movements. Admiral Sir William James' 1955 biography of Hall gives the origins of this development, which began in 1915 and which was extended by the Marconi company. Churchill himself visited Room 40 to congratulate the staff there on their achievements.

In June 1917, the busiest German submarine month, twenty seven U-Boats were located in the North Sea and Atlantic; thirteen in the Channel; fifteen in the Med; three in the Baltic; and two in the Black Sea. We also know that the "Allies developed an extensive network of direction finding centres and stations in the Med"[12]. Of these, eleven centres and fourteen stations were British; twenty were Italian; and fourteen were French.

All the literature shows that, in the words of Christopher Andrew in his *Secret Service –The Making of the British Intelligence Service*, "The main focus of Hall's covert

---

12. *Paul Halpern, Naval War in the Mediterranean 1914-1918.*

action, however, was Spain". Indeed, Thoroton's Spanish intelligence network was to persist and "reach its zenith", according to one authority, in World War II, through the Governor General Mason MacFarlane in Gibraltar itself, under Admiral John Godfrey, DNI, 1939-1943[13]. This network, based on Spain but linking closely with Morocco, and other parts of what might be termed Thoroton's Mediterranean Theatre, proved to be a far more reliable source than the Spanish government's own police and civil authorities in supplying information on what was going on in their own country. We know that Juan March, Thoroton's ace-in-the-hole, was a continuing ally of Britain up to and including the Second World War. David Stafford adds a curious rider to this certainty in his *Cavalry of St. George* chapter of *Roosevelt and Churchill*. I quote: "An intriguing post-war chapter to this story suggests that Juan March's links with British Intelligence, and perhaps even with Churchill himself, long outlived the war". This quote derives from Doris Kearns Goodwin's *No Ordinary Times* concerning a passage between Churchill and Eleanor Roosevelt at a war-time dinner in London.

There is reason to believe that the inheritors of this British intelligence service persist to this very day and this is an important contributory element to the 'locked doors' which still surround Thoroton's work.

Gibraltar, 1914 or 1915. CJT with Mr Winch (left) and Commander John Harvey (right).

13. *Richard Deacon, A History of the British Secret Service.*

Chapter 6
The Thoroton Network environment

I
n analysing intercepted enemy messages and interpreting innumerable, dissociated parcels of information from many different sources, the ability to link the apparently irrelevant into comprehensible sequences in a chain is of crucial importance. For this reason, Naval Intelligence in the Med sometimes also linked with events in America and Mexico.

It is also the case that some well-known figures, such as Mata-Hari and Wilhelm Canaris, were involved in this intelligence war along with those who are relatively unknown, such as Juan March and the Sultan Moulay Youssef who turn out to be as significant, or even more significant, than some of the better known names.

In July 1915 Thoroton wrote to Arthur Hardinge the British Ambassador in Madrid a firm description of the structure of his Network[1]:

"The scheme outlined in your letter has already been organised with the exception of the officer at Madrid and I was under the impression that Abinger[2] has told you of it. The details at present are: Head of organisation – myself at Gibraltar: North of Spain – In charge Blackwood, assistant Sullivan: 1 yacht due end of this month. South of Spain – In charge Abinger, assistants at Huelva, Seville, Malaga (post already filled). Cartagena (post already filled). Valencia (post already filled). Barcelona (post already filled), and 1 yacht. In both cases minor agents are employed, as requisite."

Thoroton employed the "War Code" as a further safeguard for security, a code shared with the FO and British Consuls[3].

'Blinker' Hall and the yacht Vergemere

From the start of the war Spain was divided in its support: to some extent anti-French, some public opinion pro-British, some pro-German. German commercial influences were strong. Madrid, with its links to Latin America, was a hotbed for spies of both the Entente and Central Powers. Spain was neutral and like neutrals generally hoped to end up on the winning side. In French North Africa the local, nationalist movements, a new phenomenon, were active against French interests and were encouraged by German agents and certainly not looked down on by the

---

1. NA, FO 185/1253, Garcia Sanz, op cit.
2. The 5th Baron Abinger was Shelley Leopold Lawrence Scarlett (1872-1917). He had served as a Major in the Bedfordshire Regt with great honour and then as Commander in the RNVR, later with BNI.
3. The First World War, Misc War Papers, secret copy of SNO al Gobernador Militar de Gibraltar, 30 August 1915, quoted Garcia Sanz.

Spanish who saw here an opportunity to increase their sphere of interest in Morocco and Tangier. In Madrid the German Embassy's wireless link with Berlin tied in with a worldwide communication system; this link was already under surveillance by Room 40. Hall recognised that knowledge of German activity in Spain and in Latin America, and indeed what the Spanish government itself was thinking, was of crucial significance and he decided that he needed more men on the spot around the Iberian Peninsula.

His first move was to organise the cruise of the yacht *Vergemere* under Sir Hercules Langrishe, an Irish baronet, handsome, brilliant at any sport, an MFH and a skilled helmsman. Money was no object, the C in C Portsmouth helped him to choose a crew of naval ratings and crates of champagne were loaded aboard. Langrishe was to be an eccentric British gentleman, perhaps rather flamboyant but nobody's fool. Lavish parties were to be given on board to convince the Germans and the Spanish that there were no shortages at home. Hall insisted that he turn on the charm with any ladies who might come aboard.

Cruising around the Spanish coasts Langrishe soon found out that the Germans were playing a similar game except from a steamer which never left port for fear of British submarines. Also, the Germans were restricted to beer for their entertaining, Berlin being rather stingy. Langrishe also investigated the attitude of the coastal population and fishermen to determine whether they were likely to assist the Germans in their plans for submarine bases. From the extensive information collected, Hall was convinced that he needed to keep an extra eye on things Spanish and this led to the addition of an on-the-sea man to supplement Thoroton on-the-land. The on-the-sea man was Mason (now a Captain in the Royal Marines) appointed in 1915 by which time Thoroton's Network was well bedded-in. Mason's first cruise was on the *Vergemere* in Spanish waters, the Balearic Islands and to Morocco until 1916. Unfortunately he left no record of his adventures although later notes, one entitled 'Gibraltar Dec 2/1916', survives and he is said to have "produced a regular digest containing detailed information of disaffection amongst the workforce and of strikes fomented by German agents". Elsewhere he writes some notes on the interception of anthrax bacilli, concealed in shaving brushes.

Mason's December notes were written after a spell of leave as he was "on his way home to England in October 1916", stopping off in Paris in order to be present at the execution of Mata-Hari. From England he sailed in Lord Abinger's yacht *St George*, a large yacht with a crew of fifty four. On board was a Herbert Sullivan and W E Dixon, Regius Professor of Pharmacology at Cambridge University, and a number of glamorous ladies to add verisimilitude. On course for Gibraltar they put in at Cadiz and, at Gibraltar, he left for Barcelona. There he seems to have been occupied on "humdrum lines" and, by the end of the year, "his usefulness in (Morocco and Spain) had come to an end". He returned to England in June 1917 on leave and for a lengthy spell of adventure writing. There is no history of any other activity in 1917, other than one or two jobs in home waters, until on 19 October he sets out for Mexico via

Washington DC (5 November) and so passes out of our immediate interest at this stage of the story[4].

The Mata-Hari tragedy

With reference to Mata-Hari (whose name means *Eye of the Morning)* she was actually Margareta Gertrude Zelle, born in Holland in 1876 of a Dutch father and a Javanese mother. At the age of twenty she married a Dutch naval officer of Scottish extraction named MacLeod, a marriage which did not endure for long and by 1905 she was an acknowledged dancer of exotic Indian dances in Paris. Berlin, London and Rome were soon to see her sometimes naked performances and innumerable high placed individuals were paying heavily for her services[5]. In July 1915 she was in Madrid, consorting with members of the German secret service, a fact undoubtedly discovered by the Thoroton Network. Early in 1916 she was returning to Holland but, putting in at Falmouth, she was taken ashore and interrogated by Hall. Failing to elucidate any incriminating evidence, Hall blocked her planned return to Germany and sent her back to Spain where it seems she remained until 1917 when she left for France. In France she was arrested, tried and executed by firing squad. Her complicated and unclear history is well described, in English writings, in Philip Knightley's *The Second Oldest Profession* but William James' account (in his *The Eyes of the Navy)* is also informative.

Further information on Mata-Hari surfaced in the Pforzheimer Collection at Yale University. MSS 489, Box 20 revealed that the idea of using this internationally celebrated dancer as a German agent came from Baron von Mirbach in 1916. Von Mirbach was head of Section IIIb in Berlin and he instructed the renowned Dr Elisabeth Schragmüller, head of IIIb in Antwerp, to install

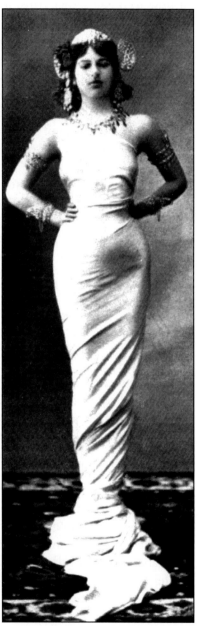

Mata-Hari, Agent No H-21 for the Germans who was betrayed to the French when the Germans discovered she was a double-agent working for the French. Shot by a firing squad at Vincennes, 15 October 1917.

---

4.   Lancelyn Green, A E W Mason.

5.   Certain writers record that she was never naked, actually wearing a body stocking for her dances.

Mata-Hari in the Hotel Frankfurter Hof in Frankfurt-am-Main and to train her on how to organise her trips, in observation techniques, report writing, the use of invisible ink and other matters. She became agent H-21. The Collection includes a letter from the German Military Attaché in Madrid asking Berlin to pay her for services rendered. Several photographs of her are in the Collection, some beautifully dressed, some beautifully undressed. She was certainly not lacking in courage: she refused to be blindfolded at her execution. As a footnote to this came an account of the proposed permanent Mata-Hari Museum to follow from the 1996 Exhibition held in her home town of Leeuwarden in the Netherlands. The Exhibition closed in 1998 and the idea of a museum was abandoned but a Mata-Hari Room is now open in the Frisian Museum.

Mata-Hari is rather "written off" by not a few historians of the secret service. Deacon, in his book, gives the opinion that she was "an extremely inefficient spy" but provides no evidence in support of his statement, whereas Knightly in his *The Second Oldest Profession* is rather more complimentary and even prepared to print her picture, understandably given her exceptional beauty. The mystery of Mata-Hari has taken a long time to be unravelled and could only be finally revealed in 2001. Even so recent a work as Andrew's 2009 *The Defence of the Realm* relies on a 1986 book by R W Howe which is at odds with later evidence. Howe recounts how a MI5 liaison officer read the Mata-Hari file at the French War Ministry and how French military intelligence had told MI5 "she had confessed to working for the Germans". Thus are myths perpetuated.

In 1915 Rex Benson, one of the "Golden Lads" and a cousin of Stewart Menzies (C of SIS), had been transferred from the 9th Lancers to the *Bureau Interallié*, the headquarters of the Allied counter espionage service. It was there that he is said (by Cave Brown in his life of Stewart Menzies) to have arranged the capture of Mata-Hari, although this does not appear elsewhere. It may be noted here that she was a double agent and it is certain that no concrete evidence of her enmity to France was produced at her court-martial on 24-25 July or subsequently. "There was not a shred of evidence that Mata-Hari had ever given the Germans any evidence at all, a fact that the French finally admitted in 1932 when the head of the *Conseil de Guerre*, Colonel Lacroix, read the file and announced that it contained "no tangible, absolute, irrefutable evidence". (Paul Allard in Knightly, op. sit.)

Her trial and execution bear all the hallmarks of a political cover-up. She slept with French Cabinet ministers and with German officers, amongst the former, probably the Minister of the Interior, M Malvy, or the Minister of War, General Messimy. It was the initial 'M', found in her diaries, which led to these two possible identifications. M Malvy was responsible for the *Carnet B*, the list of suspects to be arrested in an emergency situation and which had nearly been invoked following the assassination of Jean Jaurès in 1914. If it was General Messimy as Minister of War his would have been an even more dangerous liaison with Mata-Hari. Messimy was a violent man with a loud voice and "bright peasant eyes behind spectacles".

He had resigned from the army in protest against its refusal to reopen the Dreyfus case and he went into politics in order to reconcile the army with the nation. As Minister he inaugurated a dramatic programme of reform and had invited Gallieni to be Chief of the General Staff. Finally forced out of office during the great retreat of the French army, under the hammer blows of von Kluck's Army of one million German soldiers, he departed as a Major and served at the front until 1918, rising to General of a Division.

It had been the NID in Madrid who had reported on Mata-Hari's association with suspected German agents, thus bringing her activities to the notice of Charles the Bold. His agent, Mason, even took the vicarious trouble of attending her death by firing squad but we can find no evidence for his reason for doing so[6].

Behind the Mata-Hari legend lies a complex web of conflicting interests and it was only when Léon Schirmann published his 2001 work, *Mata-Hari: Autopsie d'une Machination* with its accompanying *Dossier Secret du Conseil de Guerre*, directed by Jean-Pierre Turbergue under the joint title *Mata-Hari – Espion ou Victime?* that the truth emerged. Schirmann's meticulous examination of all the relevant extant documents, and his painstaking examination of the truth and falsehood therein, throws the most clear light on the exotic and mysterious career of this famed dancer turned spy. It is clearly demonstrated that Mata-Hari, at the age of 41, was immolated on falsified evidence as a sacramental victim to save the crumbling reputation of the French government and military leaders. However, it is the sections concerning Spain during the period 1916 to 1917 which relate to British Intelligence interests in Madrid, Barcelona, Malaga, San Sebastian, Vigo and Lisbon in Portugal which involve the Thoroton Network.

British Intelligence first involved itself with Mata-Hari in November 1915 when she was intercepted on a voyage from Holland to Dieppe. Nothing incriminating was discovered and Scotland Yard passed this information to the French Intelligence Service. (Scotland Yard note reference MI5 E61207). Later she left Paris and travelled via Portugal to Spain, arriving first in Barcelona and then in Madrid. Other travels followed until she was recruited as a spy by the Germans in 1916 under the code name H-21. Shortly after this she was retained as a double-agent by Captain Ladoux of the French SCR (SCR = Counter-espionage français, 5° Bureau) and arrived back in Spain after a further interrogation by the British SIS in Falmouth while on a second voyage to Holland. At this point, 14 November 1916, the British Police officer concerned, George Grant, confused Mata-Hari with Clara Bendix, a known German spy responsible for communications between Hamburg and Barcelona and whose photograph, taken in Malaga, resembled Mata-Hari to some extent.

By this time the British had discovered that the French had taken her on as a double-agent, a fact which Captain Ladoux vigorously denied for fear of repercussions

---

6. *Amongst the known witnesses the only British name is that of Henry Wales, journalist with the International News Service. His account does not mention A E W Mason.*

from the British. Such an undisclosed action on the part of the French ran seriously counter to agreed Allied procedure. Later, Ladoux was arrested as being a double agent himself. (Shipman, *Femme Fatale*)

Mata-Hari had many friends in Spain. She seduced the German Military Attaché Major Arnold Kalle, who was also her paymaster, and extracted his secrets which she passed to Ladoux. Later secrets included information on the shipment of arms and agents to Morocco by submarine U-20, due to be landed at Melilla on the Rio de Oro. The Germans maintained two spy rings in Spain, the Army ring under Kalle and the Naval ring under Hans von Krohn in Madrid. In Barcelona they had von Rullan of the Army ring and Lt Fritz Ruggerberg under the orders of von Krohn. Von Krohn had been seduced by the French spy Marthe Richard whose intelligence role was unknown to him.

By 1916 the Germans had installed two radio towers in Spain, one at Carabanchel near Madrid, the other at Aranjuez, some 50 kilometers south of Madrid. These transmitted messages to Nauen and Königswusterhausen near Berlin. However these messages were intercepted by the French via the Eiffel Tower in Paris. Knowing this, Kalle falsified his messages, finally turning them into incriminating disinformation concerning Mata-Hari whom he had discovered was working for the French. At the same time, disinformation was greatly furthered by the subsidies paid to the press by the Allies: many thousands of pesetas from the French Embassy to *El Parlamentaro*, *Epoca*, *L'Imparcial*, *Correspondencia de Espana* and *El Liberal*. 24,800 pesetas per month rising to 100,000 French francs a month in 1917 ensured that the vast bulk of the Spanish press was in the hands of the Allies, all the French subsidies being augmented by those of Great Britain.

Given the inclusiveness of the Thoroton Network it is certain that much of this, if not all, was known to BNI. Three or four English officers were said to be among her lovers in Spain but these are not named and may have been just dinner companions as was frequently the case, or possibly British Intelligence agents.

In 1916 Guy de With, of the Dutch Legation in Madrid, recalled that Mata-Hari had told him of a contact of hers in Barcelona who was *"l'homme d'affairs"* of Catalan extraction. Although de With is not a man to be trusted (his evidence was found to be frequently invented) it is clear, from later research, that this was one of her Spanish lovers, the Senator Jundy, who had, to his surprise, been investigated by a French secret agent concerning his contacts with her.

Schirmann's analysis makes no mention of Hall nor of any British agents in Spain, not even of Rex Benson who (according to Anthony Cave Brown in his book on Sir Stewart Menzies) was responsible for "arranging the capture of the famous German (sic.) female spy, Mata-Hari". At that time Benson was the British representative at the *Bureau Interallie*, the Madrid HQ of the Allied counter-espionage service. This *Bureau* was responsible, in 1916, through the offices of Ladoux, for awarding a visa for France to Mata-Hari. The British protested loudly at this, not having been informed of Ladoux's 'turning' of Mata-Hari to his own ends, since it was against the rules of the *BI* for any country to accept onto its soil anyone declared as an "undesirable" by another allied country. One can only wonder what Rex Benson's role in all this really was.

Also missing from Schirmann's account is the identity of those who were "invited" to witness the execution in Vincennes. These people had arrived earlier at the Saint-Lazare prison. We know that A E W Mason was among them[7].

Sam Waagenaar's 1965 work *Mata-Hari*, in an edition adapted by Jacques Houbart (Fayard), is highly praised by Schirmann. However he points out that Waagenaar never saw the whole dossier nor all the archives, with the result that his book contains "errors and inexactitudes"; nor is he "always prudent in his choice of sources". Also, in this writer's opinion, he tends on occasion to present his own opinions as facts, attributing characteristics and thought processes to Mata-Hari out of his imagination. That said, he does contribute to an understanding of the British role in this affair.

He affirms that, for the first time, it was possible to reveal the role of Scotland Yard. For a 1965 book this is correct but the information is restricted to her arrest at Falmouth, her interrogation at Scotland Yard and the all important telegram sent by the Yard to the Dutch Legation in London and, secondly, to the Hague, giving their reasons for refusing her a visa, considering her to be an "undesirable woman" – in the security sense of the word of course. Only the name of Sir Basil Thomson figures in this text.

The Mata-Hari affair was essentially a Franco-German matter involving disinformation, betrayal, lies and double-crossing, a sordid and tragic affair driven by French political and military corruption and the government's need to distract the public from the hecatombs of the Somme, the Chemin des Dames and Verdun; the siphoning off of armament funds into the pockets of ministers and generals in Paris; the mutinies in the French army; and the widespread disillusionment of the public with the conduct of the war. A sacrificial victim had to be found and a cosmopolitan, notorious, foreign and beautiful spy was ready to hand. By failing to give her an official code name or number, Ladoux had denied her any legal protection in France, a fact of which she was unaware. Kalle handed her on a plate to the French, content that they would destroy their own agent who had betrayed Germany.

Gerald Kelly and A E W

Another of Thoroton's key agents was Gerald Kelly, later Sir Gerald Kelly, President of the Royal Academy. Sir William James, in his biography of Hall, says it was Hall who asked Kelly to go to Seville "during the last year of the war" as he had lived there for some time and knew the language.

In Derek Hudson's biography of Kelly (*For Love of Painting, Peter Davies, 1975*) Hall is not mentioned but he attributes Kelly's first interest in Spain to Somerset Maughan who, in 1911, proposed Seville as a fertile scene for Kelly's art. Hudson's

---

7. *For names of those present, see www.eyewitnesshistory.com/matahari.htm.*

book gives considerable detail on the role of *BI* in Russia, as Maughan was the chief *BI* agent there in 1917. Three of his stories in *Ashenden* concern the activities of secret agents in Spain, and are based on Hudson's accounts, thus relating to the Thoroton Network.

Of particular interest was the fact that Kelly was asked to "write a report on the whole activities of the Spanish machine" and to join Professor Dixon's staff. Professor W E Dixon was Regius Professor of Pharmacology at Cambridge and appears as Bendish in Mason's *The Summons*. (In this story he introduces a Martin Hillyard: could he have found this name through talks with Thoroton whose closest cousins were Hildyards?) Mason and Dixon had sailed in Lord Abinger's yacht the *St George* which was engaged in secret surveillance of possible German submarine bases in Spain.

Described as an "exception" in the service of Thoroton, Kelly was destined to end ignominiously when the following report was written in November 1918 by the Consul Jerome in Seville[8]:

> He (Kelly) does not understand how to handle men and has made a host of
> unnecessary enemies, which would not matter did it but affect himself, but most
> of his enemies (are) foreigners (who) are made into potential enemies of the cause.
> He arrogated himself the sole right as to the management and policy of this part of
> Spain… he showed an inclination to teach me my business… Unfortunately so far as
> I can judge, our NID service in the South of Spain does not compare favourably with
> the same service in the North, where there were men like Dawson, Mitchell, Spark
> and others with business knowledge and methods.

Well might Hall describe Mason as his "star turn" whose flamboyant spy yarns, where fact and fiction are entwined, remain virtually impossible to unravel. Mason's rodomontade is revealed in Lancelyn Green's biography where he inadvertently attributes Thoroton's reports to Mason and goes on to misquote from "manuscript notes (which) have chanced to survive". All this certainly contributed to Hall's love of panache and dazzle. Seen as a bit of a charlatan by many, Mason undoubtedly achieved not a few remarkable results and added to Hall's extraordinary ability to charm and persuade everyone he met from the President of the USA to every member of his staff who would do anything he asked of them. The glamour of Mason also provided an effective cover-up for the deeper-set, covert operations conducted by Charles the Bold. It is more difficult to penetrate the latter than to attempt to unravel Mason's 'One of Them', (fuel for German submarines in a Spanish port); 'Peiffer', (a bombing attack on the Rock); or 'The Winding Stair', (destruction of the pro-German movement in Morocco) but all show that Mason was deeply involved and very much part of the counter-intelligence scene.

8. *NA, FO 185/1478, Garcia Sanz, op cit.*

In Chapter 1 we made reference to Thoroton reading Mason's *Ensign Nightly* in 1901. However, it is Mason's *The Winding Stair* of 1923 which comes closest to underground activities in Morocco and which is widely considered to be based, in part, on actual experience. Other stories by Mason with connection with his secret service work include *One of Them* and *Peiffer*.

They were first published in March 1916 and then in January 1918 under the title *The Four Corners of the World*. By late 1917 Mason had left the Mediterranean but in January he had published *The Silver Ship*, a story based on a British deception plan to lure a German submarine to its fate in its attempt to sink an Allied ship carrying assistance to General Lyautey in Morocco. It is in *One of Them* that we are able to identify real life characters. Anthony Strange is certainly Mason himself, identifying ships chartered by a German but trading with England. (This incident we find reflected in the actual field reports of BNI in Spain, see Chapter 8, entry for 5 August 1915). Strange visits the British Consul and "was introduced to Major Slingsby in command of the Secret Service in those parts". Major Slingsby is Major Thoroton. Together they set to sea in a yacht equipped with a gun disguised as a capstan. They follow one of these ships which had taken on a load of 'bicarbonate of soda' in numerous 'heavy barrels'. In an unfrequented bay of Spain, under cover of darkness, the 'neutral' ship transferred its load of barrels to a raft and sailed away leaving it behind. Immediately Strange and Slingsby came up and broached all of the barrels. The 'bicarbonate of soda' contained in them was nothing other than fuel for a German U-Boat which in due course came to the surface in the unfrequented bay and was promptly sunk by the newly mounted gun!

In *Peiffer*, Mason and Thoroton (Strange and Slingsby) meet up with Peiffer, a German saboteur (trained in Hamburg) in Lisbon[9]. A complicated plot follows in which Peiffer 'converts' to being pro-Allied and is awarded a pass into Gibraltar. He is arrested and interned on the Rock. Hysterically he pleads to be transferred "anywhere else but Gibraltar". Thoroton and Mason smell a rat and finally run to earth a Spaniard, with a German mother, who was to carry out a bombing attack under the cover of a flying demonstration. Included in the target zone was the internment camp. The pilot is arrested but Peiffer is left in ignorance and growing terror.

Professor WE Dixon appears as Bendish in *The Summons* where his skill at opening letters and reclosing them without a trace, dealing with secret writing and so forth is by no means exaggerated. Dixon was on Lord Abinger's yacht *St George* for the cruise round Spain. Roger Lancelyn Green, in his life of Mason (*The Adventure of a Story-teller*) shows some ignorance of real events when he describes the story *The Erri Berro* and the *Wolfram* as "completely inexplicable" but compares it with *The Silver Ship*. How much of this Thoroton might have read we do not know but it is on record that he wrote to Hall concerning the trouble Mason had got into by writing some of his stories

9.   There was a Dr Eric Pheiffer, a Lieutenant in the German Navy, who had served in German Naval Intelligence during World War I, possibly the model for Mason's Peiffer (Louis Farago The Game of the Foxes). A later Pfeiffer, a Lieutenant Commander Eric Pfeiffer, was in charge of German espionage in North and South America (Sayers and Kahn). Of these three names, with similar spellings, Mason's is invented, the other two are real.

and reminiscences. Thoroton could see no harm in them himself but he was careful to leave no record of his own.

Compton Mackenzie, stormy petrel

Compton Mackenzie, the record shows, was never part of the Thoroton Network even though CJT was officially responsible for the Eastern Mediterranean.

It is evident that Compton Mackenzie knew Hall well as he has left a brilliant description of him in his *Life and Times, Octave 5*. Compton Mackenzie felt "like a nut about to be cracked by a toucan" when Hall fixed him with "a horn-rimmed horny eye", an eye which was given to high speed blinking, hence his nickname, 'Blinker'.

Later however, Hall was able to take control of the Aegean area which he put under the direction of the admiral commanding the area. While this should have terminated Monty's independence he was able to convince the admiral that he should carry on as before and wrote "...am now supreme head of all intelligence in the eastern Mediterranean", thanks indeed to his BNI cover.

Compton Mackenzie, due to the suppressed first edition of his *Greek Memoires*, was faced with a trial at the Old Bailey on 1 December 1933. There were three specific charges against him: communicating Mansfield Cumming's name and the military initials MI1 (C); giving the names of sixteen agents; and revealing that passport control was used as a cover for espionage. None of these charges stood up in court but Mackenzie was persuaded by his counsel to bring the proceedings to an end by pleading guilty, suffering the financial damages which this lead to[10].

Thoroton thought the trial something of a storm in a teacup, since then other information has emerged. It is evident that Thoroton was familiar with Mackenzie's activities in the Aegean but it is clear that he had no line responsibility for him.

Thoroton's progress from 1913

We have seen how Thoroton's career developed from entry into the Royal Marines, 1 September 1893, up to his appointment as Intelligence Officer in Gibraltar on 12 September 1913.

From 1913 onwards there is evidence of rather rapid promotion from Major to Temporary Lieutenant Colonel, September 1915 and on 23 September 1915 he is transferred to General Staff Officer (GSO) 1st Grade and is added to the List of War Staff Officers "without undergoing the usual examination". On 3 October 1916 he is promoted Brevet Lieutenant Colonel for 'meritorious services' and, the same year, we have examples of his correspondence with Marshal Lyautey, at that time General Lyautey, French Resident General in Morocco. Throughout 1913 to 1919 he is serving in HMS *Cormorant* in Gibraltar.

From 1915 onwards we can gather some concrete information from his awards and decorations.

---

10. Andro Linklater, Compton Mackenzie – A Life.

First came the Moorish Order of Ouissan Alaouite, 3rd Class, Commander in 1915 (restricted permission to wear). In 1917 this became 'unrestricted permission to wear'.

The Supplement to *The London Gazette* of 20 April 1917 lists decorations conferred by the Allied Powers on officers and men of the British Naval Forces for distinguished services rendered during the war. Vice Admiral Currey (Senior Officer in Charge Gibralter in 1915, see later) received the *Legion d'honneur* as a Commander. This was followed by Major and Brevet Lieutenant-Colonel Charles J Thoroton (temp Lt-Col) RMLI, as *Officier*; then as *Chevalier*, Captain Edward M Compton Mackenzie RM. *The Edinburgh Gazette* of April 1917 also carried this news.

Thoroton was made a Companion of the Most Distinguished Order of St Michael and St George (Additional member 3rd Class) gazetted 4 June 1917. Interestingly, Thoroton's CMG preceded Hall's KCMG by one year and there is reason to believe that the two awards were not unconnected.

He was made a Commander of the Order of the Crown of Italy, gazetted 30 October 1917. This Order ranks fifth in precedence and is therefore equivalent to Great Britain's Star of India.

Research in Rome has revealed that the Italian Consulate in Gibraltar informed the Italian Foreign Office (18 August 1915) that all the coasts of Spain were under active surveillance and control by Il Capo (Major Thoroton) "who is informed of all ship movements and re-fuelling"[11]. It goes on: "The English authority is in liaison with a certain individual Juan March, a contrabandist with control of over 240 motor ships and monoplanes (and a great fortune). In effect, this covers all ship movements (more or less licit) from the Balearic Islands. He gains political sympathy and a lot of money and his information is accurate. This is confidential to Il Capo and is not to be revealed to the French Consul. It is for the benefit of British surveillance of the Mediterranean Sea so it is to our advantage". Here we may see the reason for Thoroton's Italian decoration. To this may be added his January 1917 action in saving an important Italian steamer due to leave Barcelona, as he knew German submarines were waiting for her[12].

Also at this time, Hall was able to report on conditions inside Italy to the War Cabinet (ADM 116/1768), indicating that there existed an effective information source in that Allied country which included BNI outposts in Rome and Taranto.

In 1918 the Moorish Order of Ouissan Alaouite was finally conferred by His Imperial Majesty the Sultan of Morocco and reported in the *London Gazette*.

Reasons for the Moorish Order will become evident when we look at Thoroton's involvement with Lyautey and the Sultan in Morocco. The Order of St. Michael and St. George ranks sixth and was awarded for "extraordinary or important non-military service in a foreign country..." and, originally, for "high

---

11. *Garcia Sanz, AMAER Busta 80, translation FPV.*
12. *A E W Mason, January 1917 report.*

L.P.—No. 8.

In any further communica-
tion on this subject please quote

C.W

and address letter to—
The Secretary,
Admiralty, Whitehall, London, S.W. 1.

Admiralty,

12th October, 1917.

Sir,

I am commanded by My Lords Commissioners of the
Admiralty to forward herewith the Insignia and Brevet of
Commander of the Order of the Crown of Italy which has been
received at the Admiralty for transmission to you, and I am
to inform you that you have the King's permission to accept
and wear this decoration.

2.   The necessary announcement will appear in the
London Gazette in due course.

I am, Sir,

Your obedient Servant,

Charles Walker

Colonel C.J.Thoroton, C.M.G., R.M.

c/o A.G.R.M.,

Spring Gardens.

Letter from the Admiralty concerning the award of the Order of the Crown of Italy.

and confidential situations in the Mediterranean". These criteria changed over the centuries.

In this overview we can concentrate more closely on the top command structure for NI in Gibraltar about the time of his appointment there.

The post of Senior Officer in Charge of all HM Naval Establishments at Gibraltar was held by Vice Admiral F E E Brock (promoted Admiral in 1917). Rear Admiral Bernard Currey (promoted Vice Admiral after 1916) took over on 21 September 1915. Currey was in receipt of the CB in 1915. He was given honours by both France and Russia, the latter suggesting that BNI might have had contacts there before the end of the war. Currey's successor was Rear Admiral Heathcoat Grant who took over 19 June 1917.

Captain (later Admiral Sir Richard) Webb (1870-1950) was, between 1914 and 1917, Assistant Director of Trade Division, Admiralty War Staff. Webb later became Second in Command of the Mediterranean, ending finally as President Royal Naval College, Greenwich.

It was on HMS *Cormorant* that the Admiral Superintendent flew his flag and Thoroton would have been on the rolls of this 'ship'. Although Thoroton, as a Major, was a long way below a 4-star Admiral, his significant role in Contraband Control would have been known to Webb through his subordinate Admirals. Webb's report on Thoroton's contraband control work appears below.

We can now draw all these figures together. This is most clearly done by quoting directly from Thoroton's 'Special Reports of Service, Mentions in Despatches, etc'. (Extract from Papers CW19749/16-RM20291/16, Lt Col Thoroton).

We will start with Brock, under whom Thoroton served initially:

"Specially mentioned for duties in connection with intelligence".

Next comes Currey:

"The officers mentioned have rendered unique and valuable service at this place since the commencement of war, especially in connection with Trade, Intelligence and the Colony of Gibraltar".

Now Webb:

"At no port abroad have contraband matters been handled more efficiently than at Gibraltar (…) I can safely say that the work of this port has been excellent".

(We would dearly like to be able to fill in the omitted sentence which is unreadable in the original).

Next, Hall:

"Concur with DTD. As regards intelligence work, Colonel Thoroton is invaluable. It is largely due to his initiative that our information from Spain is so excellent, reliable and exclusive. I am in entire agreement with the recommendation of Adml Currey".

All these recommendations were, of course, signed.

We could summarise these statements by quoting from 'Comments Pertaining to Military Career':

> "Comment in record of service: <u>established intelligence organisation throughout Spain. 'Very little of importance happens without his being informed'</u>"
> (*Original underlining*)

The dates for the above are: Brock, 1915; Currey, 1916, Webb, 1916; Hall, 1916.

We can pass from here to consider a letter from Marshal Lyautey to Vice Admiral F E E Brock, from Fez, dated 20 April 1915. Lyautey makes the point that "the Admiralty ought to know…"what Thoroton was achieving in Morocco. In the margin of this letter Sir Edward Grey (Foreign Secretary) adds a note, in his own hand, that he too wants "to know what Thoroton is doing".

What, one may well ask, was the maverick quality in Thoroton's make-up which placed him in the role he was to occupy throughout World War I? Anyone familiar with the literature of those days (and it can only be largely through the literature now) will know that the extraordinary and even fantastic qualities of those involved in SIS was a crucial and, in the end, long lasting influence on the British Intelligence Services. Total amateurism characterised the early successes and failures of course. Major D S Hanker's 1965 *History of the Intelligence Corps* pin-points the situation well, albeit from the Army's aspect, which in this instance is perhaps in no way different from the Naval one. Commenting on the "green tabbed officer of the IC", his "reserve was very marked and he had an insatiable curiosity, a combination of characteristics which the average Britisher resents…and he was consequently looked upon at first as suspect".

Already noted are Thoroton's 'zealous' commitment to his assignments and to his 'originality' in choosing the Royal Marines. There are faint allusions to 'wild living' (an accusation brought against him by the Americans when they were belatedy endeavouring to set up their own spy network in Spain) and these touched upon amorous affairs. There must be something more: was there, perhaps, a steely, imperturbable quality in his make-up which, combined with his intellectual abilities, made him successful? Perhaps his character engendered devotion or commitment amongst his far-flung agents. He became the virtual confidant of that ebullient maverick, Admiral Sir Reginald Hall. One also wonders, how he was able to win over the Majorcan smuggler Juan March who, at certain times, had been inclined to the opposite camp. There was certainly more than awards involved (*à la* Mason) or even money (*à la* Thoroton, courtesy of the British Exchequer).

That said, it is from the various reports on Thoroton (contained in the National Archives, Record N° 299 in ADM 196/62) which have been quoted, that we can best gauge how he was seen by his superior officers. That and Cummings'"cut of the jib".

Chapter 7
Controversial issues affecting BNI

Although we are primarily concerned with World War I, the official history *British Intelligence in the Second World War* (Hinsley & others, HMSO 1979) sheds some light on the Great War period. It reports that the undue success of 'Blinker' Hall as DNI resulted in 1918 with a move by the Foreign Office and "by a considerable body of naval opinion" (unnamed) to abolish the posts of DNI and DDNI. It was thanks to the Admiralty that this attack was resisted. Hinsley further denigrates the "NID's standing among the divisions of the naval staff" (again, unnamed) and claims its influence on the Admiralty "was no greater than was that of the intelligence branches of other service ministries". In fact the entire drift of the official history is to write down the scope and ability of the intelligence services. It claims, for example, that "the bulk of the NID continued to be divided into geographical sections which were content to collect static or topographical information while the main sources were ports' 'consuls and ships' intelligence officers filling in NID questionnaires, usually with data quite easily available in public sources". It goes on: "The NID did little more than pass on to the naval authorities, parrot fashion, the political tit-bits handed out by the FO".

This is so self-evidently ridiculous (even if penned in 1979) as we now know that one asks the question, why?

Hinsley, one would think, would have known of the Admiralty memorandum *Reorganisation of the Intelligence Organisation 1918-1926* which delineates the work of the Intelligence Centres and which lists ten specific "normal" roles and, with the experience of war, eight new responsibilities. These include secret agents (spies); Direction Finding W/T; interception of allied and neutral messages; etc. The Memorandum reads:

> On the outbreak of war the Intelligence Centres received the majority of the telegrams of orders and information for the various Commanders in Chief abroad, and in spite of the crushing volume of work, carried out the distribution in a satisfactory manner (...)

> Apart from the normal Intelligence duties of obtaining, sifting and distributing intelligence to HM ships, and routeing of merchant vessels , the Intelligence centres proved to be of the utmost use in extraneous duties, e.g, shipping sugar, issuing Charts, bunkering merchant vessels, docking merchant vessels, assisting in censorship, arranging passages for ratings, etc whilst the actual intelligence duties expanded on lines not anticipated until war experience showed the necessity.

> Examples of such duties are:- Issue of war warnings and official press bulletins, interception of allied and neutral messages, Direction Finding W/T, secret service, personal investigations, etc[1]

We now know the criticisms levelled against BNI to be false. Major Walter (later Major General Sir Walter) Kirke of MI5 was one who represented the high opinion held concerning Hall's Spanish network outside as well as inside the Admiralty. Military intelligence, Kirke reported, regarded the Spanish set up as "a good show".

Hinsley however attributes to Patrick Beesley's *Very Special Intelligence* the much more favourable accounts of the work of the NID which appear in the official history, *British Intelligence in the Second World War.*

Restructuring BNI in Gibraltar

It was in 1914 that Whitehall issued its triple programme for the Intelligence Services in colonial areas: repression of contraband; interception of shipping movements including submarines; and the identification and elimination of enemy spy structures. Earlier in 1914, the Admiralty had telegraphed Thoroton with instructions to urgently organise a ships' Examination Service. This was based on Churchill's Secret Standing Orders of July 1914. Within five days Thoroton telegraphed London that the service had been established[2].

Towards the end of the year Thoroton went to Madrid to discuss with Hardinge a number of questions. First, the presence of the German official in Malaga, Felix Wisotzky, who was involved in negotiations between Morocco and the United States and with matters concerning the passage of submarines through the Straits. Then, the activities of the Mannesmann brothers in Malaga, Cadiz and Seville concerning the employment of Spanish shipping. Finally, Major Willis' detection of the German use of a Spanish Naval code service in Cueta, Melilla, Tetuan, San Fernando and Almeria[3].

In June 1915, Thoroton sent Hardinge a manual containing clues for identifying submarines in the context of their navigation, vitalization and refuelling. "Most consuls", he wrote, "seem to have little, if any, idea of the habits or appetites of submarines, and these notes are intended to give them a little help" (FO 185/1252) These notes numbered six in all: types of fuel required; minimum requirements; supplies required including sulphuric acid and zinc batteries; methods of transfer to submarines; need for certain analyses of substances; need to telegraph BNI in Gibraltar with information so obtained. As Thoroton was using the telegram service of La Linea de la Conceptcion, the Spanish Authorities objected. Thoroton wrote: "If the Spanish Authorities object to receiving telefonema messages in cipher so

---

1. *NA, ADM 116/1842, Garcia Sanz, op cit.*
2. *Gibraltar Archives, Garcia Sanz, op cit.*
3. *NA, Garcia Sanz, op cit.*

addressed (which is unlikely) nothing need be said except name, place, time and date: it will be understood that a submarine is meant". (ibid)

The prolongation of the war called for a re-organisation of the Thoroton Network. The proliferation of vital issues ranging widely from the manufacture of explosives (and the use of fruit and olives in their production); minerals, particularly wolfram; the drive to eliminate German spy networks; the submarine menace and other objectives, all demanded a re-structuring.

In addition to his role as Chief of Naval Intelligence, in May 1915 Thoroton was appointed Chief of Military Intelligence, a post previously occupied by the Military GSO (*War Diary*)[4]. This led to much closer surveillance of enemy agents and augmented control of mineral shipments. It also brought in the services of Captain Hope-Johnstone, of Military Intelligence, as assistant to CJT, and who had previously reported to Captain Vernon Kell, the founder of MI5.

Early French propaganda initiatives in Spain in 1915 suffered from the absence of a proper organisation and a lack of finance and technique. Henry Montague Villers wrote (in his book, *Charms of the Consular Career*) of the British experience:

> Undeniably the Consular Service gives one a pleasant opportunity of getting to know the charms of various places and peoples. The local language having been once thoroughly acquired, one can begin to understand the great difference that nationality makes – their different points of view on all great economic questions, commercial problems and methods etc. The average insular Briton seems to find it almost impossible to realise these differences, or at any rate to act, either in politics or commerce, as if he duly allowed for them. He expects all foreigners to play cricket. They do not. It was this knowledge and often local influence that made Consuls so exceptionally useful during the late Great War[5].

The Szek Affair

Michael Occleshaw, in his *Armour Against Fate*, emphasises the supremacy of Hall's NID in World War I over and above not only the enemy and allied secret services but well ahead of British Military Intelligence. He brings this out in the context of the Zimmerman Telegram and of Alexander Szek whose work for the British resulted in the deciphering of German codes, leading to the Zimmermann affair. When the time came for Szek to be extradited from Brussels, where he had been working inside the German code centre, Hall organised his journey to the Netherlands and on to a ferry for England. He never reached our shores. In 1984 Professor Michael Foot revealed that Szek had been murdered on the night ferry, his papers removed and his body dumped overboard. The reason for this is totally unknown as Szek was by that time no sort of possible, or remotely possible, security risk to Britain. Tuchman, in

---

4. *This combination of Naval and Military Intelligence at the level of the Chief of Intelligence for an area such as the Mediterranean can be considered unique.*

5. *Quoted Garcia Sanz, op cit.*

her *The Zimmermann Telegram*, can give no explanation for his death but reports that Szek's father, after the war, accused the British of doing away with him in order to ensure that the Germans never discovered that their code was compromised. Szek is thought to have been the man Oliver bitterly regretted having had killed at the cost of £1,000[6]. Roskill revealed this in his 1980 book *Admiral of the Fleet Earl Beatty* but the account of this in Patrick Beesley's *Room 40* discredits the value of Szek's work in obtaining the German code for Britain. William James' excellent life of Hall makes no reference to Szek[7].

The Szek affair demonstrates the "ruthlessness" which is said to be a feature of the British SIS. Alexander Szek was drawn into working for the NID by Hall following a tip-off from Sidney Reilly ('ace of spies') through C and Vernon Kell of MO5, later called MI5. Szek's mother was British (and lived in Croydon, Surrey) but his father was Austrian and he was, himself, a skilled wireless operator. Szek was working in occupied Brussels for the German Army's wireless wing, but he was anti-German. Through his mother, messages were sent to persuade him to steal the German wireless cipher. Some pressure was applied by Hall who threatened to have Mrs Szek and her other children interned as enemy aliens if her son did not comply. Szek complied on one condition which was that the British would exfiltrate him from Belgium to Croydon if the Germans were to discover that their cipher had been broken. Hall, somewhat reluctantly, agreed with this stipulation. At great risk Szek set about copying the code onto tiny slips of paper which he concealed in his rectum (a trick taught him by the British) and then passed them to C's agent in Brussels. Room 40 was thus able to break the German codes resulting, most spectacularly, in the decipherment of the Zimmerman Telegram.

In due course the Germans realised that a leak had occurred and that their code had been compromised. Szek was now in a dangerous situation and needed to be extradited for two reasons. The danger to Szek was obvious; for the British there was the risk that he might be caught and, possibly, give away his Brussels contact and much else besides. Szek then imposed a second condition: he refused to pass on the final clues to the German cipher until he was safely in London. Taken out of Brussels and into the Netherlands, he was soon on a ferry to Britain. As we have seen, he never arrived and no official papers make any reference to him from that time onwards. Only Michael Foot's 1984 revelation came anywhere near to explaining the mystery. No evidence seems to be available on whether there was any risk of Szek betraying England - the time for that had clearly passed - so what could be the reason for this extreme act? Might his second condition have caused worries in Room 40? Later conversations with his family reveal that they were convinced that Alexander had been murdered by the British SIS.

A semi-final, bizarre twist is given to this story by Nigel West (in his *C-C HQ*

---

6.   *£1,000 in 1917 would be the equivalent of £68,400 in 2010.*

7.   *David Ramsay somewhat adds to the confusion by quoting from Diana Preston (Willfull Murder, 2002), a source which Ramsay himself finds unconvincing.*

book of 1986) where he submits that the whole story was a cover-up, produced by Admiral Oliver, in extreme old age, as cover for the fact of the code's capture from the German Consul in Bushire (Bushehr) on the Persian Gulf coast of Iran. As Michael Foot (to whom I am indebted for this information) says, Nigel West may be right, we simply do not know.

Returning to the question; why should the official history present such a lop-sided view of the intelligence services and, in particular, of the NID? It attributes a whole range of reasons: men of average or less than average professional competence; the higher ranks of the armed forces showed antipathy to the intelligence authorities; "anti-intellectualism"; "dislike of the officer class for the un-gentlemanly aspects of intelligence work" (spying, sabotage and assassination?); resentment of its influential nature; etc.

Two possible answers present themselves: either it was an official decision to obscure and cover up the real sources and methods of intelligence gathering which produced such important and far-reaching strategic and tactical results (this was during the Cold War period); or it simply reflects the official view, at a certain level, that failures could best be attributed to the intelligence services, thus letting others off the hook. Nowhere in Hinsley do you get the slightest idea that there were spy networks on-the-ground which were providing information. Most information is attributed to "the Foreign Office". Furthermore the author positively discriminates against "naming individuals": "to have given prominence to only a few would have been unjust to the many more who were equally deserving of mention". While this is right and fair it does not relate to the descriptions of the intelligence services we have noted[8].

Ten years earlier in 1969 Richard Deacon's *A History of the British Secret Service* had been published. It is possible that officialdom was then moved to initiate the "official history". Crucial to the official history is the statement that the Secretary of State for Foreign Affairs made it clear in 1978 that he "drew a distinction between the records of the Service Intelligence directorates which will be placed... in the Public Record Office and other information, including details of the methods by which this material is obtained." Although Hinsley and others had access to "records which are not to be opened" they were restricted on "researching about intelligence techniques and with respect to individuals". Many files remain closed until 2015.

So there we have it: in a phrase, closed and locked doors.

The American intervention

It was towards the end of World War I that the Americans, who were trying to set up their own secret intelligence network in Spain, accused Thoroton of being a

---

8. *This false impression may be partly explained by David Winter in his analysis of Douglas Haig and the said fabrication of the Official History of the First World War, written by James Edmonds, and the weeding of documents to be transferred to the PRO. (Haig's Command-A Reassessment, Penguin 2001) David Winter is harshly criticised by some commentators but is accepted by Len Deighton and others.*

"loose liver". "Living with a woman to whom he was not married and certainly no teetotaller". This accusation held no significance for Hall who expressed his complete confidence in Thoroton, saying he was only interested in results which Charles the Bold was "producing in full measure[9].

Probably this was a report from agent "M.A." of the American secret service. We know the name of the woman who was living with him, it was Mrs St Aubyn Stevenson. However, the accusation seems rather naïve if it was thought that such behaviour could damage an agent's reputation or usefulness. When, during 1919 to 1923, Thoroton was head of the Federation of British Industries in Madrid it was the Spanish government which insisted on his continued services in Spain as he was able to provide them with more accurate information regarding revolutionary and subversive activities inside Spain than could their own secret service. Some American agents

Evelyn Flora St Aubyn Stevenson in Andalusian costume in Malaga.

and diplomatic staff were involved in petty skirmishing with the Thoroton Network. In London Admiral William S Sims was in command of all USN forces in the European theatre. He became a close friend of the Royal Navy and he and Jellicoe had no secrets between them. He was fully in Hall's confidence. Sims, like the US Ambasador Page and Edward Bell, who was responsible for intelligence liaison at the American Embassy, was the soul of discretion which went to the heart of the best Anglo-American relationships.

In 1918 Sims insisted on seeing all the US Naval Attachés' reports in Europe before they were forwarded to Washington so that they could be checked against the much better British intelligence made available to him by Room 40. While this was somewhat humiliating to Captain Roger Wells, Director of Naval Intelligence in Washington, it was a sensible idea. However, once Sims slipped up. The US Naval Attaché in Madrid, Captain Benton C Decker, reported that the Germans were sending wireless messages "from towns throughout Spain". Sims immediately

---

9. Alan Hillgarth once remarked, "An intelligence officer will be at a very definite disadvantage if he is a teetotaller". Ref TNA ADM 223/490 (Macintyre Operation Mincemeat).

requested the American Embassy in Madrid "that this grave matter be taken seriously with the Spanish Government". In fact only the Madrid-Berlin link remained to the Germans and this was being read by the NID. Had it been severed no more intelligence could be garnered from this source by Room 40. The catastrophe was averted.

Captain Decker was not content to remain idle however and had thrown himself into the task of building up an American spy network in Spain in rivalry to the Thoroton Network. It transpires that it was Decker who accused Thoroton of being "a loose liver" and "certainly no teetotaller" in the incident previously reported.

Beatrice von Brunner, by Bassano, London 1910. Then aged eighteen she was to become involved with CJT in Paris eight years later.

Beatrice von Brunner and 'the poisoned cup'

In 2007 we obtained a 1918 report on Thoroton from the US National Archives at College Park, Maryland. This originated from the Military Intelligence Branch, Executive Division, General Staff and shows that its source was this agent "M/A" in Spain. Under the curious heading "Thoroton, Charles. Colonel. – Army Suspect (British)" we get the report dated 23 May 1918, Paris, that is some six months before the end of the war. This report concerns the activities of the German born actress Beatrice von Brunner (1892-1955) who had been appearing in London theatres about 1910 aged eighteen and who was a theatrical associate of Gladys Cooper, Phyllis Dare, Cecily Courtenidge, Billie Burke and other glamour girls of the day. In 1911 the *New York Times* of 17 September reported that she was to appear in '*The Spring Maid*' at the Whitney Theatre in London on the 28th of that month. She was aged nineteen at that time. This appearance was to be followed by a trip to Vienna and Berlin by Mr Whitney who envisaged staging *The Girl from Maxim's* in those cities.

The fashionable photographer Bassano made fourteen portraits of her on 26 August 1910 and in America she was glamorously, and profitably, featured on cigarette cards between 1904 and 1917. (Regarding these photographs, Amazon was quoting a price of US$247 per photo in 2009.) M/A reports from Paris in May 1918 that Thoroton is "…intimate with Beatrice von Brunner, sus(pected) spy wor(ker) … used (his) influence to keep her in England when she was to be sent to USA – by Eng(land); employed her as one of his workers." (sic.) (File no. PF 13907-2, revised to PF 28825)

From this it is evident that Thoroton was in Paris in May of 1918 and the implication is that his purpose was to "keep her in England" rather than have her "sent to USA". Was she working for German Intelligence in Paris and was it his role to turn her to work for the British? If so, it would seem he was successful as he "employed her as one of his workers". It would appear that MA had the task of shadowing Thoroton when he was in Paris in 1918 and in Spain, no doubt in Madrid in 1921.

The 18 January 1921 report describes the Federation as "The Federation of British Merchants" and that it had a membership of 18,000 firms: "Thoroton is the head of it". It seems more than likely that Thoroton would have known he was under surveillance as he would have been fully informed by 'Blinker' Hall of the American attempts to discredit him. Hall and Thoroton were still very much in touch. They were to lunch together in 1932 and they collaborated over Hall's autobiography. Hall maintained an eagle eye on all matters concerning intelligence and was active behind the scenes as late as 1941 (he was to die in 1943). It was Hall who had repudiated Amercian attempts to discredit Thoroton and he would have been the first to warn him of any surveillance.

The National Archives at College Park, Maryland, then came up with an even more complete report concerning Colonel Thoroton and the von Brunner sisters.

This, a three page letter on American Embassy headed writing paper (from the office of the Military Attaché, 5 rue de Chaillot, Paris) and dated August 22nd 1918, had been sent by Major Barclay H Warburton, Military Attaché, and was addressed to the Chief, Military Intelligence Branch, Executive Division. Its subject: "Miss Beatrice Brunner".

The text of the original letter of 22 August 1918 concerning "Miss Brunner's" involvement with the American colony in Paris and with Thoroton follows.

'American Embassy, Office of the Military Attaché, 5 Rue de Chaillot, Paris

201-W.   August 22nd 1918.

(Stamped PF28825-13. Sep 17 1918 War Department 71)

From: Military Attaché, Paris, France.

To: Chief, Military Intelligence Branch, Executive Division.

Subject: Miss Beatrice Brunner.

1. Referring to our letter of June 6th 1918, subject: Miss Beatrice Von Brunner, to the knowledge of this Office the subject is still residing in England.

2. Shortly after her departure, her two sisters, Miss June Brunner and Miss Grace Brunner, who goes under the name of Mrs. Travers, took a villa at Deauville. Some weeks ago, they received an order from the French Government to leave France before the 10th of August, as they were considered undesirable aliens.

3. Immediately, the two sisters came to Paris and appealed to various people with influence. Among them, one Mr. Charles Carroll of Carrolton, who is well-known in the American colony of Paris. They met Mr. Carroll only once or twice through Frederick Hoey, a Manager of race-horses for various people, including Harry Payne Whitney and the Duke Decazes. Grace Brunner is the mistress of Hoey[10].

4. When Mr Carroll was appealed to, to aid the sisters in their predicament, he communicated with a friend at the Ministry of Foreign Affairs, who, Mr Carroll claims, assured him that the order for deportation would be rescinded and for Mrs Travers and Miss Brunner to remain quietly in Paris. On the 17th of this month, however, the Police visited the two sisters and asked why they had not left on the specified day. The Police were referred to the Embassy and to the Ministry of Foreign Affairs, neither of which, however, would admit having interfered in any way in the case. They were then taken up for trial and received 15 days in the prison of St Lazare, after which they are to immediately leave the country.

5. Attention is invited to the action of Mr Charles Carroll who, in addition to communicating with the Ministry of Foreign Affairs, wrote a letter to His Excellency the Ambassador of this Embassy, vouching for the character of the two women, whom he knew through a third person, Mr Hoey. Mr Carroll holding an important situation in the American Society in Paris, and also being an influential member of the American Cross here, would naturally have considerable weight in a matter of this kind.

6. When questioned, Grace Brunner who is the most intelligent of the two sisters, denied having any knowledge whatsoever of her sister's transactions. This cannot,

---

10. *The multi-millionaires, Carroll and Whitney, were the elite of America's financial and society world. Decazes was a leading aristocratic French businessman and racehorse owner; Hoey one of the world's leading racehorse trainers.*

possibly, however, be true as while Beatrice Brunner was here in Paris, her sister stayed with her a long time at the Hotel Grillon and when Beatrice went to Britain, Grace Brunner was intrusted with some confidential papers, which, however, have since disappeared. Neither June nor Grace Brunner, however, can be considered clever enough to carry on anything very complicated on their own initiative, and it is probable that they have only been made use of by their older sister.

7. Regarding Beatrice Brunner, a good deal of more or less reliable information has been received. For instance, referring to the enclosure of May 22nd 1918, in our letter, paragraph 3, it is now heard from a servant formerly in the employ of Miss Brunner, that it was she who tried to poison Colonel Charles Thoroton, and it was only because of fear of discovery, that she took a small dose of the drug herself in order to avert suspicion. It is also stated by the valet of Colonel Thoroton that Miss Brunner was in the habit of going through his private papers whenever the occasion offered, even going so far as to examine the pockets of his clothes when he was out of the room. The valet appears to have reported this on one occasion to his master, who, however, refused to believe it. The valet is an habitual drinker and was provided with money for that purpose by Miss Brunner in order to get him out of the way and give her more opportunity. Knowing himself coupable in this respect, however, he was afraid to insist too strongly on her actions.

8. There can be little doubt in anyone's mind who has clearly followed this case, of the connection of Miss Brunner with enemy agents, and if it had not been for the protection of Colonel Thoroton who appears to have very unusual influence with the British Admiralty, there is very little doubt but that she would have been dealt with by the French before she left this country.

9. The attention which she has brought on herself has probably forced her activity to become dormant for the present but in the opinion of this Office, she should in every way, be considered a dangerous person, more especially on account of the great influence which she has over Colonel Thoroton who occupies such an important and confidential post with the British.

Signed Barclay H Warburton, Major, Military Attaché.   JMF/MT.'

There can be little doubt but that Thoroton was more than aware of Miss Brunner's interest in the contents of his pockets. We can also well imagine who was responsible for the disappearance of the confidential papers left with Grace Brunner and that by this time they were safely in the hands of 'Blinker' Hall.

Beatrice von Brunner's attempt to poison Thoroton misfired and we are left to wonder why. Was the wrong poison employed? This would seem to be unlikely given that she was backed by the German secret service, but poison had been administered since she took some herself in order to avoid suspicion. Had Thoroton become ill, but then recovered? He was undoubtedly aware of the risks he was running with this young lady and had, perhaps, only seemed to have drunk the poisoned cup. His refusal to believe his valet's warning regarding her habit of going through his private papers we can read as suggesting he was well aware of this and his refusal to believe his valet could serve as cover for his continued association with her. Why did he need to be 'put-away'? It seems inevitable that the German secret service were well aware of the damage the Thoroton Network was doing to Germany's interests in Spain and the Mediterranean (blocking the re-fuelling of its submarines, cutting its communications, etc) and were seeking a way to neutralise him. We do not know the date of the attempted poisoning but it must have been in 1917 or 1918. By this time (27 April 1917) the German High Command had concluded that "victory was impossible on any front. It depends entirely on submarine activity". Since the Network was proving so effective in frustrating German U-Boat activity the decision may have been taken to attempt his assassination.

Towards the end of the war, Edward Bell reported to Washington that Thoroton's organisation in Spain "became immensely powerful and used frequently to give information to the Spanish Government of disaffection and strikes in Spain itself, and when a few months ago Admiral Hall started to cut down his organisation… the Spanish Government actually requested him not to do so on the grounds that his organisation was to them a far more reliable source of information of what was going on in the country than their own police and civil authorities…" (Andrew's *Secret Service*, Bell to Leland Harrison 2 May 1919, Leland Harrison MSS box 102, Library of Congress, thanks to David Khan).

No wonder that Thoroton was made Commissioner of the Federation of British Industries in Madrid from 1919 to 1923.

Chapter 8
The Foreign Office and Thoroton Network Reports

The best source of information which enables us to put together a more comprehensive idea of Charles the Bold's work out of Gibraltar, is contained in a large 17" x 13", 2 ½" thick, leather bound book in the National Archives bearing the title "FO 566/1220 Spain & Portugal 41, 1914-1917". This remained on the secret list until 1968, that is for fifty years.

The book chronicles an enormously comprehensive yet succinct logging of messages, sometimes running to six or seven in a single day, over four years of the war. In giving here a summary of some of these messages we get as close as we can to the actuality of the flow of intelligence from the Western Mediterranean theatre. In a few incidences this information is augmented by other sources.

Sources vary but the majority appear to originate from the DNI while others are labelled WO, Paris and Lisbon. Various cities in Spain are listed, Madrid, Barcelona and others, which would have come under his responsibility. Many sources are not recorded. From these almost telegraphic entries, in various handwritings, we can get a much clearer view of the work of the Thoroton Network which enables us to portray the scope, scale and significance of the Intelligence services in Spain and Portugal and their relationship to the conduct of the war. Specific sources are nowhere identified, apart from reference numbers but, more often than not, even these are absent. It is probable that these numbers refer to individual agents but it is unlikely that these would be their field numbers by which they were actually identified.

Reading through the messages one can pick up the predominant subjects and get some kind of weighting on the issues involved. Amongst the most frequently mentioned subjects are the purchase of rifles and ammunition; the U-Boat menace; political issues in the two countries; German sabotage and the action of German agitators; and the fluctuating 'loyalties' of the neutral powers (Spain and Portugal at the outset) towards the Allies and the Central powers. Cartagena as an information source figures considerably, followed by Barcelona, Madrid, Bilbao and Malaga and by Lisbon in Portugal. On a year by year basis we can follow this flow of information.

1914

The type of issue concerned here may be exemplified by an early entry, that of 4 November (Registry No. 67250, No. 152) concerning Spanish Remington rifles and 500 rounds of ammunition. Before purchasing these there is a need to see a sample, if that is possible. It will be recalled that part of Thoroton's remit lay in the Trade Division so here is a good example and we know that his work in this area was considered "excellent" by Captain Richard Webb, its Assistant Director. The purchase of Spanish rifles is a *leitmotif* throughout the four years recorded here. This is reminiscent of Thoroton's letter to Hall, 21 November 1932, when he was contributing to Hall's autobiography and where he wrote, "My pirate says the cavalry carbines were Lebel, they were packed in artificial marble columns and blocks. I think there were 2,500 and 20 rounds of ammunition for each in safari cases...(the) carbines had been captured from the French and sent to Spandau..."

Moving on from this particular example, a host of issues is recorded: Naval movements in the Mediterranean; the need for goats to feed to Indian troops in France on the Western Front; the state of the political parties in Spain, their internal divergences and inter-party power struggles; and outside influences on the Spanish government's policy.

Foreign Office files FO 4551/1220 continue for Spain and Portugal for 1914-1917, these files having been closed for fifty years until released in 1968. The first entry (No 73) concerns Madrid which had received information from Malaga on naval movements: a Spanish gun-boat had left port and the *Laya* had arrived. Tenerife was reported to be the scene of potential disturbances by the Germans there. On 14 September 1914 a Spanish artillery officer reported on German plans for the invasion of England, intelligence he had gathered in conversation with the Spanish Military Attaché in Berlin. Ref 150/122 details the searching of ships bound for the USA and Italy to remove contraband, copper being particularly mentioned. Cartagena-based agents had reported on Spanish naval movements there. A Minute to Sir Edward Grey, dated 15 October 1914, arose from King Manuel's concerns over "the recent argument between France and Portugal" and offered his services to the British. November 17 saw Bilbao reporting on local German agents making enquiries regarding arms purchases. This was followed, the next year, by similar reports from Madrid.

1915

The FO files start with the assessment of the possibilities of purchasing Spanish rifles and mules in Madrid. Then, in February, demonstrations break out in Barcelona where "offensive caricatures" are printed depicting the Allied leaders. These are reported to the Spanish Minister of State. 12 June in Huelva, BNI intercepts a letter concerning Spanish political attitudes towards the Allies. By the end of the year, German sabotage and revolutionary plots are reported for Madrid, Vigo and Seville. The first concerns the destruction of Spanish railways and, on 28 December, a quantity of wood prepared for incendiary use was discovered on the beach of Huelva and promptly disposed of. This report derives from Madrid, Gibraltar and the Admiralty.

Ref 28 reports that two suspects have been arrested and are due to be handed over to General Lyautey in Morocco. Ref 41 details the use of *feluccas* for smuggling and for carrying German reservists. In Ref 1150 Gibraltar is instructed to detain and report on all cotton shipments to Mediterranean ports with the sole exception of French ports.

The Thoroton Network is committed to a public relations campaign to improve the British image in Spain. This involves the purchase of the "goodwill" of the Spanish newspaper *La Tribuna*.

Hot on this item, Intelligence reports that American rifles are arriving in Spain which are to be shipped to Germany via Portugal (Ref No 6713). This is followed by a message detailing the "desperate need of rifles and ammunition"; 18 million rounds of Mauser are needed by the Union of South Africa. Then, 1,000 horses are ordered in Barcelona, as remounts for the Western Front, an order later cancelled as "not required". The difficulties in obtaining rifles persist and on 12 March the "services of Officer at Gibraltar" are requested to expedite the supply of rifles. 10 June: Mauser rifles are being purchased. At the same time 30,000 old sandbags are on offer to the British Army at Villagarcia.

On the political front, the Intelligence Division reports that the German cause is supported by the Spanish Right Wing Parties who have offered Gibraltar and Morocco and a free hand in Portugal to the King of Spain if he espouses Germany. Following this message there are pages and pages of negotiations over the purchase of rifles.

5 August: a German plot to blow up British ships leaving Spanish ports is discovered. Gibraltar (SIO) informs HMG that "all necessary precautions have been adopted" against the reported plot. The British agent in Bilbao also reports in on this issue. At the same time Bilbao reports that Germans are trading with British companies in the port of Bilbao and warns that such ships should not be loaded by Mr Wakonigg. The placing of explosives in seemingly innocent merchandise has been detected[1].

The involvement of the Church is significant, both Anglican and the Vatican. Madrid logs the Bishop of Southwark as reporting that the Spanish clergy is in opposition to "the infidel French government" rather than against England. This explains, in part, that element in Spanish public opinion which is pro-German. The bishop has an audience with the King and Queen of Spain on 1 October.

Information from Garcia Sanz reveals that as a result of the Naval Agreement between the Admiralty and the French Navy, the French Minister of Marine wrote:

> **I have the honour to advise you that the entire British Intelligence Service in the Iberian Peninsula is under the direction of Major Thoroton, an agent who is held by**

---

1. *Wilhelm Wakonigg, former Austrian consul for the Habsburg monarchy, was executed 19 November 1936 by the Popular Front, along with others, for sabotage, spying and the smuggling of military documents out of Spain. He is reported as being 'involved in the shadowy front of the secret services in the First World War' (Niebel 2009). Wakonigg SA trades today as a major non-iron metallurgy enterprise in the energy and building markets and is an affiliate of the International Manganese Institute.*

the Admiralty in high esteem. He lives in Gibraltar and has been advised by telegram of the coming visit of M. le Lieutenant de Vaisseau de Roucy and of the purpose of this visit.

It would be appropriate therefore that M. de Roucy gets in touch as soon as possible with Major Thoroton who will himself put him in touch with other officers of the Intelligence Service in Spain[2].

This initiative was badly handicapped for the French as Thoroton was located in Gibraltar (a British colony) while the French were based on Madrid and in Toulon in France. It would also seem that the Admiralty War Staff had reservations as to the extent to which the Thoroton Network should open itself up to their French allies in Spain. (As will be seen in Chapter 12 there were no such problems in Morocco where France did not seem to operate much of an Intelligence Service.) Later, in 1916, the French became increasingly active in Spain but remained handicapped by the self-evident problem of the geographical distance between Madrid and Gibraltar.

However, French initiatives were then further crippled by a six point *Exposé*[3] from Paris which laid an enormous burden on their agents. Too long to even summarise here, it went into such comprehensive minutiae of the work to be carried out that, as soon as their agents began sending in their reports, there was no headquarters staff available or capable of reading, interpreting or transmitting the information obtained.

In February, the only German POW to escape from England, Oberlieutenant Pluschow, had been arrested on an Italian ship in Gibraltar.

1916

At the beginning of the year, Gibraltar reports to HMG on a German plot to destroy the Spanish railways. This report comes from Malaga. Attacks are anticipated on British properties in Barcelona: this is a German inspired action designed to inflame public opinion against Britain. This is followed by a message detailing German methods of communication including codes and ciphers and the use of secret (invisible) ink.

Then, on 11 March, it is reported that Germany declares war on Portugal.

Spain is beginning to swing away from Germany towards the Allies. *La Tribuna* publishes an article on German activities in Spain. English propaganda is beginning to pay off.

Further German sabotage is reported on 28 April when bombs are placed on British ships in Spanish ports. This report comes from an agent in Madrid.

1 May: reports of German activity in the Balearic Islands and of German submarines off the Spanish coast.

24 May: Germans in Seville are overheard beginning to anticipate a German defeat. (*This is in 1916.*)

---

2.   Translation from the original French by KMTV.
3.   Vincennes, SSEA 77, 65, Garcia Sanz, op cit.

25 May: Portugal declares war on Germany. (*See 11 March entry*.) German plots are reported in Valencia.

Malaga, 17 September: reports of "Spain joining the war". Madrid reports on German West Africa and the presence of the German Consul in Cartagena is reported from Malaga in October.

For 1916 German efforts to excite anti-British feeling represent the main entry. In the Foreign Office Ref 371/2760 there is a Naval Intelligence Division report of 27 January which continues the theme of incendiarism. The *SS Salaminia* sailed for Glasgow with 5,000 tons of ore on board. While on voyage several explosions occurred and the ship caught fire. The vessel was rescued by a Royal Navy ship and taken to Gibraltar. Spanish port authorities were accordingly alerted to be vigilant concerning persons allowed on merchant ships. Then the discovery of a German bomb-making factory on board a German vessel in the USA gave further cause for vigilance and German agents were prevented from placing bombs on Allied ships in Valencia. This information was passed to the Spanish Minister of State.

A report on Spanish public opinion in respect of the Allies was communicated on 2 February 1916 (Ref. 20576). The Spanish Navy was pro-Ally but the majority of the Spanish disliked the English. The clergy was pro-German due to the anti-Catholic position of the French Republicans while the English were considered to be heretics. The Spanish clergy's views greatly influenced the general public's opinion. The King was pro-Ally. At this time, 80,000 Germans were living in Spain. The Spanish press was divided: two leading journals, one of them Carlist, were anti-Allied; five were pro-French, no doubt a reflection of the heavy subsidies paid by France, and by Britain, to influence editorial bias.

Affairs of state arose with Lord Herschell's 20 March 1916 contact with the King of Spain who told him of his desire to maintain and improve Spain's relations with Portugal. But, later on 27 May, British agents in Lisbon reported on active propaganda by German agents against Portugal's participation in the war. (War had been declared on 26 May). Portugal's secret agent organisations (the *Carbonarios* and the *White Ants*) were said to be "useless".

Then in April a company called Areco Brothers was found to be responsible for the transit of arms from Switzerland, via Genoa in Italy, to Spain, a transhipment which involved cement blocks containing arms for Morocco which were found at Malaga[4].

Widespread dissatisfaction with the high prices and unemployment caused by the war was exploited by Socialist-led demonstrations in Madrid on 8 May 1916. During this month, German submarines were observed off the Spanish coast; German purchases of arms and munitions developed; German insurgency activities increased in Spain and in the Balearic Islands; bombs were placed in Allied ships; and many other reports on German intrigues and submarine activity were recorded.

---

4. *This company continues to trade today under the name Areco Consulting & Engineering.*

However, by the end of the month Germans in Seville were beginning to say that Germany would lose the war. Such a sentiment might have been occasioned by the German failure to capture Verdun or the catastrophe of the Somme, but it seems early days for such an opinion to be voiced.

Separately from this we understand that in 1916 the German Military Intelligence Officer in San Sebastian was Baron von Colberg. It was his wife who transported two bottles of wheat germ pest to Argentina in order to disrupt the wheat harvest destined for the Allies[5].

In addition to this information from the National Archives Garcia Sanz reveals that in June 1916 Thoroton made a trip to London largely in order to clarify relationships with the head of the Special Branch, Sir Basil Thomson, and developments in Barcelona. Basil Thomson recounts an incident in his book *Queer People*, as an example of "questionable activities" but does not attribute these to Thoroton personally. He recounts how an "escorpión"[6] and the head of the Carabineros shot a suspicious character, whom they believed to be a German spy, inspecting the port facilities in Barcelona. Only wounding him, he was taken to hospital. Thomson believes that he was "finished off by British agents". There is much in this account that does not ring true but Garcia Sanz includes it to illustrate the controversial aspects of secret service work. She herself does not trust Thomson's sources, nor do other researchers. Garcia Sanz adds (private correspondence) that Thoroton rendered extraordinary services

A corner of Barcelona Docks where the shooting incident occured. The entire Docks area covered 300 acres.

5. *During the war a team of German agents travelled around the USA infecting mules, horses and cattle with diseases and hundreds of soldiers also died (Davis and Johnson, 2000).*

6. *Escorpión, etymology uncertain, seemingly a word for someone living or working in Gibraltar, often found in English sources. Alternatively, a mistranslation of espion (spy). Spanish slang for a Gibraltarian is llanito.*

to the British cause in Spain, transcending and extending far beyond that kind of "episode" due to the "dirty war on neutral arenas".

Also in the same year complications erupted in the British Consular Service as a consequence of the FO's *New Rules regarding the Secret Service Work* (NA,FO 185/13020). The Consul General in Seville, Arthur Keyser, wrote to Hardinge:

> As to Consuls employing secret agents, so far as my District is concerned, we have no employees who could be so described... As to Cadiz, it is well known to the Admiralty that Mr Calvert has, to write colloquially, the whole place in his pocket... Colonel Thoroton tells me that in accordance with these new Foreign Office instructions he must now put an agent in Cadiz as Mr Calvert's work must cease. Am I to order Mr Calvert to refrain from all intelligence work and thus strike a blow for the advantage of our enemies?

This hiatus appears to have been, finally, self-liquidating and Thoroton continued to receive intelligence from such sources as Mr Calvert until December 1918.

1916 saw strains developing between the Network and French secret agents operating in Spain. One example: France was paying the Captain of Customs in Barcelona for information which he was not providing and was passing exclusively to the British. On appealing to Thoroton, the French were met with the firm conviction that this was a matter of "absolute discretion" concerning their Customs agent in Barcelona. The French saw no alternative but to cease paying out such money and to retain it for their own direct use and not on any joint Allied efforts.

A major problem had broken out regarding the use of British Consuls in the secret intelligence programme in Spain. This turned on the legal point concerning the role of Consuls in foreign countries. The FO solution was perceived as "footling" by Thoroton who wrote (10 May 1916) as follows to the Admiralty War Staff in Madrid:

> Even supposing the Foreign Office statement had any basis of truth underlying it, the method by which they propose to deal with the danger is obviously absurd. The prohibition by the Spanish Government of the export of mineral oils from Spain would in no way prevent mineral oil being removed from one Spanish port to another.eg, from Barcelona to the Balearics or from Bilbao to the Canary Islands. If this oil was destined for some nefarious purpose, it would obviously not be cleared for Norway, Sweden, or anywhere else. Therefore what the Foreign Office proposes is mere footle. Equally footling is the other proposal. How they can for a moment consider the fixing of a ration restricting the imports of mineral oil into a country the size of Spain, could have the faintest effect on the occasional replenishing of a submarine I cannot imagine[7].

---

7. *NA, FO 185/1329, 10 May 1916, Garcia Sanz, op cit.*

1917

1917 opens with a report that the Portuguese troops in France are to be under the command of Field Marshal Haig. This decision is motivated by the French General Staff who see this as in the French and Allied interest. This is followed by a series of reports on German activity in Fernando Póo[8]. The Apostolic Letters of the Spanish bishops are reported and Vatican communications concerning Spain.

These Intelligence reports cover a wide spectrum of events and activities. International politics is one of them. The Church in Spain influenced political action and the attitude of the people. This was crucial to the 'hearts and minds' issues. The Vatican was in touch with both sides of the conflict and had, and has, both its own intelligence services and some influence, especially in the two predominantly Catholic countries in Europe, Spain and Italy. The bishops in Spain also wielded influence on the King, the government and on the people as a whole. BNI could not afford to remain ignorant of all this.

Reports of Spanish ships being sunk by German submarines begin to accumulate.

Great Britain is reported as being "unpopular in Portugal". 17 March 1917: German plots against British shipping come in from Barcelona. The SIO, Gibraltar (*Thoroton*) takes the initiative and "his action is approved". What this action was the report does not describe.

Bread riots erupt in Lisbon: many shops are wrecked and considerable casualties are reported. Martial Law is imposed in the Portuguese capital (21 May). Later, Portugal reports that the riots were fomented by German agents to prevent Portugese troops being sent to France. This is followed by serious unrest in the Spanish Army over scandals concerning promotions. An amnesty is later announced. This was fomented by "French Revolutionaries" who encouraged dissent in the Spanish Army. Extensive strikes break out, particularly in Catalonia where Catalan separatists are active and involved in directing the strikes. A major strike occurs in the Rio Tinto mines (*Juan March held a major financial interest in the Rio Tinto Company*). Later it is reported that the difficulties in Spain have been "worked up" by German agitators. Unrest then spreads to the Balearic Islands (Juan March's home territory).

In December of 1917 Revolution in Portugal is reported.

With 1917, the pattern of reportage continued much as before: Malaga agents and Major Grant in Bilbao sent in accounts and Lisbon reported, in December, on the revolution in Portugal. Malaga reported that the new Governor was pro-German and that bombs had been discovered on the Norwegian vessel *SS Glydempris*. There were anti-German demonstrations in Saragossa and Catalans were said to be in "protest at British support of the 'Catalan Movement'". While this seems to be a contradiction in terms that is how the record reads. This was a confused period for Catalonia as Martial Law had been proclaimed there following the Barcelona strike and the publication

---

8. This is now Bioko and is an island off the Cameroonian Litoral and was part of Portugese West Africa, now Equatorial Guinea. Fernando Póo had been leased by the British from local chiefs 1827-43 to facilitate the suppression of the slave trade. The Governor, 1829-34, was a Royal Marine, Lieutenant Colonel Edward Nicholls, later General Sir Edward Nicholls.

of the Catalan Manifesto. Disinformation was circulated that it was the British who were behind the strikes and further revolutionary moves were fomented in Barcelona, the Germans being said to be in support of Carlist propaganda. (All this is covered in Ref 158900/711). In May, the Thoroton Network successfully "infiltrated Gibraltar personnel" amongst the strikers, one example of the Network's *modus operandi*. Warnings were being sent to the Spanish Government concerning the threat to Spanish territorial waters by German U-Boats, backed up by warnings to the Spanish people of Germany's abuse of Spain's neutrality.

The Thoroton Network is credited (by David Ramsay in his 2008 life of Hall, *Spymaster*) with often being successful in thwarting the German shipment of anthrax and glanders bacilli. These passed through Cartagena and other ports in Spain, while on their way from Austrian bases in Cattaro and Pola to Argentina for use in poisoning cereals for human consumption and mules purchased there and destined for the Western front.

A rather unusual affair arose for Mason in the summer of 1917. This concerned a highly specialised product called an Audion lamp. The Network in Spain came across a German order for Audion lamps, high-powered valves used to receive radio signals, for amplifying long distance wire communications and as oscillators for transmissions, an AT&T product on the restricted list. NID Gibraltar discovered that, instead of being sent to Spain or Morocco as they had believed, the shipment had gone to Mexico. It was to deal with this that Hall despatched Mason to Mexico where he successfully and spectacularly neutralised German wireless communications with Berlin.

Garcia Sanz provides further extensive detail concerning the visits of Herschell to Madrid, and to King Alfonso XIII, and the work of Hardinge, Baring and of Thoroton, which had resulted in an enormous transcendence of the British Secret Service in Spain. It occupied a privileged position under which naval, military and consular services could operate. The tentacles of the Thoroton Network extended throughout Spain from the Spanish-French border to Gibraltar and augmented Franco-British co-operation in the secret war. Thoroton had no longer the need to make frequent visits to Bayonne (accompanied by Captain Dawson of Bilbao) as Franco-British co-operation had become habitual there.

The Pforzheimer Collection

Research at the Beinecke Rare Book & Manuscript Library at Yale University was due to two references to the Walter L Pforzheimer Collection on Intelligence Services contained in footnotes to Christopher Andrew's *Secret Service – The Making of the British Intelligence Community* of 1985. Andrew is one of the doyens of secret intelligence history. Through the Internet we traced the Collection to the Beinecke and, through a series of emails, discovered the scale and nature of this reference source. It turned out to be one of the world's most important collections on the subject including rare documents going back to the days of the French monarchy, the Indian Wars and the American Revolution, up to the days of the Cold War and the CIA.

Walter Pzorzheimer came of a wealthy family of book collectors, was a trained lawyer and one of the founding fathers of the CIA, steering it to its legal status under the Constitution. He was also the creator of its historical archives. He served at Army Air Force HQ in World War II, a position which took him into war-torn Europe including Büchenwald and the Reich Chancellory in 1945. He later became responsible for money-laundering for the OSS (Office of Strategic Services) which he conducted under the name *Yale Library Project*. He never married and had no immediate relations when he died at the age of eighty eight in 2003. He was the CIA's first attorney.

In this research we were not only primarily concerned with the references which concerned Charles the Bold but hopeful that other files would reveal even more.

In particular we nursed the hope that Gerald Kelly's Report might have found its way into the Collection, that trail having petered out at Burlington House. A number of hurdles needed to be overcome, the first and major of which was that the Collection was vast and consisted of no less than 92 boxes. In addition was the fact that it was almost entirely unsorted, had not been fully catalogued and much of it had never seen the light of day since its donation.

In the event, we struck gold thanks to the personal researches of Dr Kevin Repp, the Head Librarian responsible for the Beinecke, assisted by Stephen Jones. In the basement archives he retrieved five vital documents including the A E W Mason manuscripts (Box 16 in UNCAT General Collection MSS-WLP/Intelligence) consisting of *Some Services Rendered by our Organisation in the South of Spain* (A E W Mason, undated); *Contraband* (AEWM, 5.11.17); and Report N° 7 (AEWM, 3 Oct. 1916). In addition we found the three page *I reached Tangier* Report from Thoroton (Ref D9367).

To Report N° 7 was attached *Copy* dated 24 October 1916 with the note: "Reference my D.532/16 of 16/10/16". This unsigned and undated Report was authored by Colonel Thoroton as we can confidently confirm from the following internal evidence. First, the size and type of paper and the typewriter lettering are identical with the Thoroton Report D9367 and use the same layout and dropped, page-over word system. Second, it refers to Senor Moyano who was a close, personal friend as we had discovered from correspondence in the Thoroton Family Archives. He is described here as a fertilizer agent and we know, from 2007 Internet research, that the Moyanos are today specialists in bacteriology relevant to plant infections. Third, the writer is highly praiseworthy of Mason's intelligence work and fully in support of his N° 7 Report recommendations. These are characteristic Thoroton sentiments.

Neither of the above two Thoroton Reports are recorded by Andrew so it must be assumed that he did not come across them in the Pforzheimer files, a circumstance not to be wondered at given the unsorted, uncatalogued nature of the Collection in 1984 or thereabouts, a situation only marginally improved upon by the time of our visit some twenty three years later.

In his book *Secret Service* Christopher Andrew attributes what he calls 'dubious …claims' to Thoroton personally. Here he is in error as these issues are contained in A E W Mason's Report (as Andrew himself records in his Notes on page 521 concerning his Note 102) whereas the two actual Thoroton reports[9] concern other subjects and include his praise of Mason, as already noted. That said, there is abundant other evidence of the denial of supplies and information to German U-Boats and the frustration of German sabotage efforts by the Thoroton Network. For example, R V Jones' Royal Society of London talk[10] includes references to the *Goeben* in the Mediterranean; cipher intercepts in Madrid; reports from SIS spies; intrigues in Morocco; the passage of ships at Algeciras; arrangements for the reception of submarines on the Spanish coast; "and a host of things too numerous to mention", all of which relates to the Thoroton Network. When Portugal entered the war on the Allied side, the German agent in Madrid suggested that the rivers flowing from Spain into Portugal should be contaminated with *cholera bacillus*, a suggestion duly refused by Berlin.

A E W Mason reports in

We have Mason's excellent Report N° 7, written from Barcelona on 3 October 1916. Its first concern is the transfer of German wireless stations from Barcelona to Valencia under conditions "…such, that our service cannot deal with them". One station is installed in the Jesuit College "and we have no more malignant enemies than the Jesuit brotherhood in Spain". Mason includes photographs and maps (sadly not in the file) which clearly show the impossibility of observing the wireless station or those using it. The Jesuits are also "…teaching little children in their schools, to include, in their prayers to God, one for the victory of the Germans, seeking thus to inspire young Spain with an enmity towards the allies which shall still bear its fruit in a generation hence". Prophetic words. Other installations had been effected on German and Austrian vessels in the harbour and these vessels were "guarded with remarkable vigilance". The *Commandante de Marina* is himself pro-German and cannot be relied upon to take any action. The great danger posed by these wireless stations is the transmission of reports of "The movements of allied transports, allied merchantmen, allied hospital ships and of neutral merchant ships carrying lead and other contraband to allied ports" with a view to organising their destruction by submarine action. The sinking of the Spanish merchantman *Luis Vives* stirred up the Spanish authorities to even as high a level as that of the King who has issued "strict and personal instructions" that there was to be "no provisioning of submarines, in any form whatever" from the Spanish coast.

Mason submits the strongest plea for pressure on the Spanish government for the removal of the wireless installation from the Jesuit College and "to take on shore and

9. 'I reached Tangier…', 13 February, ref D9367 PHZR, and 'Copy', dated 24.10.16. in UNCAT Gen Coll MSS Box 16 WLP (Intelligence).

10. Volume 34, N° 1, July 1979, Box 21 of MSS 489.

house under guard the wireless apparatuses on the enemy ships".

His next subject is the development of English trade with Spain, "the best thing for Spain itself" in the words of Carbonell, Head of the Criminal Police in Barcelona. Here, published for the first time, is Mason's report. We do not have his five enclosures. "REPORT No. 7.(5 enclosures)

---

1. Wireless installations at Valencia

Owing to the increasing difficulties which harass their espionage in Barcelona, the Germans, a month ago, transferred some part of their organisation in that city, to Valencia. This transference makes the existence of wireless stations in Valencia, a matter of urgent importance. There are certainly two and probably four such stations at the present moment in Valencia and its harbour; and the conditions are such, that our service cannot deal with them.

The first is the wireless station on the Jesuit College, of which I enclose photographs. Photographs Nos. 1 and 2a show the school; Photograph No. 2, the dead end erected on the house of Señora Paula Merelo, Gran Via 35, Valencia, with Visconte Martiñez, the tenant of the top flat as its guardian. This Station is expressly allowed by the Spanish Government for instructional purposes, and no attempt is made to conceal it. The probability, however, of its improper use, is very great. The garden of the school abuts on the back premises of Polster and Buch, Brush Manufacturers and Buch is the German Consul. Photograph No. 3 shows the German Consulate; and the portion of the plan of Valencia enclosed, the position of the Consulate in relation to the Jesuit School. We have thus no means of surveillance. I have, personally, examined the surroundings with Lt Bruce, and we could find no building or place from which the garden could be commanded. The German Consul may have the run of the Jesuit College after dark for all we can discern, and the chances are ten to one that he has. For he is active personally, and we have no more malignant enemies than the Jesuit brotherhood in Spain. They have even been teaching little children in their schools, to include, in their prayers to God, one for the victory of the Germans, seeking thus to inspire young Spain with an enmity towards the allies which shall still bear its fruit a generation hence.

The second installation is on board the SS "Salvator", a German tug. There are three enemy ships in Valencia harbour, the "Salvator" and the "Norna", German, and the "Ana Goich", Austrian. Of all three, though they have no aerials strung between masts, complaints have been made to Commandant de Marina, in connection with the illegal use of their wireless apparatus. The "Ana Goich" was found to have a wire rigged as a stay, and passing down through the deck. This was removed on the complaint of the Consul, Harker. With reference to the "Norna", information was given by an engineer of the Correo de Africa Steamship Company, to Senor La Roda. This engineer heard the tapping of the machine in the operator's room, as he walked along the quay one night under the ship's stern. These complaints were lodged some time ago, and since then, it has been impossible to get definite information. But the "Salvator" has of late been used as a floating hotel for officers of the German Merchant Marine, it houses from twelve to fifteen of them at a time. It has become a German centre, and is guarded with remarkable vigilance. No one but a German is allowed on board, and not even a bumboatman may come alongside. We are quite unable, therefore, to get any inside information; and the Commandante de Marina, an admitted pro-German, while professing himself ready to take any steps necessary to prevent a breach of neutrality, cannot be relied upon to carry out his professions.

There are reasons which make the existence of these stations especially dangerous at this time. The capture of three wireless installations in Barcelona, and the absence of any evidence that the Germans think it worth while to try and set up another three for one thing. The latest development of the German Secret Service in the South of Spain for another. A new Chief, the Baron von Rolland, or the Baron von Bojal, or the Baron Isbert, - for he uses all three names – has superseded Albert Hornemann, in Barcelona, and Bojal is still more insistent to his subordinates than even Hornemann was, that the information which Germany is now seeking to obtain is information from ships. The movements of allied transports, allied merchantmen, allied hospital ships and of neutral merchant ships carrying lead and other contraband to allied ports, are now the chief object of the German Secret investigations. Such investigations must have for their principal aim, attacks by submarines, and their value will be greatly increased by rapid communication from shore with German submarines at sea.

Furthermore, the loss of the "Luis Vivea", has undoubtedly stirred up, at last, the Spanish Authorities to make communication with the shore and submarines as difficult as can be, if not altogether impossible. The Conde de Churruca, Head of the Arrenataria de Tobacos Filipinos, sent for Lieutenant Fava three weeks ago and informed him that he had strict and personal instructions from the King, to take care that no provisioning of submarines, in any form whatever, was made from the Spanish coast. Within the last week, the Governor General, the Civil Governor, the Captain of the Carabineers and all officials, received orders from the Conde de Romanones of the strongest kind, to the same effect, and these orders have been sent to all ports along the coast. All these restrictions increase the value of wireless stations to the Germans.

I submit, therefore, that the strongest pressure should be brought upon the Spanish Government, to remove the installation from the Jesuit College until the end of the war, and at the same time to take on shore and house under guard, the wireless apparatuses on the enemy ships, until either the end of the war, or the morning of the day they put out to sea, should they feel inclined so to do.

2. Development of English trade in Spain.

On returning from Valencia, I had some conversation with Carbonell, the head of the Criminal Police in Barcelona, and in the course of that conversation, he offered some suggestions for the future of English trade with Spain, which I think it worthwhile to repeat. For he was speaking views of his own and not views of his neighbour and had drawn them from a long experience of many parts of Spain. He started from the belief that English penetration of Spain would be the best thing for Spain itself. The best method of penetration was to be found in agriculture.

The Spanish peasant, is a man who can be trusted to be loyal to the people by whom he is benefitted. His need of agricultural implements, and wells, and machinery, is at present, very great. His methods of agriculture are, according to all modern ideas, backward in the extreme. You will still see wooden ploughs throughout Andalusia, and still more primitive methods in other parts of Spain, but there would be two necessary conditions to English success. In the first place, English firms must drop the commercial traveller and replace him with agencies in the capitals of the provinces. The commercial traveller arrives with a fixed knowledge of what he wishes to sell, and no knowledge whatever of the people to whom he is selling. Carbonell drew a picture of the commercial traveller as a grand and educated being who dealt with the farmer and the peasant in a lofty tone, sold what he had to sell and was indifferent as to the result. He would agree, so far as words went, with the Spanish purchaser, but words are not enough. The farmer is not apt at expressing what he wants, and the traveller has no insight into his mind. Thus the article agreed upon would fit accurately the words used by both the traveller and the farmer, but words would not correspond with the farmer's want. The whole trouble with the commercial traveller is, I think, not that he is educated, but that he is semi-educated. He has the conceit of small learning. If, however, there were agencies in the provincial capitals, where the purchaser could see examples of what was for sale, and could find, besides, a manager of that agency who was in rapport with him and could discuss his needs with knowledge, the opportunities of English penetration would be greatly increased.

The second condition was, facilities in the matter of payment. The Spanish farmer is not a man of capital. He can only pay by instalments. If his harvest is bad, he must be allowed to hold over his instalment for that year at a fair rate of interest. He is honest. I have never heard, since I have been in Spain, any two opinions about this. He will certainly pay, but he must be allowed time to pay.

Apart from wells and the ordinary agricultural machinery, there is a great opportunity for light motor lorries. Railway communications in Spain are not merely slow and rare: they are also extremely expensive, and were an English firm or firms to take up this question of motor conveyance, from the agricultural point of view, very good business could be done. Carbonell suggested that the motor engine, by means of a change of wheels, could be used as a plough. In such a combination of motor lorry and motor plough, he saw remarkable chances for both Spanish agriculture and English manufacturers.

A further opening awaits some foreign country, in the coal mines of Cataluna. There are great coal mines at Lérida which are not yet opened up. At the present moment, Cataluna gets its coal from Aragon, and the cost of its mere conveyance on the railway line, from station to station, is 100-pesetas per truck, which, of course, is almost prohibitive. Lérida is about eight hours distant from Barcelona by motor. Thus, the company which opened up the mines at Lérida, and also delivered the coal by motor power, could make a very handsome profit at a much smaller cost to the purchaser.

We, of course, could not discuss these subjects without getting on to the old subject of cheap goods from Germany, and the English argument that England's prestige and wealth depended on its making the best article of its kind in the world, and leaving the cheap goods on one side. Carbonell held that the Spaniard would like to buy the best article, if it was made possible for him to afford it. Thus, he would rather buy a suit of English cloth at forty dollars, than a suit of shoddy from Sabadell which would cost him from sixteen to twenty dollars, for he knows that English clothes will last him four or five seasons, whilst the Sabadell will only last him one, but he cannot afford to pay the extra price on the nail, so once again we came to what is the great stumbling block in the English and Spanish trade – facilities of payment. Agricultural Banks might solve the problem, but if British trade is seriously to take a stronger hold upon Spain after this war, it must do so by extending its payments over a period of time.

3, BRITISH DECORATIONS.

Carbonell is a type of man whom I wish to bring before your notice from another point of view. He holds a position here in Barcelona of great importance. He has worked for our service in the most thorough way. When we have denounced to him the existence of a wireless installation, he has accepted our word, and without waiting for official instructions, has raided the houses and captured the apparatuses. He brings us immediately all news that comes to his hand which may be of value to us. For instance: the news that Muley Hafid had telegraphed to the Conde de Romanoes of his intention to visit Madrid; the news that no reply was received to that telegram, and the subsequent arrest of Muley Hafid in the train on his way to Madrid; all reached us from him at the earliest possible moment. He introduced Lieutenant Fava to the Fiscal del Tribunal Supreme at Barcelona, the legal authority who controls the Carabineers and the Civil Guard throughout the whole of Cataluna, and persuaded him to put himself at our disposal; and these things he does without receiving, and indeed, while refusing to accept a farthing of our money.

But I know that he longs for a British decoration at the end of the war. He has already received the "Legion of Honour" from France, the "Crown of Italy", but nothing from us, although it is for us that he is doing the work, and not for the Italians or the French.

The question of a British decoration, is one which is becoming an urgent matter. A very great deal of work, in the hope of this particular reward, is being done for us by Spanish officials such as, Heads of Police, Captains of Carabineers, who are in a position to put a great number of men at our disposal; and I am sure that, if, at the end of this war, no such award is given to them, there will be a marked reaction amongst these people which will not be good for England. I cannot afford to say to any of them "The likelihood of your getting a British decoration is a small one", for I would strike the heart out of all their assistance. But, nevertheless, I cannot help feeling that I am getting their assistance now under something very like false pretences. It is, of course, perfectly true that England has been very jealous of giving decorations in the past, and I think it is just because British decorations, compared with the "Legion of Honour", have been extremely rare, that we are getting so much help in minor official quarters now. We are making our profit now out of past economy in the distribution of British honours, but we are only doing so because it is believed that assistance given to us in the unexampled perils of this war, will be rewarded after it is over, with an unexampled liberality.

There follows a crossed out and amended section referring to "the English in this service" and a note reading: "I am writing of course entirely of Spaniards". It then goes on:

I should feel very much easier in my mind, if I were able to believe that a list of Spaniards who have given us genuine assistance, would, at the end of the war, be likely to receive serious consideration.

I realise that there may be many difficulties in the way of extending any of the known Orders, to embrace the people of whom I am writing. But a new Order, instituted before the end of the war, and already given before the end of the war, to distinguished Englishmen in the Army and the navy and the British Public Services, so that, at the end of the war, the Order might have an estimated value, would quite meet the case.

BARCELONA, October 3rd/1916.   Signed: A.E.W. Mason."

Thoroton's commentary

Thoroton's commentary on Mason's Report N° 7 is dated 24/10/16 and is referenced "my D.532/16" of the 16th October. This, again, sees the light of day for the first time in ninety years and deserves to be quoted in full.

"Copy.   24/10/16.

…Reference my D.532/16 of the 16th instant.

Captain Mason's Report No. 7 is of its usual excellence and I have but little to add thereto. I fancy it will be only a question of a short time before the Germans in Valencia find their activities as futile as they do at present in Barcelona.

With regard to Captain Mason's suggestions as to trade: I regard these as being of very great importance. The remarks of Carbonell coincide entirely with what I have been informed by Senor Moyano, who, travelling the country as a Fertilizer agent, is in a unique position to know the Spanish farmer and his necessities. I understand that the whole trade question is in course of consideration, and I cannot too strongly urge, the matter should be taken in hand as quickly as possible[11].

I understand also that the question of British decorations is under consideration. I am in entire agreement with everything written by Captain Mason on this subject. There are many people in Spain who have been most helpful to us: there are still more who could be made useful if one was in a position to hold out the bribe of some decoration. Though many Spaniards are susceptible to the persuasive powers of the peseta, there still remains a class who look for their reward otherwise than monetarily.

I feel I cannot let this opportunity pass without calling attention to the very excellent work which Captain Mason has performed. He has never spared himself, and has often worked at high pressure when far from well. I feel myself extraordinarily fortunate in having to deal with a man of his calibre, and it is owing to his adroit handling that our work in the South has been carried on with the minimum of friction, and that we have been able successfully to combat the many activities of the Germans."

The 'Services Rendered… in the South of Spain' report

Mason's "Some Services Rendered by Our Organisation in the South of Spain" report is undated and consists of one page only. Three matters are addressed: the frustration of German Shipping Policy; Submarines; and Prevention of Damage by the Enemy.

The full text of this report follows.

"SOME SERVICES RENDERED BY OUR ORGANISATION IN THE SOUTH OF SPAIN. FRUSTRATION OF GERMAN SHIPPING POLICY.

Attempts made by the "Brasilia" and "Dusseldorff", interned German steamers in Barcelona, to escape, have been prevented.

11. A report published in The Times, 26 February 1916, fully endorsed this concern over trade with Spain, Garcia Sanz, op cit.

The Germans possessed a complete system of espionage connected with neutral boats throughout Southern Spain. This has been completely destroyed.

Information regarding movements, activities and supplies to submarines, has, on numerous occasions, been communicated to Gibraltar.

On several occasions, steamers have been saved from destruction. Thus, two English steamers and one Italian, about to sail from the port of Barcelona during this month, January 1917, were prevented because we had precise and definite information that submarines had instructions to sink these particular boats and were waiting for them. In the same way, the "Bestritza", loaded with war material for Russia, was saved from destruction.

4. Submarines

Much of our work has been connected with the prevention of supplies and information to submarines and by tracing and having information concerning all oil movements throughout Spain, we have rendered the collection of considerable quantities of oil at any one spot extremely difficult for anyone without our complete knowledge of the circumstances.

In two cases, that of the "Jugar" and the "Amalia", oil was actually shipped in a secret manner, but in both cases we prevented it being used by the enemy.

5. Prevention of damage by the enemy.

We have prevented the blowing up of a Chemical Products Factory in Barcelona. Attempts have been made on the Cebere tunnel on two occasions, but a complete knowledge of the circumstances beforehand has enabled us to prevent any damage, and in one case, to arrest the man with his explosives about him.

We have, from time to time, examined the safeguards for bridges, tunnels and piers associated with the export of minerals, in most of the big mines in the South of Spain and have, in some cases, caused additional precautions to be taken.

The S'S' "Fortuny", loaded with inoculated rags, was prevented from discharging her cargo in London."

Contraband

Gibraltar was the main contraband control base for the Mediterranean. RN officers boarded all ships entering the Mediterranean and people with Swiss passports were particularly suspect as this cover was largely used by Germans from South America and the USA.

In 1907 the Declaration of London defined two classes of contraband: absolute, which concerned military stores and conditional, which related to foodstuff and fodder for enemy armed forces. As it was impossible to prove that such material might reach the Central Powers via neutral countries, Britain was hamstrung.

Provisions made in the British Orders in Council of 1914 resulted in a serious curtailment of supplies to Germany and Austria so, in February 1915, Germany declared a blockade by submarines of all waters around Great-Britain and Ireland. This was a foolish decision as politically the British Orders had antagonised neutrals, particularly the USA, and a German U-Boat blockade would embroil Germany with every neutral power trading with Britain. On 1 May a US merchant ship was sunk and one week later, the *Lusitania* was torpedoed and sunk. Britain then organised a full blockade on all goods to the Central Powers (15 May 1915)[12]. It was against this backcloth that Thoroton and March exercised their contraband control.

The "Contraband" Report (which is only signed X and dated 5.11.17) certainly touches on the activities of Juan March but he is not mentioned by name. The *Cia Arrendataria de Tobacos*, the omnipresent and all powerful tobacco monopoly, was directed by the Marques de Comillas who is "a God Almighty…nothing bad may be breathed about him". A pro-German, the Marques was installed in Madrid. Given the complexity of the situation, only the Report itself can clarify it.

"CONTRABAND

Before the war the principle centre of the contraband business was along the south coast of Spain. Entire villages and even towns of importance were given over to this traffic. The local authorities and the Government authorities were perfectly aware of the fact, but did nothing of a practical nature to put a stop to it, the explanation being that the fattest jobs were precisely those in the contraband centres, and these jobs were obtained by patronage or influence.

By far the heaviest trade in contraband was done in Tobacco, Alcohol occupying an honourably second place. The boats used for the Alcohol contraband are models of ingenuity. Some of them have tanks so cunningly hidden that it is possible to discover them only by their being denounced by someone who happens to be privately aware of the construction. The same applies to Tobacco, which is extraordinarily difficult to get at.

Certain of the boats have been kept as Museum specimens in the Arsenals (Apostadero) of Cadiz and Cartagena, and their ingenuity is really amazing. One of these Alcohol boats which was in the year 1903 stranded near the Carraca, and was captured through a private denunciation, was found to contain a double hull, the seats round the boat were hollow, as also the masts. She took a cubic metre of alcohol and her ostensible trade was in fruit. It has been conclusively proved that both the Tobacco and Alcohol contraband originated commercial concerns with large capital, in which persons of high position and officers of the Army and Carabineros figured.

---

12. Fuller, *The Decisive Battles of the Western World*.

The professional contrabandist, at least those of the South of Spain, has a perfect passion for his work and once in the trade never leaves it. Whether he makes much or little money he goes on contrabanding and, like the gambler, cannot keep away from it. The state of things which exists at the present time is really serious. There are apparently no contrabandists, that is to say, the Tobacco traffic etc. has practically ceased; though there is absolutely no doubt whatever that the same amount of contraband traffic goes on as before; but it is of a different nature. Here lies the whole point.

The agencies in the service of the "Compania General Arrendata de Tobacos" fully confirm that they have very little to do. The contrabandists, they assert, are very few in number and it is extremely rare that a cargo of Tobacco is captured; it is also rare that these Agents are not aware of what these contrabandists are up to and there are rumours to suit all tastes. One in particular is interesting and well founded but to understand it, it is necessary to know the nature of the corps called "Agentos ge la Cia Arrendataria de Tobacos".

This corps was constituted for the express object of effectively persecuting the Tobacco contrabandists. It is well known that the Carabineros and their Chiefs can be got at. This was a sad fact, which though it did not arouse the collective conscience of the Shareholders of the Cia Arrendataria, most certainly affected their dividends and in their own material interests it was absolutely necessary to take some step. Having, then, obtained Governmental sanction, the Corps of Agents was organised. The preference of entry into this body is always given to ex-soldiers and especially to those of the Civil Guard, as far as the Land Agents are concerned; and to ex-naval men for the coast work. The Section commanders in each Port are Pilots or Captains of the Mercantile Marine. The Inspectors of each section are Captains of proved competency.

These officers have absolute command over their subordinates. They have small steamers and a large number of craft at their service, vulgarly called "Lanchillas de la Arrendataria". The crew of these boats is composed of skilled sailors and they are in charge of certified Captains (sic). It is almost impossible to bribe these people. They all observe the strictest reserve regarding their service and the discipline is of a most exemplary nature. They none of them have a legal right to register people or luggage but are entitled to be present at it; at a hint from them the Carabinero in charge of the register is obliged to make it, whether on a person or luggage (boxes, etc). The Chiefs of the sea section have their secret agents, even in Gibraltar and it is their business to find if the crews of any boat or ship make unusual purchases of Tobacco and denounce them at once. If the boat in question is a small one, balucho or the like, the Chief sends out the "Lanchillas de Caza" with orders to detain or arrest the contrabandist, and crew and take Tobacco; for the proper fulfilment of their duties the "Lanchillas" have full powers and are authorised to open fire if necessary.

These secret agents are perfectly well acquainted with the male and female contrabandists, with their ways of living, the money they possess, their accomplices etc and are correspondingly loathed by them and liable to attack on the slightest relaxion of vigilance.

As above remarked, there is at the present time practically no contraband in Tobacco. Nevertheless the Contrabandists live off another class of contraband, which is free from the risks of persecution by the Agents of the Cia. Arreriandata, and produce better results. The Agents of the Cia. Arreriandata are fully cognisant of this, beyond all doubt; but as it doesn't directly concern them, and they are not legally authorised to intervene in contraband matters outside Tobacco, they have a legitimate excuse for not interfering with them. "We don't touch them as long as they don't smell of tobacco". Hence the well founded rumour above referred to and to which this somewhat prolix description has been leading up.

Among the pro-Germans of high position in Madrid, may be reckoned the Marques de Comillas. This Gentleman is one of the principal and original shareholders of the Cia Arrendataria de Tobacos. To get an idea of the enormous personal influence which the Marques wields over the Chiefs of the Agents of the Cia it is quite sufficient to talk to anyone of them. He is a God Almighty amongst them, and nothing bad may be breathed about him. These Agents are paid splendidly and have good pensions. The Commander in Chief of all these Agents is, ex officio, the Director of the Cia Arrenataria; and it is well worthy of note that he is always a man of the Marques'. The same applies to the factory Managers, who are always Germanofile, and so on right down the scale. There may be exceptions, but it would be extremely difficult to find them.

The Naval authorities & Carabineros have no authority to extract shipping papers from the boats of the Cia Arrendataria. These enter and leave any port they like without being despatched, at any time of the day and night. They have their role but nothing more.

The rumour above referred to, is to the effect that the Agents of the Arrendataria either provide the submarines with what they need, or that they hold in their hands the whole network of the business.

Where are the Germans most to be found? Unquestionably in the South and in the sea ports; for the reason that the centre of the contraband trade is to be found there. Travelling from Malaga towards Velez Malaga, Estepona, Calaburra, Marbella etc., or towards the West in the direction of Tarifa, Barbato, Conil, Algerciras; it is no exaggeration to assert that every three leagues there is a German. Here a small vineyard, there a well cultivated piece of ground or a garden with its corresponding house. The "Lanchillas" of the Arrendataria follow the line of the coast day and night for this is their business. Those of Alicante, for example, frequently go out for 40 hours at a time and in spite of all

> this the contrabandista of tobacco does not turn up. This is the point.
>
> If special attention were given by someone who, understanding what he was doing, made a journey to study the matter, something might be discovered to put him on the track, though it is not very probable.
>
> In any case it is pretty evident that, from Seville, nothing can be done. (X. 5.11.17)"

The author of this book bitterly regrets disregarding the Thoroton/Contraband FO card files (in their original wooden filing cabinets) on his first, 1995, visit to the PRO. At that time I did not appreciate the importance nor significance of smuggling in the context of Naval Intelligence and these are the archives which have, unaccountably, disappeared from the NA filing cabinets[13].

Thoroton in Morocco

Report Ref D9367 from Thoroton concerns his visit in February, probably in 1916. His report reads as follows.

"I reached Tangier on the 13th February and saw Mr. White, the British Agent and had my passport visaed by the Spanish Consul for Cueta and Tetuan.

While in Tangier, I met an old friend of mine, Mr. Bibi Carlton, who is British Vice-Consul (unpaid) at Alkasar[14]. Mr Carlton was born in Morocco and has spent most of his life at Alkasar, where he is a person of great influence. He was instrumental in securing the release of both of Caid Sir Harry Maclean and Mr Harris. He is the only Englishman I know who has worshipped as a Moor in the Mosque of Mulai Idria in Fez and, I think, possesses unrivalled knowledge of the Western part of Morocco. He said to me he was willing to help in any way possible. He is at present taking care that no oil or arms come through Laraiche into the hills, as they could easily do without proper surveillance, but he also told me that he had friends in the Riff district, although that country is rather out of his beat and if necessary, he would be prepared to go there himself.

On Monday, the 14th, Mr Newell arrived in Tangier and together we took the steamer to Cueta on the 16th. There, I presented my letter of introduction to Sr Jose Romani of the firm Romani y Miguel[15]. This firm, besides being the agents for the Correo de Africa Steamship Line, run the motor transport from Cueta to Tetuan and are in a big way of business[16].

As far as Cueta is concerned, I think there is little opportunity for German work. It is a fortress in which, at the present moment at all events, a great many precautions are taken.

---

13. Specific references are given in the Annex B.
14. How Bibi Carlton came to be 'an old friend' is something we have been unable to discover.
15. Romani y Miguel SA was still in general tramping in 1939 (The WorldMerchant Fleets).
16. In 1917 this shipping line was merged with Juan March's Transmeditárrenea (www.wreck site).

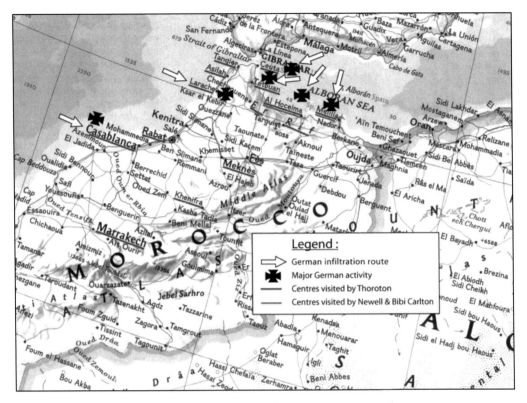

Legend :

⇨ German infiltration route
✠ Major German activity
— Centres visited by Thoroton
— Centres visited by Newell & Bibi Carlton

North Africa

The danger spot of the district is undoubtedly Tetuan and to that city Sr.Romani took us in one of his motors on Thursday morning, the 16th. We put up at the Hotel Suizo and in the dining room I saw an undoubted German, whom, from the descriptions I had received, I identified as Albert von Kros. Enquiries which we have made proved this to be the case, but the account which I had of this man differs considerably from the information I had previously received. I was told that von Kros was a Colonel in the German Army, but had escaped from an internment camp in Algeria. He has been at the Hotel Suizo undoubtedly for the last six weeks, and was only allowed to come to Tetuan on the express promise of the German Consul in Tetuan that he should not go away from that place and its immediate neighbourhood. Von Kros was certainly with the German Consul continually, and we saw that, during our stay, a third man was frequently associated. This third man called himself a Swiss. He is the representative at Tetuan of the firm, Max Tarnow, who, amongst other business, are agents for two small steamers known as the Miquellitos which ply between Tetuan, Tangier and Casablanca. I have left a man over at Tetuan who will keep an eye upon these boats, for, upon the receipt of any information that they were acting for the Germans, they could be held up at Casablanca by the French.

In company with Mr Newell and Sr Jose Romani, I visited on the Thursday afternoon, Sr Toledano, the agent for Romani y Miguel at Tetuan. I have been given

A street in Tetuan at the time of Thoroton's visit.

to understand that Sr Toledano himself, the descendant of an ancient Moorish family, had probably a more intimate knowledge of the Riff district than any other man in that quarter of the world, and that I might speak to him with all confidence. Sr Toledano assured us that he prayed night and day for the victory of the allies, but admitted that the Germans had spent and still were spending a good deal of money in the Riff district, that he himself had no actual knowledge of what they were doing, but that if he received a letter in unmistakable language from Sr Manuel Romani, the head of the firm at Valencia asking him to do so, he would put his knowledge and resources at our disposal. He was quite clear that the Germans had acquired a preponderating influence in the Riff district by their liberal distribution of money and he thought that we should have to take some similar measures ourselves if we wish seriously to counteract them. He also urged that it would be wise consistently to bring pressure on the Spanish Government. Tapez toujours, I pointed out to him that in order to tap with any sort of success, we must have precise information and it was for that for which I should hope to look from him.

He also suggested that it would be advisable for us to get into touch with traders at Melilla doing business with other traders in the Riff country. His argument was that one trader will say to another in intimate conversation, much which they would never say in reply to direct enquiry. I then asked Sr Toledano, since he admitted that he had many acquaintances in the Riff district, whether he knew the Cherif (*the Cherif's name is omitted*) and he said he did not know a man of that name. All through this conversation, we could not but notice that Sr Toledano, while professing intense enthusiasm for the allied cause, was really speaking with considerable reserve. Moreover, in an outer office, we heard the perpetual chink of silver, as though innumerable dollars were changing hands. On descending the stair-case from his office, I noticed that the front door bore a brass plate with the name of Sidi Hassan. Upon enquiry, I found that Sidi Hassan, represented by Sr Toledano, was the chief banking firm of Tetuan.

From Toledano's we then went to Juan March's agent in Tetuan, - Alberti, to whom Mr Newell had a letter. Alberti told us that he was keeping a good watch and that he did not think that anything was actually being done from Tetuan, but that the German Consul was undoubtedly sending considerable sums of money out of it. Information came to him in this way:-

The German Consul had notes of 1,200 pesetas, one of the notes being for 1,000 pesetas which he required changing into small and the German Consul's notes were brought round to Alberti, since in the course of his business, he has always a large command of small change. What became of this money he could not tell, but he was quite sure that it was not distributed in Tetuan. This statement led us to enquire into the names of bankers in Tetuan and as to how money was transmitted to the German Consul at Tetuan. Enquiries made revealed the following facts:-

There is no branch of the Banco Aleman at either Cueta or Tetuan, but the bank of Sidi Hassan which has its headquarters at Tetuan, receives money from Englehardt at Seville. This money goes over in the form of a cheque to the Sidi Hassan house at Tangier, is there cashed into Moorish silver, carried on the steamboats of Correo de Africa to Cueta, handed over there to the branch of the Sidi Hassan house at Cueta and thence sent to our friend Toledano, at Tetuan. The three bankers at Tetuan are the Banco de Estado, Theofur and Sidi Hassan. These three banks between them, imported in Moorish coinage nearly 2,300,000 during the past twelve months. Of this sum, 1,110,000 had gone to Sr Toledano.

This practice of importing Moorish silver from Tangier is something quite new and has grown up since the war began. There could, I think, be little doubt whatever that great sums expended in the Riff district by the Germans have reached them through the channel of the German Consul at Tetuan and the Sidi Hassan bank. This condition of affairs naturally explains Sr Toledano's reserve with us, but it appears to both Mr Newell and myself that in making himself the channel for the passage of the German money he was just acting in the way of business without any sentiment in their favour. In any case, he is entirely under the power of the firm of Romani y Miquel who are, of course, pro-ally.

We learnt, moreover, that at Alhucemas, one of the most notoriously dangerous places in the Riff district, there are two Spanish officials – Sota and Vancos who are the nominees of Villanueva, the Spanish Minister for Foreign Affairs.

On the way back from Tetuan, we stopped outside Ceuta and paid a visit to March's agent for Ceuta. He also was keeping a good look out and left no doubt in our minds about his eagerness to carry out his chief's instructions.

Altogether, the impression which I derived, that although we are late in the field, we must make an effort to obtain some counteracting influence in the Riff district. I accordingly made the following arrangements:-

Sr Manuel Romani at Valencia, the head of the firm of Romany y Miquel will be asked immediately to write to Sr Toledano, requesting him to put his knowledge and his resources at our disposition. This undoubtedly he will do. Sr Toledano and the two agents of Juan March will then communicate all knowledge that comes into their possession, to Jose Romani at Ceuta. He will pass this on to Valencia.

Mr Newell will proceed within a very few days to Melilla and by means of March's agent and others to whom he will take letters, try to get in touch with merchants trading in the Riff district.

The centre of this particular section of the organisation will be Valencia, where, beside Romani y Miguel, the Correo de Africa have their headquarters. The Captains of the Correo steamers which touch at Velez de Penon and Alhucemas, as well as at larger ports, will also be asked to give all information they can.

In addition, I have left a man – Zeruya, who comes from the firm of Mackintosh[17] and for five years lived in Ceuta, to give me such information as he can obtain, especially with reference to the dealings of the German Consul at Tetuan and Albert von Kros. Mr Newell himself will take charge of this particular district and I have asked him, after his visit to Melilla, to prepare for me a statement of what he thinks it will cost. I think that I shall be able to run a reasonable organisation on that coast, on what I have, but, of course, it would be impossible – nor do I think it would be useful – to compete in this respect with the lavish expenditure of the Germans. Should Mr Newell's visit to Malilla prove less fruitful than we both hoped for, I shall try to arrange Bibi Carlton to come over for a while to that country."

The maps of Southern Spain from Motril to Huelva and the coast of Morocco from Casablanca to Melilla illustrate this particular journey and the areas of concern with which it deals. This report gives a rare insight into Thoroton's work in Morocco which was of such intense value to the French, as recorded by Marshal Lyautey and which we cover in Chapter 12. It also reveals some of his most important sources of information and his long time friendship with Bibi Carlton, the liberator of Caid Sir Henry MacLean and Walter Harris, the former through his friend, Eaisol. Mr Newell was one of Thoroton's English agents. Bibi Carlton, a man of great influence, ran a "lucrative business with the natives, by whom he is much feared and respected"[18].

Bibi Carlton evidently had what the Moors call Baraka, a supernatural power which dwells in people and affects their character and capabilities. No doubt Lyautey was seen to have this and perhaps also Thoroton. All were Caciques, in the Spanish word, that is, 'big men'.

The Caid Sir Henry MacLean was one of the leading members of the English-Moroccan community, well established in Morocco long before the arrival of the French and Spanish. Tangier became 'English' in 1661 as part of Catharine of Braganza's wedding dowry to King Charles II. Members of the highest level of English society and with a deep knowledge of Moroccan life and culture, intermarried with leading Moroccan families. Some dressed as Moors and, in the case of Sir Henry, became Caids, that is local leaders of tribes (al-Kâ'id in Arabic means 'the leader') or governor of a town or prison. This would account for his ability to worship "as a Moor in the Mosque of Mulai Idris in Fez". Walter Harris, The Times correspondent, was also long-established in Morocco and belonged to the same high social milieu.

The region through which Thoroton travelled on this mission was seen as the most

---

17. Mackintosh, a household name in Gibraltar, is now M H Bland & Co Ltd (The Voice of Gibraltar Business).
18. Lawrence Harris FRGS, With Mulai Hafid at Fez: Behind the Scenes in Morocco.

dangerous area in Morocco. Not only was it the centre of German intrigue, based on Alchecima (or Al Hoceima or Alhucedras in his Report) on the coast, but it had a long history of banditry, corruption, murder and tyranny.

This description gives but the mildest impression of the Morocco of those days. Only a reading of Lawrence Harris' *With Mulai Hafid at Fez* can bring to life the real horror of Morocco at that time. Such words as degenerate... brutal... cunning... violent... corruption... tyranny and torture become almost commonplace.

Who was Bibi Carlton, also known as Bibi Bangari Carlton[19]? William Rothenstein, in his *Men and Memories 1872-1922*, gives as those present, amongst others, in Tangier, the Duke of Fryas; Cecil Hunt, the painter; Walter Harris; Bibi Carlton; and Cunninghame Graham. The latter is said to have written a life of Carlton but I have been unable to trace it. Here he is described as an adventurous Levantine Englishman whose name was known throughout the country. It was he who obtained permission for Harris to travel throughout the interior and who arranged everything: tents, a cook, three other servants, four mules and two donkeys plus two huge sacks of Moorish silver. Harris and Arkell-Hardwicke went lightly armed, only a revolver between them, and dispensed with the usual armed guards needed for such a venture. Carlton, as British Vice-Consul, introduced them to the Governor of the District and from there unfolded scenes reminiscent of the paintings of Delacroix. They were heading for Laraiche, later a point of entry for German infiltration.

Newells, Thoroton's choice for the northern coastal region, is almost certainly the Englishman pictured with Thoroton in one of our photographs.

There was no suggestion that British funds would be squandered on the locals in the unproductive way the Germans were doing. Bibi Carlton's advice to Lawrence Harris, on his exploratory mission, had been for him to use his name as a virtual password in the area and always to arrive at his destination before nightfall. Harris' guide, appointed by Carlton, was reluctant to set out but had no choice in the matter. Rounding a corner on the track they came across an appalling sight. A man, covered in blood, had dragged himself to a rock. Harris poured some brandy, provided by Carlton, down his throat in an effort to revive him but it was too late. "Muleteers", the guide exclaimed, "very bad people - kill for a few pennies". The guide's schoolboy-like reluctance to press on caused them to experience nightfall before reaching the village they were heading for. Unidentifiable shapes loomed up: were they men or shrubs? The complete silence of the village unnerved Harris, there was no sign of life. Then, a group of armed men appeared out of the gloom. They did not give a friendly impression but on the mention of the name Carlton, everything changed. They were welcomed into the village and soon provided with a feast. A similar ambiance pertained in 1916, aggravated by German subversive activities. The Alkasar of Bibi Carlton lies inland from Larache (Laraiche) where he was preventing the importation of oil and arms. (We ourselves travelled in this area in 1979

19. Correspondence between E B Carlton and Cunningham-Graham is held in the National Library of Scotland (Acc. 11335) and he is featured in association with Sir John Lavery in the description of Lavery's painting, My Studio Door, Sotherby's, 2008.

CJT on right with an unidentified Englishman, probably Mr Newell, possibly Bibi Carlton, standing beside a Calif, in Morocco.

and later in the *Jebel Touchka* when we were based on Tamrhakht, but our *toutes risques* referred only to our car insurance! Even in 1992 the Rif area still contained no tourist infra-structure).

We may well ask how it is that these unique documents (in the case of Thoroton concerning Morocco, the only two personal reports to have come to hand throughout our research) have survived and how they found their way into the Pforzheimer Collection?

We surmise that the name of A E W Mason may have preserved them because of their 'literary value' for they were featured in a sale catalogue from Colin Richardson, Booksellers, of Charing Cross Road, London (Catalogue N° 96) in early 1957. Pforzheimer purchased them and then took up two photographs from the same sale: one of a large, three masted, steam vessel, one funnel smoking, at anchor in the port of Palma, Majorca. We cannot identify the vessel but it may relate to the "Contraband" Report. The other photograph is of a street scene in Malaga, the *Camino del Palo*. This shows a broad sweep of unsurfaced road, a rail track to one side, some pedestrians and horse-drawn carts and a run of buildings to either side against a rugged, mountainous background. There must have been some significance, at least to Pforzheimer, in this photograph. On our visit to Malaga we identified this route, the *Camino del Palo*, which is, of course, today entirely altered, only the rugged mountains, named Monte San Anton, remaining unchanged. This is the road from central Malaga to Pedregalejo where Thoroton's villa stood. This *Camino* was almost certainly a smugglers' route, Pedregalejo being an important fishing village.

But how is it that these unique Reports could have turned up in the 1957 sale catalogue of a Charing Cross Road bookseller, some forty one years after they had been written? The first Room 40 official papers (ref. Nos. ADM 137/3956 to 3962) only reached the PRO in 1976. No further releases were made until the end of 1980 when ADM 137/4057 to 4189 appeared. Others followed but none of these were original field reports of the kind we have here, if the *Erri Berro* can be excepted. This would seem to have been a very rare lapse in Room 40 security.

Confusion and clarification

There is notable confusion in several histories concerning the role of certain individuals in the Thoroton Network. Like Compton Mackenzie in Greece, A E W Mason seems to enter and exit the Network, being something of a loose cannon. We need not be surprised by this, it was all part of Hall's way of working. Mason undoubtedly worked directly under Thoroton (see Thoroton's 24/10/16 Report on Mason's N° 7 Report of 3/10/16) but his earlier work, directed by Hall, may be described as somewhat on the loose side, if we may so term his 1915 cruise in Sir Hercules Langrishe's yacht *Vergemere*. As we have seen, at the behest of Hall, this involved a cruise in Spanish waters, off the Balearic Islands and Morocco, as a means of spying-out German submarine bases. It lasted into 1916. Thoroton had taken charge of his Mediterranean theatre, from the Iberian peninsula to Greece, on 12 September 1913. Mason joined the Royal Marines in the summer of 1915. That same year he made his first contact with Marshal Lyautey in Morocco (reflected in his *Winding Stair* story of 1923). We know that Thoroton was also in Morocco in 1915 and that there is clear evidence he had been there in 1914, just possibly even in the winter of 1913. Lyautey described Thoroton as "our ally from the first hour" – a reference which could only relate to 1914. Mason had joined the 19th Manchester Regiment on 19 December 1914 ("one of the finest officers in our Regiment", wrote a private in D Company, 21st Manchesters) and was, at Hall's behest, transferred to the RMLI in the summer of 1915. It was then that he set out on the *Vergemere*. While Beesley, and others, pin-point Thoroton as "the head of Hall's Spanish organisation" and quotes Bell, the American Ambassador, as stating that Thoroton's organisation in Spain "became immensely powerful…", Ramsay (in *'Blinker' Hall Spymaster*) calls this "Mason's operation" and even describes Thoroton as "a more conventional but equally effective agent" and as Mason's "replacement" in 1917. Thoroton had been responsible for the entire Network since 1913, and a confidant of Lyautey since at least 1914, whereas Mason was not to meet with Lyautey until 1915.

Ramsay provides a considerable amount of information on Thoroton's activities in Spain although he makes the already noted error of putting Mason in charge of intelligence there.

He times Mason's arrival to be one month following the return of the *Vergemere* to Portsmouth. This occurred at some time in 1915. Hall had been alerted to Mason about February 1915 while he was in training with the 19th Manchesters at Morecombe.

By the summer Mason had become a RMLI officer, following a period of "wandering about Spain and Morocco in a steam yacht" as Lancelyn Green puts it. He was recalled to London by Hall in 1917 and then appointed to Mexico, a country to which he returned for the second time in 1918. Ramsay slightly misquotes Beesley (in his footnote 15 of Chapter VIII *The Great Game I*). He attributes the American Secretary to the Embassy (sic) in London Ed Bell as congratulating Mason rather than Thoroton in what he calls a "remarkable tribute to Thoroton" in his extract from Beesley's book.

As noted elsewhere, Thoroton had the highest regard for Mason: "I feel myself extraordinarily fortunate in having to deal with a man of his calibre, and it is owing to his adroit handling that our work in the South has been carried on with the minimum of friction, and that we have been able successfully to combat the many activities of the Germans". To Thoroton "the South" must have inevitably referred to Morocco and southern Spain and in this attribution he in no way prejudices the performance of his agents elsewhere.

Lieutenant Colonel Thoroton was at this time two ranks senior to Captain Mason and was designated Senior Intelligence Officer so it is therefore hard to see how David Ramsay could have confused their roles. Noted elsewhere is the confused impression given by Christopher Andrew concerning Mason and Thoroton (ref Leland Harrison MSS box 102, Library of Congress, p 117 in Andrew's *Secret Service*) and his reference to "dubious claims" *(sic)* of the Thoroton Network[20].

In January 1917 Mason was in England, writing "adventure stories" and "saw some home water jobs". After some leave he sailed on Lord Abinger's yacht *St. George* calling at Cadiz, Gibraltar and Barcelona searching for German submarine bases until, by the end of the summer, his "usefulness terminated". On his way back to England Mason witnessed the execution of Mata-Hari on 15 October 1917. He set out for Mexico via Washington, DC where he arrived on 5 November. His Mexican adventures lie outside the scope of this narrative.

1917 saw Thoroton's staff of two augmented by up to thirty four Special Service agents; in 1918 he had four Royal Marines and up to one hundred and thirty Special Service agents in Gibraltar who he might have been able to call on plus Gerald Kelly who went to work for him in the last year of the war.

If this review is correct we can only conclude that part of Hall's "considerable gifts as a story-teller" and Mason's novelist's creativity have helped weave a web which still manages to confuse people today. In this respect it provides the necessary cover-up for the longer running and deeper intrigue wrought by Thoroton, with Hall's connivance. Nowhere is this more evident than when Ramsay (in his otherwise excellent and welcome 2008 '*Blinker' Hall Spymaster*) describes Juan March as "one of the leading tobacco smugglers in Spain" who "in later life,…went legitimate,

---

20. *These references to Mason are only included here to clear up the confusion about the relative positions of Mason and Thoroton and other uncertainties concerning the function of the Network.*

ending up as one of the richest men in the country and one of General Franco's most important supporters". As Chapter 11, "Juan March, 'The Pirate'", makes clear this is an understatement of very considerable proportion.

Overriding all these confusing accounts is the unquestionable importance of Mason's work in Spain and in Spanish waters and the high regard in which he was held by Hall and Thoroton.

The Spanish viewpoint

A Spanish research study *'Gibraltar and its Field: A Regional Study of the International Relations of Spain during World War I'* appeared in *Hispania*, Volume LXVII of May-August 2007. Its author is Carolina Garcia Sanz of the Institute of History (CSIS) and the study includes 'Counterespionage, security and international relations in Spain during World War I'. It covers North Africa as well and includes hitherto unknown insights into its subject.

She remarks that Gibraltar was the "best base for co-operation between the Allies, better than at other points in the Mediterranean" and that " the 18th century capture of Gibraltar marked the first instance of British marine hegemony against France". The saying, "As safe as the Rock of Gibraltar" then came into being as a result of British propaganda because the British knew it was, in fact, highly vulnerable: they cultivated this disinformation in order to protect it.

Gibraltar was the key point for Spanish and British sea borne trade and traffic. In the 19th century Britain spent £5 million on the docks, yet by 1914, out of four docks in all, only two could accommodate "big ships". Nevertheless Gibraltar was "a privileged place" for Allied co-operation and the centre for naval communications.

Lt Col C J Thoroton (misspelt Thoronton) is described as being "in charge of British espionage in Spain". He is also described as being, in the absence of an English Naval Attaché until the spring of 1918, the recognised RN authority in liaison with the other Allied countries. As well as information gathering, the British organised "skirmishes in Spanish territorial waters against suspicious boats (maybe carrying) military contraband".

Early in 1914 an embargo system began to emerge involving the use of blacklists by the British and French. The blacklist was a register of neutral and legal persons and companies, who were prohibited from concluding any type of business, commercial or financial operation[21].

Thoroton administered a 'White List' and a 'Black List' in order to persuade Spanish companies to work on behalf of the Admiralty. Sent to London for the final decision, a company would be allocated to one or the other list. It was a stick and carrot affair: an "amiable" rating meant that the British granted facilities for the supply of mineral coal in Gibraltar or Spanish ports – the 'White List'. The shipping line *Ybarra & Company*,

---

21. *From the manuscript British blacklists in Spain during the First World War by Carolina Garcia Sanz, post-doctorate on blacklisting.*

in the summer of 1915, was under pressure from the British who had captured one of its steam ships, the *Cabo Cervera*, en route from Malaga to the Seville region. When the Spanish Minister of State complained to the British Ambassador, Arthur Hardinge quoted recent intelligence reports indicating the *germanofila* of the shipping owners, if not also of the Council of Administration. The Marquess of Motto, Cabinet Minister of State, was placed in an awkward position if he was to maintain good relations with the Foreign Office.

British naval patrol boats off Gibraltar were seen as being somewhat hostile to Spanish shipping, even in Spanish territorial waters, and this disagreeable situation persisted until it was finally accepted as inevitable by such companies as *Ybarra* and *Transatlantic*, both of which had been placed on the 'Black List'. On the other hand the *Compania Valencian of Steam of Africa* (owned by the Liberal party Senator in Valencia) and the powerful *Association of the Mediterranean* (owned by José Juan) maintained friendly relations with Hardinge and the British naval command in Gibraltar and so continued to prosper. In autumn 1915 the British recognised "the important services" such shipping firms gave to the Allies. These included intelligence services undertaken by the *Steam of Africa*.

The Thoroton Network was implicated from the outset. Their first consideration was the control of the sea; then guaranteeing British and French naval and commercial communications and the frustration of the enemy's. The Strait of Gibraltar was the key area and on 19 November 1914 Thoroton had an interview with Sir Arthur Hardinge concerning the activities of the Mannesmann Brothers who held important mining concessions in Morocco and were active in Spain. A German officer, by the name of Felix Wistozky, had arrived in Cadiz in September (some one and a half months before the outbreak of hostilities) and was in contact with a score of German officers who had arrived in Malaga from Morocco and the USA with the purpose of laying underwater mines around the Rock. The prevention of acts of sabotage around the naval base was a priority for the Network in the very first weeks of the conflict.

Henry Montague Villiers and John Morrison of the Consular Service in Almeria found that wolfram was being exported to Holland in barrels labelled "grapes". A E W Mason was one of the Network agents sent to investigate this situation. Another example concerned the export of figs to Europe which had increased by 1,300% compared with 1913. Figs were an important element in the feeding of soldiers. Excessive exports of olive oil, used also in the manufacture of nitro-glycerine, spurred the Entente to action. Another disturbing element was the use of German submarines to intercept naval communications between Bilbao and Wales. Coal, oxides and many other commodities, including shipping, came under the microscope. While much of the British action in this field was conducted by the Consular Service it was also dependent, to a large extent, on information from the Thoroton Network.

Contraband activity was of very great significance and this links back to the now unavailable FO card files at the National Archives. These had dealt with Thoroton's involvement in the smuggling game. Naval patrols, interfering with the *Compania*

Arrendataria de Tobacos (CAT), (which was the government based tobacco monopoly owned by March) raised problems for the Spanish government. British boats protected Juan March's contraband runners, even acting as escorts to his *faluchos*. The Spanish were confused by this because they knew that Juan March was also trading with the Germans. A man named Verga, in the text, is identified only as one of Thoroton's "confidential agents". Verga is the code name of Juan March. Senora Sanz goes on to comment that Admiral Hall, in London, viewed March favourably and March's use to the British continued into World War II.

In spite of all this, at dawn on 19th August 1916, a British (RN) boat "frustrated the activity of a March owned boat" (possibly part of March's *Transmediterranean Line*, which was connected with the shipbuilding firm owned by Jose Juan and Dominé) "which was attempting to unload tobacco". The CAT Inspector, José de Arminan, reported that such patrol boats should be covered by Spanish law but the matter was left by default and no explanation of the British action was given. We may assume that this was a case of mistaken identity on the part of the naval crew. Arminan suffered as a result of his protest in this affair, becoming a "failed civil servant". At this time, 500 boats were loading and unloading in broad daylight at the mouth of the Palmones River which runs into Algeciras Bay just north of Algeciras, opposite La Linea, and this in full view of the controlling customs authorities.

The study names two main targets of German espionage at Gibraltar: first, monitoring of merchant ships moving through the Straits; second, sabotage activities. Amongst the companies targeted were the *Red Company of Huelva; the Sulphur & Copper Company* and *the Society of Mining Metalaga*. Some 8,000 to 9,000 daily workers were involved in Gibraltar. On 24 November 1914 a German was arrested at Algeciras attempting to enter Gibraltar in disguise (*The Times*, 28 Dec 1914).

The German Mannesmann brothers were active in the north of Spain, in Malaga and in Africa[22]. In September 1918 *The Times* headlined: "German agents caught red-handed – Another Morocco Intrigue". In 1918 and 1921 the Bolshevik Triennel fomented strikes in Spain.

Restrictions on Spanish seaborne trade were published in *The London Gazette*. The Spanish government became fearful of the British Secret Service when they discovered the SIS had placed a seemingly neutral officer on Spanish soil to direct activities concerning Gibraltar. The sinking of four steamers and smuggling activities were reported in *The Times* of 8th and 26th November 1918. The sinking of the *Brittania* by U-Boat U-50 on 9 November 1918 off Cape Trafalgar caused considerable dismay.

Señora Sanz's 34 page "Regional Study" provides extensive additional material on the Gibraltar scene and is especially interesting as a Spanish source and as representing a Spanish historical perspective. That Britain and Spain enjoyed much closer liaison than did the Germans becomes clear. German submarine sinkings of Spanish vessels reached a high point from February 1917 onwards. By August 1918, one fifth of

---

22. *Mannesmannröhren-Werke is now Salzgitter Mannesmann, associated with Krupp.*

Spanish tonnage had been sunk, much of it in areas outside Germany's own decreed attack zones, and some of it even in Spanish home waters, with considerable loss of life. This led, finally, to the Spanish government deciding to take over German shipping interned in Spanish ports. The somewhat heavy handed approach by Germany would seem to have been counter-productive to its own interests.

A further document, *Los servicios de inteligencia britanicos en Espana durante la Premier Guerra Mondiale* by Elizade Pérez-Grueso, includes an organigram for the Embassy in Madrid and reports the secret correspondence from Thoroton to Lorraine referring to the liaison established by the Naval Attachés "of other countries" with the Network. It also emphasises the supreme significance of the Gibraltar Centre as being free of the restraints imposed on "foreign" activities within Spain itself. Such an issue was, in 1917, the German Wireless Company's activities in Spain which had established coded radio communications with South America, Central America and Mexico involving the Canary Islands and Cadiz. The neutralisation of this service was another task for the Network. This paper (prepared under the aegis of the Spanish Ministry of Defence) gives a comprehensive analysis of the interaction between BNI, the British Embassy, the FO and the Admiralty relating to France and Portugal in the field of secret intelligence.

HMS Brittania, King Edward VII class battleship, sinking off Cape Trafalgar after being torpedoed by UB-50, 9 November 1918. This disaster was not revealed until long after the war.

Chapter 9
Last year of the war, 1918

A further source of information at the National Archives was listed under the reference "ADM 223/758, DNI's Secret Telegrams" (Volume 1504.) Here a more detailed set of documents was found. These too give an idea of the Thoroton Network's activities but spill over into allied areas of activity, particularly into South America which, it will be recalled, was an additional region covered by Lord Herschell at Room 40. Volume 1504 is not a handwritten ledger of the kind we have just looked at. It is a file containing original telegrams, letters and typewritten reports.

A good example from Volume 1504 is a lengthy report from PISCATOR dated 22.7.18. This is addressed to "N". It refers to the activities of "F" who had left Buenos Aires on 2 December 1916. At a meeting with the Kaiser in Germany on 10 February 1918, "F" was questioned by the Kaiser on a number of issues, particularly concerning Argentina. The Kaiser wanted details of the condition of the railways there and of the activities in that country of the British whom he referred to as "an octopus". "F" was later instructed in the use of secret ink and, as a secret agent, allocated the field reference AR10. In Madrid the principle German agent was called 'STRIPS' (?), commonly known as Son Pedro, of the German Steam Lines. "F" was given a number of pens, nine chemically prepared handkerchiefs and three towels. By 23 February he was in Barcelona from whence he went to Madrid. The report runs to several pages of close typed text. Later he was subject to an assassination attempt, his life being saved by his dog. Considerable detail is given and he finally dives for cover (Ref DNI 2).

Another example concerns Italy. Nigel de Grey, who is in Rome "on loan to Italian Naval Intelligence" warns Hall on 20 July 1918 that INI has informed the French Secret Service in Spain that the Germans have developed another code and of their knowledge of the positions of Spanish steamers and of the position of German submarines in the Gibraltar area. This is seen as a dangerous lack of security on the part of the INI. (Ref DNI 1530).

Touching upon such security indiscretions over the leakage of secret information, there is a separate incident when the then head of the French Secret Service was invited to England for a session with the NID. He recounts, in his autobiography, how he had expected to be given some sort of red carpet reception by Admiral Hall. Instead, he found himself wisked off to a house in Sussex where he was greeted by Admiral James and his wife. They served him "an execrable meal" and he refused to drink "the wrong wine served with it". James took him to task over certain leaks which had occurred in Paris and which had been reported back to the NID in London.

"If it had been one of our men we would have stood him up before a firing squad in no time" James told him. The Frenchman left, "grateful", he wrote, "not to have suffered a similar fate" himself.

We pick up again on 'Secret Telegrams' with PISCATOR (a British agent) who surfaces in Buenos Aires on 29 June 1918 and reports to the Admiralty that he has identified the location of the German Legation Conference and that contraband supplies are being hidden by the Germans for despatch by ship. These supplies are stored in oil tanks or oil drums with double bottoms and are placed underneath the engine room. This information is also passed direct to SEIFFER in Barcelona and to JANSSON in Madrid. (Might these be the names, or rather code names, of Thoroton agents in these two cities?)

We can identify one British agent who was active in Buenos Aires, Argentina in World War I. His name is Lloyd Hirst, already mentioned as part of the Thoroton chain who, between the two World Wars, went on to set up a radio station under British government and Marconi Company auspices (*BBC Radio 4, 13 Sep 2008*).

On 11 July 1918 Gibraltar reports the bearings of two merchant ships and the call sign of a third (Ref No 874). From Malta, on 3 July 1918, more German submarine call signs have been identified.

> **Admiralty to SNO Gibraltar, Ref No. 562, dated 28.4.18. British Naval Intelligence telegram contents have been leaked by a British Naval Officer in Madrid, after he left Gibraltar, giving information on the expected arrival of German submarines and on the destruction of a German submarine on 19 April near Gibraltar. "The officer is to be identified but no action taken which could alert the Germans that we are aware of the leakage. Any measures you take should be such that Germany will not suspect..."** (DID). The identity of this miscreant is not revealed, nor are what measures were taken to neutralise him.

Innumerable other messages, reports and telegrams (some of the latter in cipher) are included in Volume 1504. While some refer to the Thoroton Mediterranean network (the Malta message of 3 July 1918 is an example) they also demonstrate how the Thoroton network was also in receipt of British intelligence, as in PISCATOR's 29 June and 22 July 1918 reports, when these applied to Spain.

ADM 223/75, Box 3 (Ref A/R 47 396) continues this part of the history. Two serious intelligence leakages were reported from the Admiralty to Gibraltar, one on 28 January 1918 and another concerning Malta on 9 August 1918. At this time an estimated twenty telegrams were passing between the Vatican in Rome and the Papal Nuncio in Madrid as was previously reported in 1917. In none of these cases are the contents recorded. PISCATOR re-surfaces on 22 July 1918, reporting on 'N' and on agent 'F' where reports on F's movements in Spain show he was very closely shadowed.

ADM 223/767 (A/R to 735A) are handwritten reports to be read by Ewing, Denniston, Herschell, Paish, Curtis, Anderson, Norton and Lister of Room 40. These concern cipher messages, wireless jamming activities and anagrams to be used in decrypting messages.

In a folder entitled 'Treaty Italy Files 175-10723' there is a report of the 7 January 1918 award of the Order of *St. Maurizio & Lazzaro*, with the rank of Commander, to Rear Admiral W R Hall. On 30 September the Order of the Crown of Italy, with the rank of Commander, was awarded to Lt Col Thoroton RMLI "The form of particulars…", duly completed by Lt Col C J Thoroton, RMLI, was returned by him ("under the authority of Mr Secretary Balfour of the Foreign Office" sic) on 2 October. Regretfully, no copy was kept at the FO and our enquiry to the Italian Embassy and Consulate in London elicited no response. No doubt "the form of particulars" would tell us why this award had been made.

To conclude this late period of the war, the FO Index for 1918 reports on Colonel Thoroton's plan for loading ore on fruit ships from Spain. The Index comes to an end with an account of the *SS La Salmiera Españôla* which is said to be smuggling metals, hidden in cargoes of salt, shipped from the Balearic Islands to Iceland. Thus we come full circle with smuggling activities and can look forward to the participation of Juan March in Chapter 11.

Sir Basil Thomson of the CID

In this context the anecdotal reminiscences of Sir Basil Home Thomson (1861-1939) throw more light on the work of Charles the Bold. Sir Basil, the son of the Archbishop of York, was born in Bishopthorpe Palace and educated at Eton and New College, Oxford. His varied career began in the colonial service in the South Pacific, initially in Fiji and Tonga. He met with Robert Louis Stevenson in Samoa. Later he was appointed a prison governor and became Governor of Dartmoor Prison.

By 1913 he was Assistant Commissioner of the Metropolitan Police and head of the CID at New Scotland Yard. When the war broke out his office provided a service to the Admiralty and to the War Office because his was the unique responsibility for arresting spies. Neither the Admiralty nor the War Office had this capability. This brought Thomson into the world of secret intelligence. His first involvement with Room 40 was his meeting with Captain Hall, Director of Naval Intelligence, on 20 February 1915 when Hall informed him that he was in the process of buying the Dardanelles forts from the Turks. Five days later the Allied fleets launched their attack. Then, on 23 October 1915, he began his first contact with the Thoroton Network. Thomson had arrested "a Swiss girl named Brunner, who was carrying a message to an Englishwoman, Hilda Howsin, the daughter of a Yorkshire doctor, and Anna Brandt, a German, who pretended to be the wife of an Indian revolutionary named Vishna Dube".

This incident arose as a result of a conspiracy to assassinate Sir Edward Grey and Lord Kitchener by means of postal bombs. (The agents involved were also striving to generate insurrection against the British in India). The girl "named Brunner" was one of the von Brunner sisters, probably Beatrice von Brunner whose later entanglement with Thoroton has already been described.

On 18 May 1916 a Dane, in the pay of German Intelligence, was crossing from Southampton to Le Havre after a series of transits between Copenhagen and Madrid carrying German communications in Spanish Embassy bags. Alerted by the Thoroton Network in Spain, Thomson's agents removed the bag at Le Havre when the Dane had inadvertently left it in a passageway.

26 June 1916, I quote in full from Thomson's war diary:-

> "The great success of our secret service in Spain is due to the ability of Major Thoroton, who secured the service of the chief smuggler in southern Spain. He lives in the Balearic Islands and has an income of over 10,000 Pounds sterling a year and a staff of over forty thousand men. He keeps the government quiet by bribing officials and occasionally permitting captures of cargo, but he turned over the services of his staff to watch the coast for German submarines. The Germans offered him money, and he replied they might as well offer him an elephant, and then they tried a decoration, and he said he could buy things to hang on his coat whenever he wanted them. Then they tried a lady from Hamburg, who first would and then would not, though he offered her 30,000 pesetas. This infuriated him. Thoroton had told him she was a spy. He said he did not care what she was. He meant to have her. Thoroton became nervous, but early this month he (the smuggler) returned triumphant from Madrid with a scratch across his nose inflicted by the lady, who resented having received only 1,000 pesetas. Now the smuggler is in harness again".

We may speculate as to the identity of this lady from Hamburg. Might she have been Beatrice von Brunner? That "a Swiss girl named Brunner" had been arrested by Thomson in 1915 is no valid reason for not thinking she may have been free in 1916: her services were too valuable to be kept locked up.

The following day, 27 June, comes an analogous report concerning "a German lady much visited by officers". I quote in full:-

> "Last year I received complaints that the occupant of a house in Regent's Park was a German lady much visited by officers. She proved to be a German-American variety artist with 3,000 Pounds sterling a year of her own, separated from her husband. I sent word to her that she must return to America, whereat half the army and navy secret service and an MP or two came to intercede for her. In the end she was sent to Spain by the Admiralty Intelligence. She lunched with the governor of Gibraltar and travelled about making herself agreeable to German agents. At last they (the German agents) tried to poison her. A Spanish doctor prescribed for her, and she had the sense to try the remedy on her maid, who became very ill. The doctor had the effrontery to advise her to dismiss her English maid, as he knew a very nice German one to take her place".

This poisoning incident is highly reminiscent of the attempt to poison Thoroton by another young woman.

Three days later Thomson is recording a further incident concerning Spain. Just after his first awareness of Churchill's "land battleship" – the tank – he writes:-

> "Another secret thing is being made at Stratford, Bow, which is to be a surprise for the Germans. On the staff of the British secret service in Spain is a Cambridge professor said to be the most expert toxicologist in Europe. He has entered thoroughly into his new business and says he never knew what life was till now. He is past fifty. It is impossible to imagine him sitting down again in his lecture room".

This is Professor Walter Ernest Dixon, FRS, and since then it has proved virtually impossible to discover more on his naval intelligence work. Others, who have written about Dixon in the past, have experienced the same problem.

Although his name was not "wrapt in mystery" it seems much of his work remains so. This was confirmed when Professor Alan Cuthbert, Emeritus Shield Professor of Pharmacology at the University of Cambridge and now of the Department of Medicine at Addenbrooks Hospital, wrote to us in 2007. His 2001 Paton Memorial Lecture was entitled *The Man Who Never Was*, playing back to *Operation Mincemeat* in World War II when the body of a false Royal Marine was washed ashore near Huelva, Spain, in an elaborate deception plan to divert Axis troops from Sicily to Greece prior to *Operation Husky*, the invasion of southern Europe via Sicily. The role of Sir Bernard Spilsbury in this affair may be said to echo in some respects the role of Professor Dixon on board the *St George* in World War I. Cuthbert's lecture emphasises that the contribution made by the so-called Major William Martin RM 'The Man Who Never Was', (actually a Welshman by the name of Glyndwr Michael) was of incalculable value, "yet his name is lost in the mist of time. So it is with the person about whom I shall speak…". *Operation Mincemeat* was conceived by Captain Ewen Montagu of the NID of the Admiralty and required a Royal Marine as the subject as appropriate cover and a surname beginning with a letter after L as the Germans had acquired the Royal Marine lists of serving officers from A to L. The body was identified as that of a Roman Catholic to avoid any post-mortem being performed in Spain. A post-mortem might well have revealed that the man had died from causes other than drowning. British Intelligence were also aware of the identity and character of the German agent on that stretch of the coast and that the local Spanish authority was pro-German. To date we cannot evaluate Professor Dixon's role in Spanish waters in any more detail than we have given here, even though some ninety years have passed as compared with the sixty or so years since *Mincemeat*, the secret of which was first revealed in 1954.

On 15 October 1916 Thomson met with Lord Herschell on his return from Spain and Herschell gave him an account of his successful visit to the King.

127

Separately, we found that King Alfonso XIII was in contact with the Spanish Embassy in Berlin concerning Germany's intensification of the submarine war and on the retrieval of documents from a submarine off Cartagena. Coded diplomatic correspondence on reparations to be made to Spain by Germany were intercepted. The quid pro quo required was that Britain would be obliged to cede Gibraltar to Germany.

Other intercepted communications concerning North Africa revealed France's intentions for the region, enabling British agents to be more anticipatory regarding possible future developments. The main interception centre was Gibraltar which monitored Cueta and Madrid traffic including communications between Madrid and the Spanish Military Attachés in Rome and Berlin (*Statewatch UK/Spain/Gib*).

Eighty per cent of the population of Barcelona were reported to be "now pro-Ally", a triumph for the French and for Thoroton's subventions to the Spanish press. Herschell reported on various incidents he had participated in including the Germans' use of a red light hoisted on interned German ships as a signal to passing submarines. The chief of police had the light put out. Then the Gemans put up a new wireless. "Our agents got to know all about it and waited until the morning when the first message was taken down. Then they got the police to rush the place, and there, in damning evidence, was a message intercepted by the Germans between the Spanish man-of-war and the Admiralty in Madrid. The Germans said plaintively, "but we only started it this morning". Nevertheless they were sentenced to imprisonment for taking down the Admiralty message.

The Germans erected a kiosk in the public gardens, on which they displayed the German communiqué in Spanish. Our agent went to the police and applied for a site exactly opposite.

'What do you intend to display?' asked the police official.

'Only a notice that everything displayed on the other kiosk is a parcel of lies'.

'There would be a riot', said the governor.

'Then have the other kiosk closed'. And this was done".

On 13 January 1917 Thoroton was able to enlighten Thomson regarding the real identity of Jelks Leroy Thrasher, an American. Thrasher had been identified in Spain as Captain Boehm of the German army. His perambulations demonstrate the complexity and extent of such a spy's movements: from Germany to the USA by submarine in 1916; from America to Holland by ship; overland to Germany and on to Madrid in Spain. From Madrid he sent wireless despatches to Berlin while Thoroton Network telegrams were going from Gibraltar to England. Then he left Spain by ship only to be intercepted at Falmouth. Under interrogation by Thomson, Boehm broke down and admitted he belonged to the Political Section of the German General Staff.

Later, Thomson records various incidents concerning German submarines, one of the most vital issues facing the Royal Navy and British Intelligence around

Brigantine of Erri Berro type, The Lady of Avenel. No photograph of the Erri Berro exisits but this brigantine (163 tons) was built in 1874 and later re-fitted.

the Iberian peninsular. Help in this respect came from the French. The French had developed 'sabotage bottles' designed to be placed on German submarines by British agents and we may detect here a further contribution by Juan March's numerous employees.

On 27 April 1917 Thomson reported that Ludendorf had written to the German Admiralty to say that victory was impossible on any front. "It depends entirely on submarine activity".

129

The situation in Spain was described at this time by the Spanish Ambassador, the Marques Merry del Val, brother of the Cardinal, former Secretary of State to the Pope. He said that the unrest in Spain was "largely fictitious", in great part due to inter-party political rivalry and in part to German subversive activities. The Catalans wanted home rule (having "always been bankers and merchants"); the infantry officers wanted more pay and quicker promotion; and, finally, the Revolutionaries wanted a Republic. In Barcelona the workers wanted the war to continue because of their high wages; the people of Malaga wanted it to stop so that they could export their fruit again. "None of these factions will work together".

Thomson's work with Room 40 comes to an end on 30 October 1918 when he has a discussion with Hall on the peacetime future of secret intelligence. Hall approved his plan for four departments in a future Room 40: naval, military, foreign and home, but told him he was thinking of retiring and standing for Parliament. In the event Thomson moved into the role of Director of Intelligence of the Special Branch in Scotland House opposite Scotland Yard. In 1921 he was forcibly retired, for political reasons, at the age of sixty, in spite of the defensive pleading of his old friend Hall[1].

---

1. *Other writers attribute his "resignation" to a nocturnal encounter with a prostitute in Hyde Park, He subsequently took up wrting detective fiction. (Roland Chambers, The Last Englishman).*

Chapter 10
The Adventure of the Erri Berro,
Wolfram running and Germ Warfare

The story of the Erri Berro forms the greater part of Chapter 12, *Cloak and Dagger*, of Beesley's *Room 40* which goes on to detail wolfram running and the smuggling of anthrax germs. This chapter is reproduced here.

'The story of the Erri Berro really starts on 15 September 1917 when Mitchell wrote Herschell a long letter dealing with the wolfram problem, voicing his suspicions of a Spaniard, one Lauriano Diaz, who had previously been Krupp's agent in Bilbao and still had a German assistant named Morse, and another undoubted agent Pasch. Mitchell had been keeping in close touch with Thoroton, and he was satisfied that between them they would quickly discover any moves by the Germans to smuggle wolfram out of Spain, or to effect a break out by any of the German merchant ships interned in Spanish Atlantic and Mediterranean ports. The next pièce of the puzzle to fall into place was provided by the Admiralstab in Berlin, courtesy of Room 40's diplomatic section. On 2 October Room 40 decoded a message to the German Naval Attaché, Madrid, which read as follows: 'The Ambassador informed me recently that there is a possibility of shipping wolfram ore in a submarine. The execution of the plan is perhaps possible in November in the neighbourhood of the Canary Islands. Report in detail as to the proposal.' The Ambassador was the aged and aristocratic Prince Ratibor, and the Naval Attaché, from 1916, Korvettenkapitän Krohn. Krohn was only a reserve officer and, moreover, had a French mistress, Marthe Regnier. If Krohn made himself unpopular with the Spanish authorities by his unneutral and illegal activities in organising espionage and sabotage, his relations with his ambassador and the rest of the Embassy were even worse. Prince Ratibor, when approached by Krohn denied all knowledge of any such suggestion, but the Naval Attaché liked the idea and on 16 October informed Berlin, and incidentally also Room 40, that it might be possible to make a transhipment in the Bay of Biscay, but the Canaries presented greater difficulties. He also considered that something could be achieved in the Mediterranean. Within three weeks Mitchell was able to report that he had discovered where the wolfram was stored in Bilbao; one of his agents had got into the warehouse on the pretext of trying to recover a dog which had run away from its blind owner! Mitchell asked if he should inform the French, as it seemed obvious that an attempt was going to be made to ship the ore in fishing boats and transfer it to a U-boat. Hall at once telegraphed him to use every endeavour to prevent the ore leaving, and to report all developments immediately.

'Four days after this, however, on 7 November, the Admiralstab, ignoring the alleged difficulties of getting a ship from Bilbao to the Canaries, signalled their Naval Attaché that, 'U-cruisers 156 and 157 can be at the Canaries on (group corrupt? 24 November). Each can take about 40 tons of wolfram ore. If you are still certain that the plan can be carried out safely, please report details and meeting place can then be settled.'

'Hall at once saw the possibilities not only of capturing the wolfram but of sinking two U-boats as well, and urgently cancelled his previous orders to Mitchell; he was now to do nothing to prevent the wolfram leaving but should report the name and time of departure of the ship carrying it. The whole matter was discussed with Oliver and the 1st Sea Lord and consultations held, through Heaton-Ellis, with Admiral de Bon, Commander-in-Chief of the French Navy, who was content to leave matters to the British. It is possible that the French were also reading the Naval Attaché traffic; if they were not, de Bon was certainly kept fully informed by Hall. On 19 November Hall assured the 1st Sea Lord and Oliver that Mitchell's reports could be relied on absolutely, and that agents were watching the warehouse where the wolfram was stored. This, combined with Room 40's expertise, obviously satisfied Hall's superiors because immediate orders were sent to Admiral Bayly at Queenstown to make two E Class submarines with experienced commanding officers available for a special operation, on the understanding that two replacements would be supplied by the Grand Fleet. They were to sail for Gibraltar as soon as possible. Not content with this, Oliver, who as usual drafted every signal personally, ordered the Commander-in-Chief Mediterranean, despite his anguished protests, to send two more E Class boats from the Adriatic to Gibraltar. A collier was also provided to act as mother ship. To deal with the capture of the ship carrying the wolfram to the Canaries, Commander-in-Chief Devonport was ordered to sail the ocean-boarding vessel Duke of Clarence to St Jean de Luz, where arrangements had been made with de Bon to provide a stock of coal. A second boarding vessel Woodnut was to be stationed at Lisbon. Duke of Clarence was to be provided with a prize crew of two RNR officers and eight hand-picked ratings accustomed to handling small sailing vessels, and with a hemp or manilla towing hawser suitable for sailing vessels of up to 200 tons. All these measures show the importance attached to the operation and Hall's confidence in being able to continue to supply the necessary information.

'In the meantime, Mitchell had reported that it seemed likely that the wolfram would be shipped in the San José, 'a staunch wooden brig', capable of carrying 400 tons. He was, however, worried about maintaining communications with San Sebastian and St Jean de Luz because it was almost impossible to obtain petrol for his Lancia car, and he begged for the urgent supply of 500 gallons.

'Excellent as were Mitchell's arrangements, it is doubtful whether the British would have been able to achieve much had it not been for the unwitting co-operation of the Admiralstab and the German Naval Attaché. On 15 November Krohn reported as follows: 'The carrying out of the plan is assured. The sailing vessel will receive sealed instructions concerning recognition signals. When sighting a U-boat at the rendezvous she will lower and furl her sails and hoist a Spanish flag as well as blue and yellow pennants under one another. At night she will show a blue and yellow light. . . Request immediate instructions concerning the rendezvous and whether further particulars are necessary.'

'Two days later Mitchell telegraphed that he believed the sacks of wolfram would be concealed inside sacks of saw dust. He was continuing to watch the re-packing of the wolfram carefully. However, all this proved to be something of a false alarm, as on 18 November he had to report that San José had sailed with only iron ore on board. It is not clear whether the Germans had ever intended to use her, or whether, for some reason, a second vessel had to be substituted for her. In any case, all doubts were resolved on the 19th when the ever helpful Krohn signalled, 'The sailing vessel is a brigantine of 170 tons, both mast-heads of equal height painted white. Fore and aft the Spanish flag is painted on both sides and between it the ship's name Erri Berro. In front of the main mast a large red water tank. I propose if necessary the further distinguishing mark: a Spanish flag sewn on the schooner's sails. Vessel will put to sea about 26 November. Please let her bring the post and German newspapers.' Presumably, the last request referred to her return passage after her meeting with the U-boats.

'Two further pieces of information were required by the British if they were to make a successful attack on the U-boats - the exact position and date of the rendezvous. Within a week the always accommodating Germans had supplied the missing links. On 24 November the Admiralstab informed the Naval Attaché that 'two U-cruisers will be at U.Platz 30 about 25 December'. But where was U.Platz 30? Neither the British nor the Attaché knew! Admiralstab once more obliged with the information; it was on the south-west side of Ferro Island (Hierro), the most south-westerly of the Canary Islands. To this Krohn suggested that a safe time for the meeting would be from 31 December onwards, a somewhat vague suggestion which did not please Berlin, who signalled back that he was to report immediately what date could be fixed with certainty. This was all very well, but small sailing ships were subject to the vagaries of the weather, a fact the gentlemen in Berlin seemed to ignore. With a favourable wind the 25 December might still be possible, but what, asked the harrassed Krohn, was the latest date that could be arranged?

'In the meantime, Mitchell and his minions had located the Erri Berro and had reported that she had sailed from Corunna for Bilbao on 30 November, and that the stevedore engaged to load her with115 sacks of 'cement' for the Canaries was being paid over the odds, and estimated that the work would take two days. Arrangements were being made to notify Duke of Clarence in St Jean de Luz, whose endurance was limited and so had to keep her coal bunkers full. The four E Class submarines, now at Gibraltar, could also only stay on patrol for a limited period, and there were some doubts about the range at which they would be able to receive and transmit wireless messages. Fortunately, the wireless transmitting sets of British submarines had been considerably improved in the last two years, and a trial run showed that reception was now possible up to at least six hundred miles. Two submarines were kept on patrol off the Canaries, while the other two rested and refuelled at Gibraltar. All seemed to be ready on the British side.

'But the Germans were not ready. The captain of the Erri Berro was unfit or for some other reason unsatisfactory, and had to be replaced. A German supercargo also had to be found, but this was not particularly difficult as a considerable number of Merchant Navy officers were living on board one of the interned merchant ships in Bilbao. Johann Haberstock, formerly 1st Officer of the Hamburg America steamer Phonecia, had not seen his wife and children in Hamburg for three and a half years and was anxious to get back to the Fatherland, although he was apparently not informed that he would have to be rather more than just a passenger in order to do so. The next delay was caused by a decision that a further sixty tons of wolfram should be loaded, but in reporting this on 12 December, Mitchell warned that this might merely be a ruse to disguise an earlier departure. On the same day Berlin wirelessed that the Erri Berro was to be at the rendezvous from 20 January onwards. From the British point of view it was vital to have accurate information as to when she did sail, and even more vital that this information reached the Duke of Clarence promptly. The chain of communication between Bilbao, San Sebastian and St Jean de Luz does not seem to have been too reliable, but Mitchell had got his petrol and arrangements were made for Bilbao to inform Dawson at San Sebastian by telegram, and for the information then to be rushed across the border by car to St Jean de Luz. Dawson was an officer who was not afraid to act on his own initiative and, in case Duke of Clarence was at sea when the news came, he detained a British merchant ship, the SS William Ball, in order to be able to use her wireless to send the code word 'All's Well' to Duke of Clarence to indicate that Erri Berro had finally sailed (a very sensible move which aroused the anger of the ship's owners and for which he was subsequently required by the Admiralty to 'submit his reasons in writing'!)

'On 15 December Mitchell reported to Hall that he had 'telegraphed Duke of Clarence that the brig [she was in fact rigged as a brigantine] should complete loading at midday. 'Anticipate she will sail today. No reliance can be placed on the original description of her painting. Also she may cross a foreyard after leaving here. Up to date the flag has disappeared and the hull is black. Two narrow white lines above and below letters of name and one yard square. Grey paint either side of stern.' Everyone, German, Spanish and British, must have been keyed up, but on the next day Mitchell had to report that defects had been found in Erri Berro's lower masts' rigging (she does not seem to have been a very well found ship) and these would have to be made good. Mitchell deduced from such unusual fussiness that the rendezvous, of which he was of course quite unaware, must be a distant one and was worried about Duke of Clarence's limited endurance.

'The repairs took some days, but on 26 December Mitchell was able to tell Duke of Clarence that a tug had been ordered to tow Erri Berro out of harbour, but that owing to a gale she had not been able to put to sea. He suggested that, when intercepted, gear should be thrown overboard to give the impression that she had foundered in heavy weather. A very smart idea, but one which filled Hall with horror. He immediately wired Mitchell to 'Do nothing on lines suggested. It is important that Germans should think brig has safely sailed with every prospect of arriving at destination.'

'And then, on the last day of 1917, Erri Berro finally got to sea. She sailed at 4 p.m. and by 6 p.m., thanks to the speedy Lancia, the news had reached St Jean de Luz and Duke of Clarence had been unleashed after her unsuspecting prey. It was now up to those at sea. Krohn also reported Erri Berro's departure to the Admiralstab, adding, perhaps rather irritably, 'arrangements cannot be altered. Vessel will be at rendezvous on 20 January.' What, of course, he did not know was that Erri Berro had only been under way for a few hours when, at 0030 on 1st January, she was intercepted and boarded by Duke of Clarence. The crew were taken off, a tow line secured and a course shaped for Plymouth.

'Hall was delighted and, such was the importance attached to the capture, that instructions were immediately issued for four destroyers to sail forthwith from Devonport to bring her in under conditions of the utmost secrecy. Then, after all these careful and so far successful plans, came the first setback. In manoeuvring to get the tow line secured, Duke of Clarence, according to the Spanish captain, struck Erri Berro a glancing blow. With a better found ship it might not have mattered, but as it was, unknown to the prize crew, the brigantine sprang a leak and by the evening the prize crew had to be taken off and the already sinking vessel despatched with a few rounds of gunfire. Hall was bitterly disappointed. It was a triumph to have deprived the Germans of their wolfram, but he had wanted to cap that by securing this valuable booty, without cost, for the British. Whether it was poor seamanship, or as the British believed, because Haberstock had scuttled the ship (which seems very doubtful), Hall was highly critical of the final outcome.

'However, there were still the two U-boats. Obviously the Spaniards and Haberstock must be held incommunicado for the time being; the Erri Berro carried no wireless and therefore no anxiety would be experienced either by the crew's relatives, or, much more important to Hall, by the Germans for the next two or three weeks. He therefore requested the Commander-in-Chief Devonport to 'send the five Spaniards under friendly escort to London to be handed over to the Commandant Cromwell Gardens Barracks [a Prisoner of War detention centre off the Brompton Road in London], care being taken that they have no communication with their consul or anyone at all. The German should be sent to the same address under separate..[but apparently not necessarily "friendly"] escort'. There they remained for the time being, the Spaniards, at least, very satisfied with their treatment.

'In the meantime, E 48 and E 35 sailed from Gibraltar for the Canaries. One submarine in turn was to maintain diving patrol at the rendezvous while the other kept well out of sight of land to charge her batteries and rest her crew. U156 had left

Germany on 18 November and had occupied the time while waiting for the arrival of Erri Berro by bombarding Funchal, Madeira, and sinking merchant ships, but, by 17 January, had arrived at U.Platz 30 and lay peacefully and all unsuspecting on the surface. The first news of subsequent events was a short despatch from Tenerife to The Times reporting an engagement between a 'British warship and three German U-boats'. Two German sailors had managed to swim ashore but claimed that their boat had escaped. Both Hall and the Germans must have been on tenterhooks, because no report from either submarine was received. It was not until 4 February, when the British submarines returned to Gibraltar that Hall learned that E 48 had fired three torpedoes at a U-boat at the rendezvous on 17 January; two had missed and one had hit but had failed to explode! The U-boat had crash dived, leaving some of her men on deck. No other U-boat had been seen or heard on W/T, and it is still not clear what U 157 was doing at this time (for U 156 was the boat attacked). Both U-boats eventually returned safely to Germany, U 156 in March and U 157 in April.

'Hall was bitterly disappointed that after all his efforts the coup had miscarried and this may have been the occasion, recounted by his daughter, when he displayed one of his fits of blinding bad temper. Returning early from the Admiralty and anxious to blow off steam to his wife, he found her entertaining a number of ladies to tea. Hall usually charmed and was charmed by the opposite sex, but on this particular occasion, he glared furiously at the assembled company for a moment and then, deliberately kicking over one of the tea tables on his way, strode out of the room banging the door behind him. Few wives, even in those days, would have put up with such an outrageous display of male chauvinism, but Lady Hall adored her husband (and he her), and this squall, like so many others, quickly blew itself out.

'In any case, there was now a good deal of tidying up to be done. The Senior Naval Officer Gibraltar, who had made good use of his four submarines while they were waiting there, was told sharply that they must be returned to their former commands, and the fate of the Spaniards had to be settled in a way that would avoid an international incident, and allay any suspicions which might have been aroused in German minds about the security of their arrangements. This latter task did not prove too difficult. On 25 February Krohn had signalled Berlin that he was 'expecting a written report from Las Palmas in a few days by special messenger as I do not consider the ordinary post reliable. The two shipwrecked men are quite certain that U 156 escaped. Their statement before the Spanish judge was not compromising in my opinion; an interpreter who was friendly to us having been engaged. The grounds for lying at anchor were on account of repair to machinery. The ore sailing vessel according to news received was stopped by the English on her return journey, but before she could be searched she had been sunk by her crew. The English appear to be very badly informed. At the suggestion of the ship-owner, who was not inimical to us, the Government effected the release of the crew in England. The vigorous campaign of our local Press misled the English and veiled the affair.'

'It is true that when rumours of the fate of the Erri Berro first began to circulate in Spain, there was something of an outcry against the British, but Hall was prepared for this. The crew had been closely interrogated, and the captain had made a sworn statement admitting that he had been working for the Germans in an attempt to smuggle contraband. The Foreign Office, however, had to be informed and placated, and Hall wrote to Lord Hardinge, explaining incidentally that all the information leading up to Erri Berro's arrest had been obtained from his agents in Bilbao and that the planned transhipment to a German submarine 'has been confirmed from a French female source'. Marthe Regnier at least provided a good cover story: a typical Hall touch!

'On the 21st he blandly informed the Spanish Consul-General in London that five Spanish seamen had been rescued from Erri Berro by one of His Majesty's ships and were now lodged at the Military Barracks at Cromwell Gardens 'at the expense of HM Government'. It was desired to repatriate the shipwrecked mariners, and he begged to enclose his cheque for fifty pounds which he understood would cover the costs, if the Consul-General would be good enough to make the arrangements. The Consul-General was delighted and forwarded to Hall a receipted bill from Thomas Cook & Son Ltd as follows: 'Inclusive arrangements London to Irun with travel, Hotel and Meals. 5 @ £5.8.6 = £27.2.6 + Telegram @ 5 shillings. Total £27.7.6.' The Consul-General added that he had taken the liberty of handing the balance to the men to cover the cost of their travel from Irun to their homes.

'The arrival of the crew in Spain quickly changed the tune of the Spanish Press. The men not only made clear the circumstances of their capture but expressed themselves very pleased with their subsequent treatment. It was the Germans who now came under attack for their activities in a neutral country. Doubts began to arise even in the mind of the Naval Attaché, and he reported on 2 March: 'The investigation into the matter concerning this affair has as yet yielded no certain data for undoubted betrayal nor in connection with the fight on 17 January.'

'Poor Krohn. He was now in real trouble with everyone; the Spanish authorities, Prince Ratibor and the Admiralstab. He was recalled in disgrace, and left Spain. Two days later, Bell, 2nd Secretary of the American Embassy in London wrote to his superior, 'I understand that at the Spanish frontier an anti-German demonstration took place when he passed through. My friends in the Admiralty cannot understand how this occurred, and deplore such an outburst of popular feeling against a worthy and gallant officer. (Oh Yes, they do!)'

'There we must leave the files on the Erri Berro, which have distinct echoes of Hornblower and Jack Aubrey, combined with a foretaste of Hillgarth and Gomez-Beare, twenty-five years later.

'The story of the Erri Berro may have had its comical side, but it was nonetheless a serious episode in the constant war waged by Hall to ensure the total economic blockade of Germany. The Germans, for their part, strove ever more desperately to strike back at Britain and her Allies. Having been the first to resort to poison gas as a weapon against men in uniform, it was scarcely to be expected that they would refrain from attacking animals which, either as beasts of burden or as a source of food, were serving the Allied cause. If Britain prevented fodder and fertilisers reaching German farmers, Germany would retaliate by the use of germ warfare against livestock in neutral countries. Sometime in 1916 the General Staff decided to attack three targets which they thought they could reach; the reindeer which were sledging British arms from North Norway to Russia; the Romanian sheep being supplied to southern Russia; and the Argentine sheep, beef and mules (the last named for the use of the Indian Army in Mesopotamia) which were shipped every week from Buenos Aires. The animals were to be infected with glanders or anthrax in tiny ampoules concealed in cubes of sugar beet.

'These plans were, however, betrayed; betrayed as usual by German overconfidence in the security of their communications. The glanders germs to be used against the reindeer were sent to Christiania (Oslo) in the German diplomatic pouches, but this was detected by Room 40. Hall informed the Norwegian Government, which, unlike that of Sweden, was not prepared to act as a German stooge. Ignoring diplomatic protocol, the Norwegians seized a German diplomatic bag, opened it and confronted an embarassed German Minister with yet another example of his Government's abuse of neutrality.

'When Romania suddenly, but rashly, declared war on Germany in August 1916, the German Military Attaché in Bucharest had to get rid of his incriminating evidence in a hurry; he buried it in the Legation's garden. Unfortunately, he was seen in the act by the Romanian under-gardener who told the American Chargé d'Affaires, Brand Whitlock, as soon as the Americans took over German interests in Romania. Intrigued to find out just what the Germans had been trying to conceal, Whitlock had the gardener dig up the airtight container and a large supply of ampoules and papers, making clear the purpose for which they were to be used, were revealed.

'Hall was well aware of German ideas about germ warfare. On 7 June 1916 Madrid had cabled Berlin as follows: 'In order to close the Spanish-Portuguese frontier and to make communications difficult between Portugal and the Allies. I [Krohn or Prince Ratibor?] suggest contaminating at the frontier, with cholera bacilli, rivers flowing through Portugal. Professor Kleine of the Cameroons considers the plan to be perfectly feasible. It is necessary to have two glass phials of pure culture, which please send when safe opportunity occurs.' To be fair, Berlin replied the next day declining the proposal, but if the German authorities still had some scruples about employing germ warfare against humans, they had none about attacking animals in this way.

'However, to supply germs to South America was less easy. It was decided to ship them by U-boat from Pola to Cartagena in Spain where the luckless Krohn would arrange for their onward transport to the Argentine. The U-boat concerned was almost certainly U 35. In June 1916 she is known to have reached Cartagena with a personal letter from the Kaiser to the King of Spain (although to Prince Ratibor's annoyance she did not bring him the new codes which he had requested). Four months later U 35 was back again to collect Leutnant zur See Wilhelm Canaris, the future head of Hitler's Abwehr, who had been trying to establish U-boat fuelling points in Spain. We do not know if U 35 carried supplies of anthrax and glanders germs on these two trips, but on 14 February 1918, when she landed two agents off Cartagena, she almost certainly did so. Hall had alerted the Cartagena Chief of Police, who was pro-British, and the consignment was seized, but had to be sent up to Madrid. However, the policeman arranged with Hall's men that one of the twelve cases which contained the sugar and the germs, should be thrown off the train at a given point. It reached Hall not long afterwards, and when he considered the moment most suitable he sent Herschell with some of the sugar cubes to show

Navy Lieutenant Canaris about the time he became "Reed-Rosas" working undercover in Spain with the German Naval Attaché, 1916-1917.

them personally to the King of Spain. Hall claims that this led to the recall of Prince Ratibor, but it is more probable that it contributed to the downfall of the wretched Krohn, whose responsibility it was. Paymaster Lloyd Hirst, head of the Intelligence Division's South American desk, recounts that Krohn, who could not take his French mistress with him to Germany, persuaded her to carry a supply to Buenos Aires; she sailed in the Spanish liner Reine Victoria Eugenia, but Krohn must have reported the arrangements by wireless to Berlin before he left. Hall knew exactly what was happening and even the lid of the particular trunk in which the germs were concealed. Unfortunately, although HMS Newcastle was detailed to intercept the Spanish ship, she missed her in a fog, and Marthe Regnier was able to hand over her lethal consignment safely to Herr Arnold, Germany's most dangerous agent in South America. Arnold lost no time; he managed to infect two hundred mules which were being shipped on board the SS Phidias, and they all died. A second shipment was similarly lost. Sir Reginald Tower, the British Minister, took a sample cube to the Argentine

President, Hipólito Yrigoyen, and dissolved it in a cup of water before the President's eyes to reveal the ampoul. Yrigoyen refused to take any action, with the specious excuse that the British could not prove that the mules had been infected on Argentine soil rather than at sea. Arnold and his merry men were therefore able to continue this clever if very unpleasant campaign for some time longer, until finally checkmated by combined British and American action.

'The generally pro-British attitude of the Norwegians also enabled Hall to gain an insight to Swedish opinion. At the beginning of February 1917, he obtained a reply to questions he had asked about Swedish reactions to a possible invasion of Denmark by Germany. The Norwegian General Staff, who worked closely with that of Sweden, were unwilling to supply all the information requested, but did make it clear that in the event of a German attack on Denmark the Swedes would refuse all co-operation and would adopt a posture of armed neutrality. Any request for the passage of German troops through Sweden would be resisted by force if necessary. It is interesting to note that Hall's agent had to promise that he would not repeat this information to the British Legation in Oslo. Further evidence of Norway's partiality for Britain, to be shown again so gallantly in World War II, was the suggestion that a Norwegian coastwatching organisation be set up to follow and report on the use made by U-boats of Norwegian coastal waters. This suggestion, made in January 1918, was to depend on the supply to the Royal Norwegian Navy of the latest British hydrophones and other equipment, but was in the end rejected by the British in favour of recruiting more and better trained agents. This too is interesting because, again in World War II, it was found that even the bravest amateur could not supply accurate reports about naval and mercantile movements without thorough training in recognition techniques. In World War II, however, agents could report by means of small wireless transmitters; this was not possible twenty-five years earlier, and all reports had to be sent by cablegram. The Germans, taking a leaf from Telconia's book, more than once cut the Norwegian-British cables, but, lacking command of the sea, were unable to prevent their repair.'

That such a full description of just one incident, that of the Erri Berro, is available certainly indicates how much is missing from the Thoroton record. Just after this part of the record, in Cloak and Dagger, is a description of "Hall's men" in Cartagena seizing German smuggled anthrax germs which were finally shown to the King of Spain by Lord Hershell. These had been landed by U-Boat U 35 on 14 February 1918, the same U-Boat as was used by Lieutenant Wilhelm Canaris while he was endeavouring to establich U-Boat fuelling points in Spain.

Beesley concludes his chapter as follows:

'It would require a whole book to chronicle all the exploits of Hall and his private network of agents which ranged from India to America and back to Europe. Unfortunately, the British authorities still seem to regard the release of all the records which survive (and many, like Thoroton's, have doubtless been destroyed) as likely to endanger the security of the nation in the 1980s, and so they remain locked away. Perhaps enough has been said in this chapter to give some idea of Hall's ingenuity and the exceptional sources of information which he organised and used to such great advantage.'

Chapter 11
Juan March, 'The Pirate'

In 1958 my wife and I made our first visit to the Balearic Islands, quite unaware of her grandfather's connection with them. We spent our time on Ibiza, at that time quite unspoiled, undiscovered and very beautiful. We stayed at Sta Eulalia del Rio. Had we visited Majorca and walked in Palma from the Plaza Libertad to the cathedral we would have passed between the Palace of the Almudaina and the modern, castellated Palazo March. According to the information available at that time, Senor March was reputed locally to be the fourth richest man in the world, with "an interesting career behind him". Let me quote from the information we were given then.

"He started life with little or no capital, but he first came into financial prominence during the 1914-1918 war, after which his rise to great riches was rapid. It is suggested that on more than one occasion he played an important part in the political affairs of his country and that it was largely due to his support that General Primo de Rivera was able to become President of the *Directorio*.

In Majorca he is spoken of with some pride as the local boy who has made good, and many tales are told of his generosity to his humble associates of the past. He is considered something of a card, and there is a legend, real or imaginary, that when he was interned by the Republicans before the Civil War, he escaped by the simple expedient of bribing all his jailers and taking them with him to Paris at his own expense.

Whether this escapade is true or not, it is an unending source of amusement and pride to the Majorcans of all shades of opinion. Being islanders, they delight in any form of success over the 'continentals', as the people from the mainland are called".

Still in Majorca, we could have journeyed on to the centre of the island to Lloseta (pronounced *Closet* in Mallorquin) a village with "nothing to distinguish it" except there is one of the numerous country houses belonging to Senor March. Our guide says, "It has spacious gardens with statues and topiary, but it is perhaps a little too formal for my taste".

From here the history of these two men of such different origins, March and Thoroton, begins.

Juan March, the Majorcan tobacco and hashish smuggler, is perhaps the most intriguing and in some ways most enigmatic of Thoroton's protégés in the secret war. Of March, as of Thoroton himself, it may be said that he would seem to be surrounded by firmly closed and locked doors, although more recent research has revealed much more.

For example *Speroforum* of 5 June 2003 reported March in 1916 as founding

Juan March in Gibraltar after his March 1933 prison escape in conversation with Raimundo Burguera (considered as his son).

his shipping company Transmediterranea SA, which, to cover his smuggling activities, sailed under the British flag. Here is a direct link with the Network.

Mason has March appear as José Medina in *The Summons* of 1920.

To Thoroton, March was, affectionately, "my pirate". To the world at large he was Spain's richest man: 'the Rockefeller of Spain', a political wire-puller, a financier; an industrialist whose behind-the-scenes activities played a major role in the creation of modern Spain. In this sense he was an *eminence grise* dealing with the leading figures of that country including Primo de Riviera and Franco; and with those of Germany, Italy, France and Morocco. Today the March Foundation (*Fundacion Juan March*) stands as a solidly constructed cultural, social, historical and political manifestation of his philanthropic enterprise. Founded in 1955 it is a family-run institution organizing art exhibitions, conferences and seminars. It administers the Spanish Library of Music and Theatre along with the Cuenca Spanish Abstract Art Centre and the Centre for Contemporary Art of Majorca. Later, in 1986, it founded the Centre for Advanced Studies in the Social Sciences, specialising in research and teaching. It is a gleaming modernistic multi-storied ediface located at Castello 77, Madrid.

It is curious how the super-rich seem so often to veer towards the arts and 'culture', creating Foundations and Institutes: the Carnegie Institute, the Rockefeller and Ford Foundations, the Guggenheim, the Gulbenkian Foundation, the various Nobel Prizes and so on spring to mind. Some of the more doubtful aspects of their rise to financial eminence seem to become obscured in the process.

The beginning of the Triangle

In May 1915 a secret meeting was planned between Juan March and Thoroton by John MacNaughten "a British agent in Valencia". By means of a coded letter to G Nicholson at the British Embassy in Madrid, this meeting was to take place in Paris to confirm and co-ordinate the collaboration of March with British interests and to combat rumours which were circulating that March was collaborating with Germany. The French were particularly taken up with this issue as they distrusted March and had impounded two of his ships which, they thought, were being used to provision German submarines. By 1915 March, although at the start of the war more pro-German than pro-Ally, had become convinced that his best interests were served by the Allies. The meeting took place in Paris in June 1916 with Juan March and Thoroton representing the Allied cause and was attended by the chief of the *French Bureau No 5* and Colonel Goubert, overseen by the French Minister of War and the Minister of Overseas and Finance. The fundamental issue at stake was "the economic war".

The matter was further complicated by the French being convinced that they could never trust March and, while he might be pro-English at that moment, he was certainly never pro-French. The chief of the French military in North Africa was convinced March was dealing in clandestine supplies to German U-Boats. Innumerable messages had been sent by the French to their Embassy in Madrid and to Paris asking for information on this matter but to no avail. The matter was even further complicated by the French Post Office in Oran intercepting a letter from Juan March, to one of his associates in Paris, in which he wrote that it was inevitable that German submarines would be located in the seas around Majorca and the eastern seaboard of Spain but that no petrol had been nor would be supplied by him. Was this, the French asked, true or false or was March hiding something? "Paris was confused".

The impounding of the two ships meant that March's transhipment of tobacco could not be released and the meeting, in part, sought the unblocking of the ships and the enablement of March to pay the custom duty due. More importantly, agreement was also reached that Juan March would be working exclusively with the Allied secret services. All he asked for was that he would receive help with his tobacco shipments. The French finally came round to this position because they also depended on his services in respect of supplies that they needed and which were transported by his ships. All this was accomplished by March and Thoroton working with the Ministers in Paris[1].

By this time, in accord with the English secret services, Juan March had installed a "service of vigilance" on the coasts of Spain and the bribery of Spanish fishermen to obviate any aid they might be tempted to provide to the Germans.

In the case of March it was his original smuggling activity which provided the basis of his wealth, quickly to be augmented by the British tax-payer when he entered into the service of Thoroton and the NID.

We can only surmise on how Thoroton came into contact with March originally. It is evident that he did so quite early on. Various names come to mind: Senor Carbonell,

---

1. *Curiously, much of this information comes from the* Special State Archives of the Soviet Union, Moscow, 3rd Section; *the rest from the* First State Bureau of France 1916-1917. *(Canverga, Juan March 1880-1962, Cabrera, 2011).*

the head of the Spanish Secret Police in Barcelona; Bibi Carlton; perhaps even via Lyautey who would have certainly known of his smuggling activities; possibly Walter Harris of *The Times*; or, it may have been contacts in Gibraltar itself, men familiar with the smuggling runs (Thoroton was responsible for Contraband Control and performed exceptionally well in that field); or, it could have been through Harbour Masters on the Spanish coast who were sympathetic to the Allied cause. Most probably it was through Bibi Carlton, described by Thoroton as "my old friend", and who was credited with having the closest intimacy with affairs in Morocco and it was from Morocco that March ran his tobacco and hashish smuggling.

It was while perusing the files of the PRO (now the National Archives) at Kew that I came across the following statement:

SPANISH POLITICAL PERSONALITIES, March 1941-March 1944

File ref: HS-6/966 Secret Appendix B: Spanish personalities.

Ref: 10-6-42

MARCH Juan

Born 1880 of humble parents. Leading financier and industrialist. Has interests in tobacco, coal, iron, timber, chemicals, etc. Owner of BANCO MARCH, Palma da Malorca. Has financial contacts throughout the world. Pro-German during last war. Vital link between France and Germany during the Civil War. Is reported to have subscribed more than £3 million to Franco during his fight for power[2].

Whereas Juan March was most closely in support of the Allied cause in World War I, the reference to his pro-German interests (recorded in the above PRO file) may now be seen to be a gross misconception.

There can be no doubt whatsoever that March's pro-German activities were well recognised by the FO. In April 1915 an "alarming report was sent by the Consul in Barcelona to the Foreign Secretary reporting March's provision of hiding places and petrol dumps for German submarines; his bribery of the authorities and employment of lawless crews; etc using ships, some registered in Gibraltar and flying the British flag. Then, in June, Thoroton confirmed his "treaty" with March, writing "As you rightly surmise, I intend to keep an eye on Don Juan (March) in spite of our treaty. Treaties are of small value nowadays, though I expect Juan is more to be trusted than any Hun".

This was the "General Agreement" referred to in Cabrera's *Juan March*, which

---

2. *Above extract taken by the author at PRO. The "last war" seems to refer to World War I but, if so (see date 1941/1944) this would seem to be inaccurate given his liaison with Thoroton and his refusal to be seduced by the German's 'femme fatale', partly or largely due to British financial incentives and the rapport established by Thoroton. Note by Philip Vickers, 23 July 1998.*

was made between them in their "secret meeting" in the Consulate in Barcelona at the end of May 1915. The Network agent in Valencia, JamesMcNaughten, was instrumental in organising this event.

As a result of this collaboration between Thoroton and Juan March, the triangle emerged geographically as the Balearic Islands, Gibraltar, Tangier, Oran, Algiers. In this immense area of sea, Thoroton's incorporation of March into his Network gave him the virtual guarantee of control of the Western Mediterranean[3].

Although March's prime loyalty remained with the Allies, his pro-German activities were recorded by Georges Bernanos in his *Essais et édits de Combat* published by *La Bibliothèque de la Pleiade*. For March, Bernados writes, the overriding loyalty was always to his personal money-making and profit. He had acquired 'respectability' as a smuggler when King Alfonso XIII made him Director of the Tobacco Monopoly. Bernados goes on: "He had made his fortune during the war of 1914-1918 through his revictualing (particularly with fresh food and diesel fuel)" of German submarines and then in the construction of the railways of Santander, activities which had given rise to a financial scandal. Then, "as President of the Central Bureau of Spanish Industry, he benefited from the confidence this engendered in the world of European affairs, and he went on to finance everything in Spain concerning the anti-Republican movements and in particular the *Falange*". Other sources show he definitely sold arms to the Republicans as well even if, on occasion, they only received scrap iron instead of the fifty anti-aircraft guns they had thought they had purchased and which were needed urgently for the defence of Barcelona. These had been paid for in pounds sterling and by two chests filled with jewels stolen from the Sanctuary of Our Lady of Guadalupe and monstrances from other churches.

It is thought that it was on March's visit to London in 1936 that he negotiated, in favour of Franco, with other international financiers and possibly met with Lord Bute. The Marquess had sold his vast freeholds and coal mines in South Wales and Cardiff for a sum which exceeded the entire French military, naval and air force budget for a year. Much of this money Lord Bute donated to the Nationalist cause. For this information we are indebted to Charles Pelletier Doisy, whose family were very close to Lord Bute, living as they did in Morocco, Charles' grandfather accompanying Bute on his extensive tours of the Holy Land. Pelletier Doisy thinks it likely that these two wealthy men would have known of each other in Morocco, particularly in the light of their joint support of the Nationalist cause.

The submarine menace

Reverting to the German submarine support provided by March, we know of at least one German U-Boat which, damaged by an aircraft attack, made Cartagena harbour and was interned. As to revictualing ports on the coast of Spain, Valencia is a possible candidate by virtue of the pro-German elements known to be found there.

---

3.   NA, Garcia Sanz, op cit.

Los Barcos de March Sumistrando a los Alemanes en 1915. After re-fueling a German submarine one of March's merchant ships leaves to a salute by the U-boat crew.

It is difficult to draw a balance between the denial of Spanish facilities and the report of March gaining "a fortune" in World War I by such activities. Smuggling and British Intelligence funds certainly played a more than significant role here.

In the context of his supplying German submarines, there is a remarkable painting (courtesy of Senor Monjo) which shows the crew of a German submarine saluting the departure of one of Juan March's merchant ships which had been replenishing them with either food, water or possibly fuel oil. This was a typical activity of March on behalf of the Kaiser's fleet but there was a sting in the tail. Part of the information March was passing to the British were details of the German submarine routes in the Mediterranean and, in addition, further information on how the British could find the U-Boats. March had "a Phoenician mind" (indeed he might well have had Phoenician blood in his veins as Majorca had been part of the Phoenician empire, as had been Catalonia) and to have such a mind means that for services rendered he required appropriate recompense. He was asymetric in his approach to the field of capital investment and the time and risks he incurred in its management and, most particularly, in the services he rendered. One example of this will be seen later. To return to the painting, it reveals, I fear, part of the darkest side of his character. March had been paid by the German submarine commander for the supplies he had provided; the crew salutes; and the supply ship departs. However, the location of the unfortunate U-Boat can now be passed to the British, ending perhaps in its destruction by the Royal Navy and the loss of all hands. For this information too 'the Pirate' extracts his pound of flesh, but from the British this time. Asymetric thinking has paid off yet again.

Thus we could see then (1998) that Spain, Morocco, England and France were linked in the Thoroton/Lyautey/March consortium. Other countries too could be linked in: Germany and Italy for example.

Political ramifications

For further research we turned to the Internet and we found the following information from Wikipedia.

Juan March Ordinas (1880-1962) was a Spanish financier and British agent on the side of Francisco Franco's forces during and after the Spanish Civil War. He was born in Santa Margalida on the island of Majorca and initially he was involved with the business of smuggling tobacco between North Africa and Spain. During World War I he was supplying goods to ships of both sides, avoiding the blockade.

His power and influence increased during different Spanish governments and during the reign of King Alfonso XIII. Convicted and imprisoned by the Second Spanish Republic, he organised an escape to Gibraltar where he would be protected by his status as a British agent. Later, he became a main organiser and financier of Franco's rebellion, personally financing the Italian planes that carried the colonial troops from Spanish Morocco to Southern Spain. He did this by acquiring a majority holding in the *Savoia* aircraft factory outside Rome in 1936. This enabled him to dominate the supply of bombers to Franco and ensured continuing profits. Previously he organised the flight of the Dragon *Rapide*, Franco's aerial transport from the Canary Islands to Morocco, to lead the coup.

At the end of World War II he was the seventh richest man in the world, yet another example of how war, and armaments, are a major engine for financial gain, as Professor Galbraith and others have pointed out. In February 1948, through various contacts, he managed to buy the power company, Barcelona Traction, which had been founded in 1911 by a Canadian, Frederick Stark Pearson, much of the finance coming from Belgium. The company was worth £10 million but he bought it for only some half a million pounds sterling by a subterfuge involving the printing of counterfeit shares.

In 1944 March started the promotion of Don Juan de Bourbon, who had turned pro-Ally, to the Spanish throne. He also had investments in newspapers and political parties, mines, shipyards, steel plants, power and oil companies, chemical companies, Spain's principal brewery, and a *Coca Cola* bottling plant. He owned and controlled Spain's tobacco and gasoline monopolies and a major bank, Banco Centrale. He also held an important stake in the *Institute Naccional de Industrie*, the state-owned agency for industrial development that controlled and invested in private industry using state capital. Outside Spain he controlled holding companies in London and New York. "I have no need of banks" he once bragged, "the bankers need me". By this time he had become the chief financial adviser to the Spanish Jesuit, Dominican and Benedictine orders.

According to recently declassified documents, during 1941 it was decided in the Cabinet to create a hostile attitude towards Spain's entry into the World War through gifts of money. A group of top Spanish generals was approached by March, and his arguments were supported by a sum of US$ 10,000,000 which were put at their disposal by Winston Churchill's government[4].

Other clues concerning Juan March come from the report that he held a major financial shareholding in the Rio Tinto Company based at that time on its original site in Huelva in Southern Spain. The Tinto River flows into the Gulf of Cadiz at that point. The Rio Tinto Company, always a leading mining company, is today the fourth largest in the world. It was established by Hugh Matheson of Jardine Matheson in 1873 and financed by the Rothschilds and other international bankers. It was re-established in 1905 under British control with Rothschild backing. Its Huelva site worked the ancient copper mines. In December 1915, Thoroton wrote to his Embassy in Madrid advising them that he had drawn in agents from the Spanish Security Services to protect the Rio Tinto mines from sabotage.

March was a Freemason, or a *chueta*, as Majorcan Jews used to be called. Freemasonry was an important factor in the Spanish Civil War. Franco had been selected as leader of the Nationalists in July 1937 in part due to his distance from Freemasonry whereas other candidates were known to be Freemasons. Evidence of

---

4. Five Spanish references relate to this information: Manuel de Benavides, *El ultimo pirata del mediterraneo*, Barcelona, 1934; Ramon Garriga, *Juan march y su tiempo*, Barcelona, 1976; Bernardo Diaz Nosty, *La Irresistible ascension de Juan March*, Madrid, 1977; and Pere Ferrer Guasp, *Juan March, la cara oculta del poder*, Palma-Illes Balears, 2004, and his 2008, Barcelona, *El hombre mas misterioso del mondo*, but we have not been able to study these in any detail.

his position in the Masonic orders is provided by Mercedes Cabrera in her biography of Juan March. In 1931, threatened with an extradition order by the Republican government, he boarded the transatlantic English ship *Scrachard* in Gibraltar bound for Marseilles. He was accompanied by his close friend Ruiz Albeniz. His departure was signalled by the Masonic Lodge in Gibraltar to the Grand Master of the Orient Lodge in Madrid in a letter dated 8 November 1931[5].

March and Thoroton

We now return to Juan March and his direct involvement with Thoroton. When we published the photograph of Thoroton with the Sultan of Morocco in the 1998 *Globe & Laurel* we were not sure of the identity of the second European: was it March or Mason? Later it was definitely identified as being March. This is the only photograph which exists of Thoroton and March together and comes from the TFA (Thoroton Family Archives.)

During the Rif insurgencies, German agents were active in both the French and Spanish zones which had been initiated by the Treaty of Fez in 1912. The Sultan's Police Chief was Abel-el-Malek, an Algerian, and he may be present in the accompanying photograph. In Tangier itself the principle German agent had been identified. (This is possibly Baumann, the "short, stockish Alsatian" as described by Mason in *The Winding Stair*.)

Then, in 2001, we were able to up-date the 1998 article in a letter to the Editor dated 26 November.

Even though the original article had invited contributions from readers, none had been forthcoming. In point of fact the 26 November 2001 letter was never published so we reproduce it here[6].

Sir,

Charles the Bold – RM Secret Agent Extraordinary

The Jan/Feb 1998 issue of *The Globe & Laurel* carried an article under the above title, giving a description of Lt Col C J Thoroton's career and invited further information if this might be forthcoming from other sources. In the event, nothing more arose, until now. It seems that Charles the Bold's "pirate" Don Juan March, who later came to control the economy of Spain itself, was active again in 1916. Readers may be interested to hear in what way.

---

5.   *Grand Archive of the Civil War, Salamanca, leg. 1204.*
6.   *The RMHS and Sheet Anchor would have been the right medium since The Globe & Laurel concentrates on the serving Corps, hence the lack of response.*

In 1916, Wilhelm Franz Canaris (future Rear Admiral and chief of the ABWEHR under Hitler) was in Cartegena, Spain with the rank of Captain and had begun his long career as a secret agent and his entanglement with the British SIS. At stake was the control of the Mediterranean, of Suez, the Arab oil wells and our communications with Empire. Captain Menzies (the future "C", chief of MI-6) was despatched to "kill or capture" Canaris.

Juan March was able to locate Canaris and inform Menzies. Two French submarines, *Topaz* and *Opale* , were to torpedo the German submarine, U-35, which was coming to rescue him. They failed: Canaris and his companions escaped by means of a fishing smack which, coming alongside U-35, enabled them to leap aboard. U-35 then submerged and ran fast for the Adriatic.

Don March was later to report to "C" on Canaris' support for the Franco forces and then to reveal the existence of the *Schwarze Kapelle* (the 'Black Orchestra'), the German resistance to Hitler of which Canaris was a leading light. March warned Menzies that Canaris was "a man to be watched, cultivated and possibly won over… as a sleeping partner of British espionage". Even in 1940 March was assisting Canaris in deception moves to frustrate Hitler's attempts to draw Franco into the Axis at the Hendays meeting. No wonder Thoroton's work in Spain was credited with its "vital" role in World War II.

CJT and Juan March with Sultan Moulay Joussef in Morocco during the Great War. The only photograph showing the two agents together.

The mystery of March

It needs to be explained here why so much information is provided on Juan March and how he is inter-related so significantly with Thoroton.

First, Juan March is virtually unknown outside Spain. In terms of secret intelligence his work with Thoroton is well chronicled by Beesley and David Stafford. However, there is also much incorrect and misleading information, for example Richard Deacon's *History* and in Ramsay's more recent *'Blinker' Hall – Spymaster*. These errors are largely due to a lack of primary sources and an over-reliance on previously published accounts. Even Andrew (in *Secret Service*) casts unjustified doubt on some of the Network's authenticated achievements, an issue which I took up with him in a letter dated 9 January 1997[7].

Inside Spain a security blanket has overlaid Juan March for decades and he might well be described as the world's most opaque billionaire. More recently Spanish historians such as Mercedes Cabrera, Carolina Garcia-Sanz and Dolores Pérez-Guesco, amongst others, have brought March into the limelight. This has not happened in Britain.

Most importantly, March's services were at the disposition of both the British and the Germans at the start of WW I. It was Thoroton who won this battle and secured March's unique services in the Allied cause. March's smuggling, commercial and maritime empire provided some 40,000 agents to the Network. Without this, the war in the Mediterranean would have taken a very different course with some catastrophic results for the Allies. Instead, it was the German U-Boot menace which was neutralised. In addition, March's services in WW II were welcomed by Admiral Godfrey, by Churchill and Hillgarth, all beneficiaries of Thoroton's conversion of March.

Research at the *Instituto Cervantes* in Paris and in Tangier revealed that the Bartholomew March Foundation had its headquarters in Palma da Mallorca and that it was run in a way similar to the Rockefeller Foundation. The famous March Library is in the March Foundation in Madrid but I was informed, 'little would be gained from these quarters'.

Important source material on Juan March is available on the Internet. Robert Duncan, of *Spero News*, reported on three historians and journalists who had been working on this subject: Dolores Genovés, responsible for directing a documentary film for *Catalunya TV*, "*TV3*"; Mercedes Cabrera of Madrid's *Computense* University, who at that time was writing her biography of March; and Pr Ferder Guasp, of *El Mundo*, whose doctoral thesis was on Juan March. *Spero News* reported that March was supposed to have been guilty of the murder of one Rafael Garau in 1916. This Garau was the son of one of March's business partners who had been accused of having an affair with March's wife, Leornora Severa Melis.

---

7. *See for example p 117 of Secret Service.*

It has been stated that March never returned to Majorca after this affair[8], but this is not certain. Some say he returned to the island but did not live again in Santa Margarita. Juan and Leornora had two sons, Bartholomé March Severa and Juan March Severa, the latter said to have "the habits of an English lord" and who died in 1973, leaving two sons, one being Juan March Delgardo. This March is a Director of *Banco March SA*, a Director of the International Carrefour Foundation and is an Associate of the Council for Foreign Relations (CFR) which is at Number 58, E68[th] Street, New York. The CFR is reported as "being at the heart of the American Establishment" and to be "the most influential foreign-policy think tank" in the USA. It was founded in 1921 and now numbers some 4,200 members. He is Spain's representative to the Trilateral Commission. Today ALBA is the March worldwide Investment Company. (ALBA: Corporacion Financiera Alba SA)

Juan March died following a car accident on 10 March 1962, at the age of eighty two, "near Las Rozas, Madrid". Las Rozas, on the Madrid-El Escorial road, had been the scene of heavy fighting in the Civil War 5 to 9 January 1937 and we drove past the site on our way to El Escorial in 2008 while researching the March environment. Whether his was a genuine traffic accident or not seems to be a matter of speculation. That the accident involved no bad play is generally accepted but, in the course of his long life, he must have inevitably made some enemies, this thought perhaps fuelling the rumours which include reference to a garage engineer's report on the damaged car and that no investigation into the accident was ever undertaken. As with so much concerning this man, there are those who consider this out of the question and others who reserve their doubts.

The most surprising feature of the website of the Council of Majorca, under the title *Coleccion Can Verga*, is its frontispiece, a somewhat crudely drawn, caricature type picture featuring a whole galaxy of men who are shown surrounding March who is, himself, welcoming Franco[9]. Spanish *grandees* are shown, coming up behind March with bags of money, arms and tobacco loaded onto a horse. A pirate flag flies over them. The March Foundation, and family, are quite extensively featured on the Internet and a series of portraits and photographs are displayed in the March archives, one even of the crib in which he slept as a baby. His mature portrait, by Ignacio Zuloaga, is instructive. Grey haired, bespectacled and dark suited he leans back in an armchair, a cigar suitably clasped in his right hand. The background is sombre, rather menacing, and seems to show a Majorcan landscape. The sitter looks straight ahead, not at the viewer.

These men carry a bewildering array of banners inscribed: *Aucona, K Benson, Banca March, Casa Del Pueblo, GESA, Credito Balear, FESCA, Informacienes, Transmediterranea, CAUBET, El Dia* and others. Over on the left, behind Franco,

---

8. *Speroforum.com, 5 June 2003.*

9. *The cartoon is based on Velasquez's painting* La rendición de Breda *which shows the surrender of the city's key by the Dutch general Frederick Henry to the Spanish general Spinola. This was a highly honourable moment for both generals. In the cartoon Frederick is Franco and Spinola is March.*

Album de Photos, cartoon featuring Franco being welcomed by Juan march in the presence of Spanish grandees.

similar banners are inscribed: *Dictatura Primo de Rivera, II Republica, Dictatura Franco.* Just behind Franco is a man, who may be Don Juan de Bourbon, accompanied by a horse.

The Council of Majorca, which is partly responsible for this site, tell us that the *Coleccion Can Verga* is based in Santa Magherita, Majorca. The proprietors are named Miguel Monjo and Francisco Ferragut. Later on we were to be introduced to Don Monjo, as will follow.

Also adding to our information was a *TIME* magazine article of 1943, under the heading 'Rickety Bandwagon'. Then, *TIME* on 14 April 1961, described him as the 'Iberian Croesus' and as "the richest man in Spain at the end of World War I" who was, after World War II, worth US $ 1 billion "having financed both world wars on both sides". This $1 billion was said to be the equivalent of the US's entire foreign aid programme to Spain. An October 1949 article was quoted entitled 'The Second Battle of the Ebro'. This is a reference to the fateful battle of July and August 1838 which cost 135,000 casualties. The TIME article is emphasising the relationship of March's immense profits to the fate of some half a million casualties in the course of the war.

Enough has been said here to emphasise that Juan March Ordinas, known as "my pirate" by Charles the Bold, brings us into such a tangled web of intrigue and cover-up that perhaps only Winston Churchill (who well knew of him) is capable of describing, as he did in his 1932 book *Thoughts and Adventures* concerning the world of the secret services: "tangle within tangle, plot and counter-plot, ruse and treachery… true agent, false agent… subterranean labyrinths…"

No history of BNI in the Mediterranean in the two World Wars which omits detailed information on Juan March can be considered as being complete.

March correspondence: France and England

When we met Mercedes Cabrera Calvo-Sotelo in June 2008 in Madrid two important developments followed.

The first was that she had in her archives a letter written by Juan March (from his address, Plaza de Las Cortes, 7M) on 15 May 1927, to Don Juan Carreras who was the Director of his tobacco factory in Oran. This letter made direct reference to Thoroton and, from reading it, Mercedes Cabrera formed the opinion that the two men were on close, personal terms. What is especially interesting is that Juan March seldom, if ever, signed anything and had all his papers and records regularly destroyed. For the most part the only 'documentation' which remains are legal papers held in the Justice Department. A few newspaper reports exist but some of these journals were owned by March *Le Libertad* in Madrid and *El Dia* in Majorca, for example.

Addressed to 'My dear friend', the letter concerns a 'notarial act', signed by Thoroton, and a letter 'authorised by a notaire', which March and Carreras were to take with them on a visit to Paris on 2 June 1927, staying at the Hotel Continental. This type of 'power of attorney' concerned March's activities on behalf of the Allies during the Great War and describes how he and Colonel Thoroton had met a French Admiral and the Chief of Intelligence at the War Ministry in Paris in order to come to an agreement on "how I was to contribute" and the actual services he rendered to the Allies. Colonel Thoroton is described as being in charge of the English Intelligence Service in Gibraltar for the Western Mediterranean during the war. March calls these documents "very, very interesting for our purpose." He goes on, "Not to lose time I send it directly to the lawyer Senior Bencour so that he will have it translated and join it to the dossier". The meeting in Paris will be attended by the lawyer, Sr Bencour. A Sr Alemany will also be with them. Because Sr Leblanc is ill, it is important that Sr Carreras be present. The date of the proposed meeting is 2nd June. The notarial act referred to is not available but it is thought to be still held in the French War Ministry.

The rest of the letter, headed *Otre asunte*, concerns the poor quality of the tobacco products coming from the factory in Oran and on the urgency for this deficiency being taken in hand. This is the only letter reproduced in Cabrera's biography of March, fig. 11.

This is a unique document. That a man of Juan March's stance should describe it as "very, very interesting" shows that it was of particular significance for him. Part of his very considerable fortune had come to him during the Great War as a result of his collaboration with the British. We do not know what sums of money were involved.

Regarding the financing of secret service work, actually very little is known. Jeffrey in *MI6* provides some figures concerning Cumming's SIS; in October 1919 a sum of £295,256 (the equivalent of £9.7 million in current money) was accounted for, of which £235,700 went directly to the Secret Service. In 1910 Cumming had paid his principal Agent (B) nearly £1,500 (the equivalent today of about £110,000) for himself and three sub-agents. As to whether these sub-agents actually existed Cumming had his doubts. Another Agent (WK) received £200 (equivalent to £15,000)[10].

"Money should be spent freely", said Churchill, in order to obtain information from railway workers in the Balkans to provide intelligence concerning ammunition shipments to Turkey. In 1915 Hall had personally promised the Turkish government up to £4 million if they would allow peaceful passage for the Gallipoli landings, a scheme which aborted when Fisher revealed he had already issued orders for the naval assault. When, in World War II, March handled the $10- $13 million payments to the Spanish generals he undoubtedly took a worthwhile percentage cut. In another case we know he took 5% (not unlike Mr. Gulbenkian) so his takings here were likely to be of the order of between half a million American dollars and $650,000. The significance of Thoroton's 'notarial act' may be that it was intended to help clinch the deal between the French government and March in any forthcoming set of circumstances which would require such collaboration. This would have arisen during the Civil War and during World War II, thus guaranteeing a profitable income to March from the French, on top of his British subsidies. Alternatively it may have been seen by March to have been of assistance to him over a judicial process in which he was involved in France in the 1920s.

Mercedes Cabrera explained the difficulties surrounding research on this subject. The family is not only the richest and most important in Spain but are very polite, reserved and correct and have no wish for his war time and smuggling activities to be voiced in public. One book which was published on him was quickly taken off the market although it was subsequently re-published and they were not able to quash it again. March himself would buy up all available copies of books about him. So little original material is available and accurate research is rendered difficult and time consuming. If this be true of professional historians in their own country, Spain, how much more so for others outside Spain and unversed in Spanish politics and intrigue?

There are no published books in the English language. His name did not even become public in England until after his death in 1962 although James had referred to his activities, but without naming him, in his *Eyes of the Navy* seven years earlier.

What may we make of this understandable dilemma between his origins and the position of his family today? From a patriotic point of view we are bound to be grateful for his success in smuggling and in his business transactions as these

---

10. Other secret agent expenses are revealed in Jeffrey's MI6 for the World War II period where he quotes $250 a month for "Cynthia", and between £150 - £160 each a month for some 16 or 18 agents in Chile.

provided the basis for the huge network set up and run by Charles the Bold. Without this, and if March had fallen in completely with the Germans, the task of BNI would have been set back severely. From the point of view of winning the war we can echo Churchill's comment concerning the bribery of the Spanish generals in World War II: "the fact that...he made money by devious means in no way affects his value to us at present". (ADM 223/490). In this scenario it must be said that the British gold sovereigns (known as the 'Knights of St. George') may well have ensured that Spain kept out of World War II and, for this, the Spanish nation can also be grateful. At the outset of World War II March offered his services to Rear Admiral John Godfrey, DNI, an offer which was gratefully taken up: possible echoes of the 'notarial act'.

To underline the opaque nature of much of the available information on Juan March, and the way in which he and his family have avoided the limelight, reference may be made to some of the English histories of modern Spain which have received high acclaim. Of special interest is Paul Preston's *Franco*, a 1,000 page, somewhat official biography, Preston being Professor of International History at the LSE and an internationally recognised authority on Spain. Spending some of his research time living with the Franco family (the book was published in 1993), Preston only mentions Juan March in a footnote where he is credited with paying £2,000 for the Rapide from the Olley Air Service of Croydon "through the Fenchurch Street Branch of Kleinwort's Bank". No other reference to his financial affairs is made and only Luis Bollin 'of ABC' is credited with organising the *Rapide* flight. In a later work, *A Concise History of the Spanish Civil War*, dedicated to the International Brigades, Juan March is described as "the millionaire enemy of the Republic" who with "other well-to-do bankers" financed Gil Robles' CEDA Party election funds. Paul Preston is in receipt of the Orden de Mérito Civil, awarded by King Juan Carlos for services to Spanish culture[11].

Charles Powell, a Research Fellow at St. Anthony's College, Oxford, comes up with a revealing title, *Juan Carlos of Spain – Self-made Monarch*, but there is no reference whatsoever to Juan March. David Gilmore (Modern History at Balliol) writes *The Transformation of Spain – From Franco to Constitutional Monarchy* but, again, no reference is made to Juan March's involvement. Ian Patterson, *Guernica* and *Total War*, again, nothing. With the publication in 1998 of Gerald Howson's *Arms for Spain – The Untold Story of the Spanish Civil War*, one could reasonably expect to see Juan March quite extensively featured. The closest Howson comes is to tell us that Primo de Rivera granted a monopoly of oil sales to CAMPSA (*Compania Armendatoria del Monopoleo de Petroleo S.A.*) and "a group of banks", who also owned "nineteen oil tankers".

March's anonymity is more than matched by Thoroton's.

In our meeting with Senora Cabrera she was able to give us other information concerning Juan March during the Republican period, his escape to Paris, and of the

---

11. *Even as recently as 2009 Paul Preston published We Saw Spain Die with no reference to March.*

time he lived in France. Whether more could be uncovered concerning his work for the Allies, or for the Germans, in the Great War is problematical but from time to time new information surfaces, often from the most unlikely quarters.

The second important lead Senora Cabrera gave us was an introduction to Don Miguel Monjo Estelrich, a relative of the Marchs who was building up a March archive, the *Coleccion Can Verga*. Again, we received a warm and encouraging reply to our letter in which he offered help, if he could, with any specific questions we might have.

March, Hillgarth and Churchill

March's role in the British financial subversion of the Spanish generals had raised questions on the part of the Treasury which were promptly rebutted by Churchill in the memorable phrase already quoted. In September 1939 March went to London and, during his visit, intended to meet Churchill but "March slipped out of London before he could see him personally". Churchill had commented on March: "This man is most important and may be able to render the greatest services in bringing about friendly relations with Spain...The fact that during the last war...he made money by devious means in no way affects his value to us at the present time or his reputation in Spain as a patriot..." (David Stafford in *Roosevelt and Churchill, Men of Secrets*). Might it not have been that Churchill's enthusiasm for Juan March had been sparked by his knowledge of Hall's and Thoroton's involvement with March in the First World War?

On March's return to Spain he re-established his contacts with Alan Hillgarth. Captain Sir Alan Hillgarth, as he later became, was the pre-war British Consul in Majorca and the British Naval Attaché in Madrid. Here he operated as an Intelligence Officer and became a very close adviser to Winston Churchill.

Stafford goes on to say that Hillgarth fully recognised March's unscrupulousness, trickery and ruthlessness - "He has already had two German agents shot in Ibiza, though I did not ask him to do so..." - but the fact that March's organisation was wholly Spanish, and under March's sole control, meant Hillgarth only needed to deal with one man "thus saving Hillgarth from getting his own hands dirty". (See ADM 223/490).

To some extent the concerns raised by the Treasury are rather surprising. As far back as 1803, Spain was paying gold to Napoleon in order to stay out of the war he was launching in Europe and this cannot be the only such incident in the history books. This was followed by considerable largess by Britain to continental powers opposed to Napoleon and gold to Nelson to pay for information from his agents.

In this clandestine operation March played the major role which also involved Morgenthau, the US Treasury Secretary; Hugh Dalton, Head of SOE; the British Treasury; Kleinwort's Bank in London (which, according to Jaime Comas Gil, March had taken control of in 1936, and in which he certainly held considerable assets); the Swiss Bank Corporation in New York (March held a 25% interest in the international *Societe de Banque Suisse*); Ian Fleming and others.

March's first contact in London was with his closest associate in Kleinwort's, José Mayorga, and then with Sir George Mounsey from the Ministry of Economic Warfare. Meeting with Mounsey, March immediately reminded him of the information he had supplied to the Admiralty in World War I concerning German submarine activities in the Med. He explained that he was ready to continue such collaboration and informed him that he had under his control the provision of fuel oil in the Canary Islands and throughout the coastline of northern Morocco. It would not be long, he said, before he would have complete control of all petroleum products throughout the whole of Spain. He went on to emphasise that, since he was the majority shareholder in the marine company *Transmediterranea* and the *Mid Atlantic Steamship Company* , he was very well informed on the movements of all ships in Spanish harbours and that the harbour authorities reported back to him. He reassured Mounsey that he had all the elements required to prevent and frustrate any supplies to German submarines in Spanish waters. Furthermore he would pass all information of military intent to the Military Attaché at the British Embassy in Madrid, Mr Hillgarth, whom he knew when he had been Vice-Consul in Palma during the Civil War.

What were to be the profits he thought he might obtain in return for such secret collaboration with the British? The Admiralty did not have very long to wait before they learnt what he wanted. March informed them that, in the Spanish harbours, there were fifty five ships amounting to 219,000 tons, some of which were petrol tankers, which he was interested in buying...

Not surprisingly there are some uncertainties concerning the transactions

War material being loaded onto one of March's Transmediterranea merchant ships.

concerning the Spanish generals. Denys Smyth quotes a figure of US$13 million and says the operation was carried out through the offices of 'Wild Bill' Donovan in New York where Donovan's Co-ordination of Information (COI) was "in effect, if not in name, the American counterpart of British Security Co-ordination (BSC)" under 'Intrepid', Sir William Stephenson. The other figure quoted, in David Stafford's account, is US$10 million, the sum placed in the account of the Swiss Bank Corporation in New York. The pay-out was to be effected by March in instalments and we know that, of this sum, US$2 million went to General Antonio Aranda Mata, Commander of the Spanish War College. The High Commissioner and C-in-C of Spanish Morocco, General Luis Orgaz y Yaldi, was another grateful recipient . As Stafford writes, the "Byzantine SIS manoeuvres - ... still remain secret" in the year 2000.

It was Hillgarth's liaison with Juan March which was the final key and, in this, Hillgarth was Thoroton's beneficiary[12].

The leading histories of the Spanish Civil War written by British historians and which enjoy both Spanish and international acclaim (Hugh Thomas' *The Spanish Civil War* and Antony Beevor's *The Battle for Spain*) both consider deeply the origins of this conflict and take us back into Spanish history. The ramifications of Allied and Central Powers' espionage however are barely touched upon apart from the role of Admiral Canaris as head of the *Abwehr*, although Thomas emphasizes the importance of March. Thomas reports Canaris as being active in Spanish Morocco in 1916 where he was attempting to set up a supply base for German submarines and had set up a system of observation of Allied ships in the Mediterranean. He was also involved in efforts to stir up the Rif tribesmen against the French. All this was frustrated by Thoroton and his men in close liaison with Lyautey and the Sultan.

The closest possible link to Thoroton that Beevor mentions occurs in 1939 where he writes of Antonio Rodriguez Sastré who was Chief of Republican Intelligence but had actually been a double-agent and had been working for Franco. He later became Juan March's principal lawyer (and business associate in the Barcelona Traction Company affair) so from this we may conclude that he could have had dealings with British Intelligence through the Thoroton Network, not only then but, perhaps, earlier during World War I.

Reverting to the Canaris link brings us to another aspect of Juan March's relations with Germany and Britain.

About 1927 he played a role in forming an intelligence network in Central Europe and the Balkans and co-operated with the British against communist threats to provoke revolution in Europe. The anti-Hitler group, under Canaris, selected Monsignor Kaas as the first courier to the Vatican in this connection. The code name *Schwarze Kapelle* was taken from the Black Chapel in Rome. However, it is better known as 'The Black Orchestra' as *Schwarze Kapelle* is a German pun on the *Rote*

12. *Hillgarth features in Jefrey's MI6 but March is not mentioned.*

Kapelle, the Soviet spy ring known as 'The Red Orchestra'. Both names were invented by Reinhard Heydrich, head of SS Intelligence. Finally, these two rival services, the one Nazi, the other Communist, were merged into one, controlled ultimately by the Kremlin. Thus both German intelligence and the Vatican were penetrated by the Soviets as was MI-5 by 1940.

In Spain in 1947 an anti-communist group was formed under the name of the 'Continental Union' with the purpose of attracting *emigré* leaders away from the British controlled *Intermarium*. To what degree, if any, was the *Intermarium* linked with the old Thoroton Network? The *Intermarium* is described as "one of many long and witty British intelligence operations" by Anthony Cave Brown in his book *The Secret Life of Sir Stewart Menzies* which acknowledges the existence of many such 'long-standing' British Intelligence fronts.

As Richard Deacon has noted (in his *A History of the British Secret Service*) Spain was seen as the major country for espionage and for developing contacts on all sides. Here the chief contact was Juan March "who had been won over to the side of British Intelligence in World War I", by Thoroton. Sir Basil Zaharoff, the international arms dealer ('The Merchant of Death') was a long term friend of March's and was also familiar with Admiral Canaris. Both men, it transpired, had a fondness for Spain and Greece. It had been Zaharoff who had first interested Canaris, through Juan March, in the need for underground aid to eliminate Republicanism in Spain. The NID are said to have had a hand in the rescue of March when he escaped from Republican Spain in 1933. Zaharoff and the NID are reputed to have facilitated his escape from the Alcala de Henares prison.

There is an instance where Juan March "wrote to a Naval Intelligence friend in Madrid" (Thoroton?) in 1934, saying that Canaris was "our best ally in Europe at this moment". March not only provided the link to Canaris but initiated SIS contact with von Kleist, of the German High Command; the industrialist von Thyssen; and Beigbeder, the Spanish High Commissioner in Morocco. Deacon also brings Dom Gómez-Beare into the scene and describes him as "one of the acutest minds in the Gibraltar Section of British Naval Intelligence". Gómez-Beare was close to Juan March and, as Naval Attaché in Madrid, was March's conduit for Canaris' thinking to the British government. The multiple ramifications of the March-Canaris-BNI spider's web go beyond the needs of this account which simply indicates Thoroton's possible involvement at the time he was still living in Madrid and Malaga, even though he was no longer working officially for BNI.

Speculation concerning the Thoroton Network, and such front organisations as the *Intermarium*, is reminiscent of other such British intelligence structures which are far more definitively described in such a work as Peter Hopkirk's *Great Game* for example. In the case of Charles the Bold we have nothing comparable to the detail available to Hopkirk (no less than 16 pages of bibliography) but certain parallels may be drawn. Referring to Soviet histories and archives N A Khalfin ("a leading Soviet authority") is quoted as claiming there was "a wide network of British military-political sources of intelligence" in Central Asia. This was said to include the mission station of the British & Foreign Bible Society in Orenburg on the Ural River in Russia itself. We have also seen elsewhere how seemingly innocuous or well intentioned organisations were either the covert creation of the intelligence services or were penetrated and used by them.

In attempting to relate the March/Thoroton co-operation we have, inevitably, been led into the snake's pit of espionage in Spain and Morocco and we have perhaps not succeeded in escaping the pit ourselves. However, the essential point here is that this co-operation was fundamental to Thoroton's success and that, without their mutual collaboration, it is undeniable that the achievements of BNI would not have been as outstanding as they were. There was certainly no doubt in Churchill's mind as to the value of the services Juan March had rendered to England and, without Thoroton, March would not have been as committed as he was[13].

13. "Documents in London, confirming March's fame as a supporter of the Allies in WW I, caught Churchill's attention", Mercedes Cabrera, Speroforum.

Chapter 12
Morocco and Marshal Lyautey

Underlying the significance of Thoroton's arrival in Morocco and his liaison with Lyautey is the fact that since 1913 the war against the Berbers in the Middle Atlas massif was extremely dangerous and destructive to the French. German agents were well-established and active. This Moroccan campaign continued throughout the First World War.

The first definite information we have on Major Thoroton in Morocco dates from 1915 but there is evidence that he may have made his first visit there in 1914[1].

He was first despatched to Morocco by Vice Admiral F E E Brock SNO, Gibraltar. In a letter from Brock to the Secretary of the Admiralty, dated 19 June 1915, he says that he sent "Major Thoroton to visit General Lyautey in Rabat on duties in connection with our co-operation with the French Intelligence Centre in Morocco" on which occasion he was presented to the Sultan by General Lyautey personally. In November 1915 Lyautey went to Gibraltar to seek the lifting of embargoes on Spanish foodstuffs.

On 26 April 1915 General Lyautey, the French Resident General in Morocco, had written to Brock stating: "the Sultan Moulay Joussef has expressed his desire to confer on Major Charles J Thoroton RMLI a Moorish decoration".

Marshal Louis Hubert Gonzalve Lyautey (1854-1934) was, and still is in certain quarters, regarded as France's most outstanding colonial administrator and one of France's greatest soldiers. He held posts in Algeria, Tongking and Madagascar, the latter under Gallienei, where he reformed the administration. His most brilliant work was undoubtedly done in Morocco, where he was Resident Commissary-General from 1912 to 1925, with a break from 1916 to 1917 as French Minister of War in Paris. The development of Casablanca as a seaport was but one of his outstanding achievements. I received the following acknowledgement of Lyautey's qualities from Profesor Keith Jeffrey when he wrote to me in the context of his official history of the SIS: "Years ago I did some work on 'colonial warfare' and was impressed by Lyautey's very constructive approach to colonial 'conquest', anticipating Sir Gerald Templer's 'hearts and minds' strategy in Malaya by very many years".

Thus, the purpose of Thoroton's visit to Morocco was to further Franco-British intelligence operations in that country and along the Barbary Coast.

We had hopes of uncovering more on the Lyautey/Thoroton relationship from Monsieur Le Reverend who had studied his correspondence for his book *Un Lyautey Inconnu – correspondence et journals inédits, 1873-1934* but, regretfully, Monsieur Le Reverend had died a year or so previously.

---

1. *See Chapter 8.*

Lyautey portrait inscribed 'au Major Thoroton bien cordialement Lyautey Rabat mars 1915'. (Photo by Eug. Pirou, Paris.)

It is therefore that our family archives provide the closest insight into this relationship. There are six letters in all from Marshal Lyautey over the period 1917 to 1933. The later letters refer to post war activities by Thoroton. The first letter is dated 1st January 1917 and is from the Ministère de la Guerre, Paris; the second is dated 20.10.18 and is from Le Général Lyautey, Résident Général au Maroc; the third and final one in this series is dated 12.1.19 and is from the same address. In addition we have a signed portrait of Lyautey by Eug. Pirou of Mascre, rue Royale, Paris which is inscribed: "Au Major Thoroton bien cordialement, Lyautey, Rabat mars 1919".

The first letter is dated 1st January 1917 and is addressed from the Le Ministre RF, Paris, Ministère de la Guerre and we have translated it and give it in full here.

My dear friend,

I received your letter of 13 December and I thank you for your congratulations. The way is rough and I have need of the goodwill of allied collaborators such as you to bring it to a good solution.

Huot passed me recently one of your letters. I read it with the greatest interest. Do not hesitate to let me have such sensitive information directly or by your intermediaries when that is possible for you and believe, my dear friend, in my very affectionate sentiments.

Lyautey.

This underlines the importance of Thoroton's information to Lyautey in the third year of the war.

A letter dated 20 October 1918 from Lyautey in Morocco presents CJT as "Not only (are you) a friend of Morocco but also a family friend, truly one of us…" showing the depth and longstanding nature of their relationship.

Lyautey's letter of 12 January 1919 is much the same and reads:

General Lyautey speaking at Rabat, 11 November 1918, reminiscent of his speech with reference to CJT.

> "Thank you for your sympathy on the death of dear Bettian. I have lost one of the most sure and the best of friends and his death is a disaster for French Morocco. You appreciate him. You will know what he was worth and you understand my pain. I would be very happy to see you again. You would do me so much pleasure if you came to Rabat."

The lead to Monsieur André Le Reverend (which was given by Charles Pelletier Doisy along with several other important references) was to provide new insights into Colonel Thoroton's work in Morocco in association with Marshal Lyautey and Colonel Bettian.

First: Colonel Bettian, referred to in Lyautey's letter of 12 January 1919, where he comments on Bettian's unique and crucial contributions to French Morocco. He was Director of Native Affairs for the Maghreb and an intimate friend of Lyautey dating from 1903 at Ain Sefra. In 1918 he was responsible for French intelligence in Meknes and Casablanca and subsequently in Rabat for the whole of Morocco. His knowledge and understanding of the Moroccan peoples and culture was second to none and his was the inspiration for the creation and development of the friendship which evolved between the French and the Moroccans. At Christmas 1918 Lyautey wrote from Rabat to one of his nieces, Marie-Therese de Kerraoul:

"…the death of my dear Bettian, for whom I have the most beautiful and the warmest affection and whom I love like a brother".

He goes on to describe his time with him up until the end. He writes movingly and in depth of the anguish he experienced with the death of his friend, emotions reflected in his letter to Thoroton.

Only a year previously, in November 1917, Lyautey had made a public speech at the opening of the third, great economic fair to be held in Rabat during the war.

He said:

"Finally, I am delighted to see close to me, during this day, Colonel Thoroton, chief of Admiralty Intelligence at Gibraltar (i). He also is one of our collaborators from the earliest days, and its quite impossible for me to speak, without indiscretion, of his vital information on our behalf. It is enough for you to know that the service he has given to Morocco, during three years, has been one of the guarantees of our security. Thanks to the service which he directs, which is completely integrated with mine, I cannot tell how many affairs we have been through together, how many perils we have escaped. In thanking him I am happy to render homage to this Great Briton who has been our ally from the first hour, with whom we are linked in an indissoluble way, with whom we march hand in hand, heart against heart, without any possibility of any kind of fissure between us right up to the final triumph."

The footnote (i) reads: Colonel Thoroton directs the official, diplomatic service concerning the known and suspected movements of German submarines[2].

The photograph we reproduce shows Lyautey speaking at a similar event in Rabat on 11 November 1918.

If we go back now to the time of Thoroton's arrival at Gibraltar in 1913, Lyautey had been Resident General in Morocco for a year and had been elected to the Academie Francaise. He had begun his "pacification of Morocco" in 1912. Then, in 1913, he undertook, at the invitation of the King of Spain, an official mission to King Alphonse XIII who admired his work in Morocco and was seeking a way to harmonise Spanish and French interests in that country. He remained in Morocco until December 1916 when Aristide Briand appointed him Minister of War in Paris. Opposing Neville's disastrous offensive plans for the Western Front as unacceptable and unachievable (the Chemin des Dames which resulted in 120,000 casualties the first day and the final collapse of the French Army) he was to remain as Minster of War only until 14 March 1917 when he was dismissed by Parliament ("des indiscretions criminelles de cette Chambre") for refusing to make public certain military orders which he judged could only be revealed to the benefit of the enemy. Returning to Morocco he was to complete his thirteen years there as Resident General in 1925. Thus, effectively, his six years of close and active involvement with Thoroton were only interrupted by a five month absence in Paris, even during which time they were in correspondence together.

Since Lyautey was such a close friend of Thoroton, and since so much more is known of the former than of the latter, to what extent may an appreciation of Lyautey provide clues to Thoroton's personality?

Lyautey, as the author of the 1891 article *La rôle social de l'officier*, which was published in the *Revue des Deux Mondes*, was not far removed from Thoroton in

2. *This extract comes from Jean Louis Mieg's Lyautey – Paroles d'action, Editions de la Port. Rabat 1995.*

so far as identifying with indigenous cultures and peoples was concerned. Equally, his vision of the officer as someone unique in the French Republic, in that he was the sole person who was in direct contact with the people, might be said to parallel Thoroton's ability to work with the whole range of people and to have the help of fishermen, harbour workers and, indeed, contrebandiers, in his intelligence gathering as well as members of high society. It is pertinent to note that this essay has been republished as recently as 2009 and is considered to have remained as relevant today as it was over one hundred years ago.

Through a review of Le Reverend's *Un Lyautey Inconnu* we can see that Lyautey emerges from his correspondence and journals as a highly complex man, torn by the contradictions of logic and faith; stifled by the routine rigour of much of army life; intrigued by Islamic beliefs and less Catholic than Catholic (but finally reconciled in 1930, four years before his death);driven by the desire to direct men and events and his recognition that this was a barrier to love and marriage; and many other conflicting considerations. He also had a great capacity for friendship and a deep understanding of the human heart. In addition, he was a foremost analyst and intellectual of colonialism and interpreter of the developing social, political and military events on the stage of Europe.

In sum, this highly intellectual, far-seeing and enlightened soldier and administrator, a man given to deep interior questioning and the pioneer of rational, beneficent "colonialism", was a man who was able to win over his Moroccan subjects to an allegiance with France through a colonial policy dedicated to the genuine advancement of peoples, devoid of rapine.

This tells us at least something of Thoroton in the sense that the two men saw eye to eye and appreciated each other's qualities. It is not that we can suppose that Thoroton shared Lyautey's semi-mystic approach, nor his religious scruples, but there are evident points of convergence: marital problems, albeit of different kinds; a scrupulous attention to detail (Lyautey had "l'esprit methodique qu'il applique a toutes choses"); fidelity to the cause and to their comrades; integrity; courage; persuasiveness.

At the National Archives in Kew the Foreign Office file (Ref 372-091), headed 'Treaty Morocco', concerns the award to Major Thoroton of the Order Ouissam Alaouite Chérifien. The Foreign Office needed to know (5 July 1915, Ref 89229) "the nature of the services which it is designed to recognise". The War Office does not know the "precise position held by Major Thoroton in Morocco" and the Foreign Office has "no record of his services at the FO". Considerable correspondence was evoked by this dilemma, viz.: "Sir Edward Grey would be glad if the Lords Commissioners of the Admiralty would be good enough to inform him in what capacity Major Thoroton is employed in Morocco and also as to the nature of the services which the Sultan..." wishes to reward. (15 July 1915).

On 19 July, Vice Admiral Brock wrote from Gibraltar explaining that he sent Thoroton to visit General Lyautey at Rabat in order to establish co-operation with the French Intelligence Centre in Morocco and was introduced to the Sultan by General Lyautey personally. He feels it is advisable to give Major Thoroton permission to accept and wear the Moroccan award. The SNO in Gibraltar then writes (21 July) that Major Thoroton's services were not to the Sultan but to the Allied cause. Vice Admiral Brock's recommendation is that he should be granted "private permission to wear" it.

Finally it needed to be established whether this Moroccan Order was an 'Order of Chivalry' or not. It was found that it had been created on 23 May 1913 and that it was such an Order. As a result the Foreign Office gave the go-ahead for acceptance on 23 September 1915 and Sir Edward Grey wrote, on 28 September, that he wanted Thoroton "to be informed directly". Thus ended happily the award of this splendid Order.

Morrocan scene drawn by Frank Thoroton while on a visit with CJT.

Chapter 13
Between the wars

The usefulness of the Thoroton Network did not cease with the end of the war. Concrete evidence of this emerges largely from information provided by Warwick University's Modern Research Centre; the historical writing of David Stafford, Dolores Pérez-Guesco and others; from our meeting with Mercedes Cabrera; and Thoroton's correspondence with Hall and with Churchill.

In his book *A Man called Intrepid*, William Stevenson notes that 'Blinker' Hall in 1918 was on the look-out for "the handful of youngsters he wanted to coach for a new world of secret intelligence". Hall was indeed looking ahead and he recognized the significance of the changing times. He was to cast a long beneficent shadow over the post war period becoming involved with BSC and with "Intrepid" (Sir William Stephenson) who had met Hall in France in 1917 while flying with No 73 Squadron RFC. BSC was the precursor of the OSS and the CIA.

Of the 1920s, we read: "Admiral Hall sent word that Stephenson should return to London... Hall had retired into the shadows. The British intelligence community had been drastically reduced, and Hall tried to keep it alive through groups of civilians in politics, international affairs, and scientific development." By the 1920s, the SIS itself only maintained 'a skeleton network' under business cover in Madrid and Barcelona. The Thoroton Network had become the 'Skeleton Network'.

We know from Churchill College Archives that Hall was in close touch with Thoroton over his biography at this time and Thoroton was writing to Winston Churchill on the Fleet Air Arm and the role of the military and of the Navy in the defence of Empire bases overseas.

The story of 'Intrepid' in Stevenson's book reveals the 'skeleton' continuance of Thoroton's Network in the BSC organisational chart which was shown to President Roosevelt. We reproduce the 'simplified version' where it figures under the title IBERIAN SUBSECTION – Spain and Portugal: neutral territory intelligence. During WWII, BSC sent agents into France using Spanish ships entering the ports of Bilbao and Santander.

Thoroton as Commissioner

The work that Thoroton took on in the Federation of British Industries in Madrid[1] from 1919 to 1923 was a continuation of his wartime work but for commercial, financial and political purposes. This type of work is described as commercial or industrial intelligence.

1. *Address: Montalban, 22.*

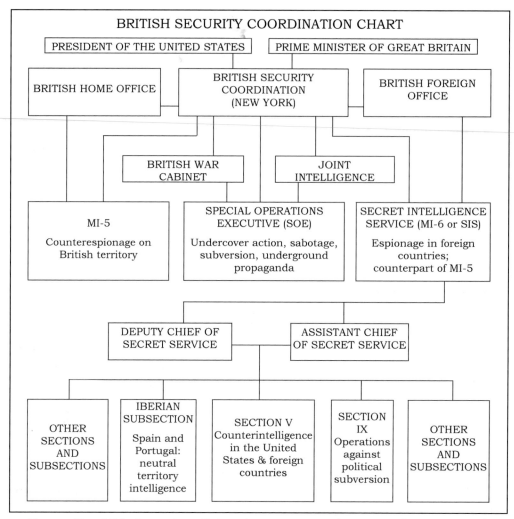

BRITISH SECURITY COORDINATION CHART

PRESIDENT OF THE UNITED STATES | PRIME MINISTER OF GREAT BRITAIN

BRITISH HOME OFFICE | BRITISH SECURITY COORDINATION (NEW YORK) | BRITISH FOREIGN OFFICE

BRITISH WAR CABINET | JOINT INTELLIGENCE

MI-5 — Counterespionage on British territory

SPECIAL OPERATIONS EXECUTIVE (SOE) — Undercover action, sabotage, subversion, underground propaganda

SECRET INTELLIGENCE SERVICE (MI-6 or SIS) — Espionage in foreign countries; counterpart of MI-5

DEPUTY CHIEF OF SECRET SERVICE | ASSISTANT CHIEF OF SECRET SERVICE

OTHER SECTIONS AND SUBSECTIONS | **IBERIAN SUBSECTION** Spain and Portugal: neutral territory intelligence | **SECTION V** Counterintelligence in the United States & foreign countries | **SECTION IX** Operations against political subversion | OTHER SECTIONS AND SUBSECTIONS

From a Royal Marine point of view this is pertinent because it demonstrates how Marines, who are at the service of their country in both war and peace, are a benefit to the nation in other ways than are more obviously appreciated. Here for the first time, to the knowledge of the author, is described the important spin-off of Room 40's Gibraltar based Network in the period between the two World Wars.

It was in the spring of 1918 that Lorraine and Josseline C H Grant, Military Attaché in Madrid, recommended the creation of a Commercial Propaganda Bureau. Its purpose would be to augment the British image in Spain with the strategic objective of developing a post-war "community of industrial, commercial and financial interests between Great Britain and Spain". Lord Beaverbrook, Minister of Information, charged Lorraine with organising this with Eric Hambro, responsible for propaganda in neutral countries[2].

2. *NA, WO 106/5128, Elizalde, GMCC No 26, op cit.*

Pérez-Gruesco writes that British Intelligence would have an important role to play in such an initiative.

The Federation had been founded in 1916 so it was three years later that Thoroton joined it as Commissioner for Spain in Madrid. This followed his retirement from active service on 1 April 1919 at the age of forty four. On 3 November 1919 he was granted permission to reside in Spain on retirement. His tenure with the Federation lasted for four years, ending in 1923. Thereafter he lived in Malaga thus maintaining his Spanish links and friendships. We discovered that Warwick University held the archives of the Federation in its Modern Research Centre. Our investigations there uncovered the existence of two files with reference to Spain, both of which directly concerned him. The then (1919-1920) Director of the Federation in London was Roland Nugent and he was in correspondence with Thoroton at that time and was also the author of a confidential report on the Federation in

CJT as Commisioner, Federation of British Industries, in his Madrid office.

Spain which he had prepared for the President under the title of "On the Overseas Organisation of the Federation", following a visit to Madrid in December 1919.

The first letter on file from Nugent to Thoroton is dated 11 November 1919 following "a long meeting of the Management Committee and I hasten to give you the results". Nugent had submitted a development plan, in part his own concerning possible commission arrangements, in part Thoroton's regarding the funding of local organisations involving a subscription in return for their seeking help from a local Federation. Other questions concerned banking and freight. Nugent considered that the meeting had been a satisfactory one and wrote to say that ways and means of raising money for the Overseas Services was also part of the remit. He proposed to come out to Spain "as soon as possible" and hoped to "bring Springer out with me if he can possibly be spared from here".

This letter is followed by his "Overseas Organisation" 13 page report dated 8 December 1919. The significance of this report, and attendant correspondence, is important as it describes the work of the Commissioner's Office abroad and lays down the corporate strategy proposed in order to further the role of the Federation both at home and internationally. In fact, so impressed was Nugent by the work being carried out in Spain he now saw the role of the Federation as being on an even more important level than hitherto. While he had been thinking along these lines before he went to Spain his views "have been very greatly strengthened and confirmed by my visit".

Relating specifically to Thoroton's work, "the Federation has built for itself... (an) extraordinary position...in those countries in which it is represented". He goes on: "In regard to Spain ... it is literally not too much to say that the Federation Office is in the eyes of all Spaniards an infinitely more important place than the British Embassy". Nugent then enumerates the Federation's achievements and status in Spain and refers to "the personal deference shown to any official of the Federation in the country not only by the heads of the big commercial houses but by Ministers, Government officials and others". The Commissioner is consulted on the most important issues by the leading authorities in the land. He writes, "We have obviously got in the Federation's Overseas Organisation not only potentially the most wonderful instrument which has ever been formed for the strengthening and pushing of British trade, but the nucleus of a tremendous international force which, properly handled, may play an immense part not only in the commercial future of this country, but in almost every sphere of international relations. This instrument, however, cannot possibly be properly developed unless we are enabled to go on as we have begun, employ only men of the highest possible calibre as our Commissioners with absolutely first rate staff, good officers, and generally speaking, every assistance not only for doing their work efficiently but for making a good appearance and filling a big position in the countries in which they are employed. This is being done adequately at present in Spain".

The Federation is hereby positioned as the spearhead of England's commercial prosperity abroad but, also, as something beyond that, namely in "almost every sphere of international relations". This clearly takes the Federation into the realm of diplomatic relations ("infinitely more important...than the British Embassy") and into the potentiality of industrial espionage, a field in which Charles the Bold would have felt quite at home. Nugent wants his Board to realise that the Federation has done things "on the grand scale and...any attempt to 'cheese-pare' would create a very bad effect. The complete disappearance of the Federation from any of the markets in which it is established would without exaggeration probably be the worst blow that British prestige and British commerce have ever received. It is to my mind not merely a matter for the future of the Federation, but very literally a matter concerning intimately the future of the country that our organisation should be continued and developed on its present lines and spread to as many further countries as possible".

The Federation as worldwide organisation

A considerable amount of the remaining thirteen pages is devoted to ways and means for ensuring the continued development of the Federation both at home and abroad, and the inter-action between them, and contains numerous concrete proposals. The status of the Federation at home in London compares unfavourably with its status in Madrid: "When one has visited a Commissioner abroad and has seen the position which the Commissioner occupies and the estimation in which he is held by the leading people in the country, one realises that it cannot but have a most unfortunate effect on those people when they come to England and find the senior officials of the Federation who are nominally that Commissioner's superiors, unable to keep up a position which (is) in any way comparable with that of the Commissioner". Taking Spain as the yardstick for development elsewhere, Nugent lists Portugal, Scandinavia, Greece, the whole of the Middle East, Italy "and probably the Balkans, probably most of South America".

There follows correspondence between Thoroton and Nugent, starting 1st March 1920, that is three months after the Director's report. Thoroton considers his proposed "subscription" for "Overseas Associate" as not being "unduly high". It was high, and was intended to be so: "We do not want to be bothered with all sorts of cheap people". As a result of his writing to a range of ninety firms in Spain "two of the largest firms in the country" had already accepted and twelve others had applied for participation plus "3 possibles", "a most satisfactory state of affairs". A canvassing operation, which should be accompanied by a publicity campaign, was next envisaged from which he expected a further rich haul. Thoroton can ensure wide scale newspaper coverage in Spain of any editorials published in England, "a valuable recruiting agency. The Spaniard loves publicity particularly abroad". He then refers to Senor Albeniz, whose return Thoroton is awaiting while he is recovering from a bronchial attack which had delayed his writing to Nugent. Senor and Senora Albeniz were on a trip to Barcelona with Springer. "I have no doubt Springer has told you all about my cottage. When I saw him last he was in good health and spirits, but since he was accompanied to Barcelona not only by Albeniz, but by Madame A, I will not answer for the state in which he reached England" [3].

Madame A might be supposed to have been a somewhat forward person, this perhaps accounting for Springer's anticipated possible state on his arrival in London.

When Nugent replies (Personal & Confidential) to Thoroton's letter, he writes on business affairs: Thoroton's suggestions are all accepted and the London Country & Westminster Bank is "frightfully keen on becoming one of (our) approved Bankers", something which should ginger-up the "rather slack" Anglo South American Bank. However, he also comments on our friend Springer. Springer, it transpires, "enjoyed himself very much and seems much better for the change", so all ended happily after all.

---

3. This Albeniz was Alfonso Albeniz, the son of Isaac Albeniz, the famous Catalan composer (1860-1909). Starting in the early 1900s as a footballer with Real Madrid he had become a diplomat and it was in this capacity that he was known to Thoroton. (Cecilia Sarkozy, née Ciganer-Albeniz, is the great grand daughter of Isaac Albeniz. Albeniz family connections link with King Alfonso XII, through his support of the composer and, more recently, contacts with NASA, AXA and Crédit Foncier, including Publicis through Cecilia Sarkozy's liaison with the Moroccan businessman Richard Attias. Publicis is owned by the March family.)

Thoroton's contacts in Madrid

The last letter from Thoroton is dated 28 April 1920 and describes the first meeting of the Federation lunch club in Madrid. This was established as a once a week lunch at a reserved table at the Ritz, "anybody who wishes can roll up". Seventeen attended and he was very pleased to welcome General Sir Horace Smith-Dorrien, the Governor of Gibraltar, "our first really important guest…the whole affair was very merry and bright".

Smith-Dorrien needs some introduction here. It was he who had been in charge of the first successful battle of the BEF with the Germans at Mons in 1914; had had a previous distinguished career but suffered greatly in the Second Battle of Ypres in April 1915 by the French failure to fulfil their commitment to a supportive, flanking attack. His clashes with Field Marshal French over this, and associated strategic issues, effectively brought his career to an end although he went on to take command in East Africa. The Army was the loser, French's own record being the poorer and ending with his debacle at Loos in 1915.

Smith-Dorrien's previous soldiering had included India, Egypt and South Africa where, in the Zulu War of 1879, he was one of only five British officers to escape from the massacre of British and African troops at the battle of Isandhlwana. He was later on the North West Frontier; in the Sudan at the battle of Omdurman; and in the South African War. He had, after that, taken over the Aldershot Command, 'home of the British Army', just before the Great War broke out. He was an outstanding general and, as he was senior to Haig, he might well have been given command of the BEF, when French was sacked, if illness had not overtaken him. No wonder Thoroton was pleased to have him as his guest.

Thoroton regretted that the head of Sanderson Brothers & Newbold Ltd, Colonel Brittain, was prevented from attending due to ill health but he had invited his wife to come. The company was involved in metal processing, including the manufacture of bayonets. He expected the local press would report the event even though it was just a private function. However he was "rather overshadowed by the presence of Joffre here". Thoroton was unhappy at the thought of having "to shake hands with Joffre at tea time much against my will". What might have occasioned this reluctance? BNI had provided the first definite information on the coming German onslaught on Verdun in 1916, Operation Gericht, as a result of a January Berlin cocktail party, thanks to the indiscrete talk of a high German official. One wonders which British agent was present there[4]. However, Joffre had chosen to ignore this report: French Intelligence had suffered a severe re-buff with the loss of over sixty of their agents behind German lines, led by a courageous French woman, Louise de Bettignies. Furthermore, the French had failed to send out patrols through No-Man's-Land. Joffre had been responsible for the plan (his "war of attrition") on the Somme in 1916

---

4. In a BBC News interview, 21 September 2010, Keith Jeffrey spoke of agent TR16, Dr Karl Krüger, who worked in Germany in WW I. The agent at the cocktail party may have been Dr Krüger, who ended up "presumed dead" at age sixty, at the start of WW II.

CJT at Stella Maris with, probably, Henryano Kerchaer, his agent and witness to his will.

which had resulted in the loss of some 400,000 British and Empire men, of which number 95,675 had been killed, along with a further 50,756 Frenchmen. Knowledge of these losses, which had achieved virtually nothing, must have occasioned Thoroton's reluctance to shake Joffre's hand.

In a long article in *Epoca* 1 May 1920 it is reported that Thoroton, as the head of the Federation, was ably supported by two consultants, Señor Moyano Kershaw[5], on engineering matters, and, on trade and business, by Alfonso Albeniz, the son of the famous composer. Thoroton was reported as expressing his appreciation of the help and friendship proffered by the King of Spain Alfonso XIII for his close interest in the work of the Federation. The Federation interests in Spain relate to trade developments with Brazil, Holland, Italy and the Orient and to co-operation between Spain and England in naval construction (*Sociedad Espanola de Construcción Naval*), largely involving British capital and expertise. The development of mineral exploration; the exportation of Spanish fruit and manufactured articles are also of mutual interest to the two countires. All this, the paper concludes, is the result of the sympathetic and intelligent initiatives of the Federation in Madrid.

After mentioning that the Ritz keeps the cost very low for the Federation, Thoroton concludes with a characteristic compliment and flourish: "I may say that the whole idea was originated over a meal I had with three of our Overseas Associates here, who thought it would be a capital thing and would probably end something like the American Lunch Club at the Savoy". Nicholas Scheetz, of Georgetown University, in a letter to the author, surmises that Thoroton would probably have met with Joseph Willard, the wealthy American Ambassador to Spain, 1913-1921, most probably in the post war years.

Warwick University holds other archives on the Federation in Spain including the Foreign Office Committee on commercial intelligence in foreign countries, the Spanish tariff and commercial treaty and the appointment of a Liverpool company representative in Spain. No doubt some of the other entries (amongst the 17 listed – one of which refers to 'the Russian situation') may also concern Thoroton but enough has been given here to highlight his Federation career. It is evident that his performance at the Federation was in every way comparable with his work as a Naval Intelligence chief during the Great War.

Retirement in 1924

By 1924 he had retired from the Federation but was still circulating in social circles. *El Imparcial* (owned by March), for 7 June 1924, reports on his presence at a "splendid aristocratic and diplomatic occasion". Written by Prince Alfonso de Hoheniche, the article tells us that Lady Rumbold's guests included Baroness Langwerth von Simmern, the Duchess of Victoria, the Viscount and Viscountess of Era and various Ministers from China, Czechoslovakia and Portugal. Colonel Thoroton was the British representative.

Who's Who for 1925 gives his address for that year as Jenner 6, Madrid. This is two years after his retirement as Commissioner in Spain for the Federation of British Industries.

---

5. *Also spelt Henryano Kerschaer and shown with Thoroton in accompanying photograph. Señor Kerschaer was a wartime agent in the Network.*

At Stella Maris, Frank Thoroton, Mrs Stevenson, CJT, Levett and Edith Thoroton, circa 1930s.

We know that Thoroton was in England in the early 1930s but still visiting Spain, no doubt at his house in Malaga. In 1931 he would have been fully aware of the looming Civil War when churches in Malaga, Valencia and Madrid were set ablaze by the anti-Catholic Popular Front and numerous believers were murdered.

Thoroton told Hall in March 1933 that he had not been able to get to Malaga "this year" but that he had had a good let. His April 1935 will makes no reference to specific properties but we do know that in 1936 he still owned the villa, vide his letter to Winston Churchill from Villa Stella Maris, Pedregalejo, Malaga. He died on 17 January 1939 but we do not have the date of his last visit to Spain which he probably left in July or August 1936. The Spanish Civil War can be said to have started on 18 July 1936 and to have ended on 31 March 1939. Whether he left before the outbreak of the fighting, or during, it is in no way certain that he would have sold the villa. By July of 1938, Republican Spain was limited to Catalonia, Madrid and parts of New Castile, Valencia, Murcia and the eastern part of Andalusia. Thus his home province was free: might he have been tempted to return and see for himself?

Thoroton has been credited with having laid the foundations of the British secret intelligence network in Spain, Portugal and Morocco which was so valuable to the UK in World War II. This can be seen in Admiral John Godfrey's welcome of March's offer of assistance and Churchill's and Hillgarth's continuing reliance on and use of Juan March. Garcia-Sanz and David Stafford both make reference to this in their books.

The preservation of the Thoroton Network in Spain after 1918 was enthusiastically welcomed by the Spanish government as the Network provided more information on events in Spain than did their own police and secret services. In this too we can detect the hand of Juan March. This contribution to intelligence was "to reach its zenith"[6] in World War II with the Governor of Gibraltar, General Mason MacFarlane, and Colonel W F Ellis in Tangier as controlling bodies.

1927 to 1930 saw a dark period inside British Intelligence with the appointment of Admiral Sir Barry Domville as Director of Naval Intelligence. He was a member of the sinister pro-German organisation The Link and was finally arrested in 1940 under Regulation 10B on account of his having been the founder and Chairman of this society. The wide-ranging pro-German and pro-Nazi elements in British society were a continuing bugbear to Winston Churchill and his government. They have been chronicled in William Stevenson's *Spymistress* (2007) and included the Duke of Windsor, the Duke of Westminster, Lord Trenchard (RAF and London Metropolitan Police chief), Lord Lothian, Lady Emerald Cunard, "Chips" Channon and many other notables of the society world. While there are reservations concerning some of these names, Andrew, in his *The Mitrokin Archive*, confirms Halifax's 'pro-German' viewpoint, with some slight reserve. Richard Deacon adds to the list, Lord Stamp, Lord Lymington and others.

Enter the Nazis

Thoroton was still living in Spain when in 1933 Hitler's SS/SD agent Walter zu Christian arrived there to develop espionage against the Rock of Gibraltar. Zu Christian was a specialist in British affairs as Head of the Reich Security Main Office, having joined the SS in 1931. He evaded the Allies at the end of the war and was not finally tracked down by Comer Clarke in a suburb of Innsbruck until some time in the late 1950s to early 1960s. In an interview zu Christian revealed his deep involvement in all aspects of espionage and subversion against Britain. He spoke both English and Spanish. Himmler had told him, "Always bear in mind that our greatest enemy will be Britain". He was posted to Spain and arrived in Madrid in the early 1930s. Posing as a commercial salesman his prime target was the Rock of Gibraltar. In addition he was to learn from British officers as much as possible about British defence plans and strengths in Britain and elsewhere in the British Empire. From such sources he claimed to have obtained intelligence on the underground arsenals and fortifications of Gibraltar and photographs of military defences. Within a few months he was appointed chief of German spy services in Spain and Portugal. Then, in 1936, he was recalled to Berlin and assigned to Department VI, the Foreign Department, ultimately responsible to Reinhard Heydrich. Here, zu Christian's exclusively Iberian responsibility ended but one of his agents, a Dutchman, moved to Portugal and flew regularly to Britain, officially representing a Portuguese firm.

---

6. *Deacon's History, p 223.*

Cartagena harbour with submarines being refuelled, photographed by Bartolomé Ros during the Civil War.

The appointment of Rear-Admiral John Godfrey as DNI in 1939 brought success back into the scene. Working along the old Hall lines he brought such talent as Ian Fleming (later Assistant to the DNI), Sir Norman Denning, Ewen Montagu, Patrick Beesley and Frederick Wells into play. Fleming studied the dossier on Sir Barry Domville of The Link. He was also aware of the preoccupation of leading Nazis with astrology and the occult. Combining the two elements he set out to recreate The Link in such a way that it could be seen to work towards the overthrow of the Churchill government and to negotiate a peace with Germany. By 1940 agents in Lisbon, and in Berne, were shaping events which were to lead to one of the most dramatic incidents of the war: the flight of Hess from Germany, on the night of Sunday 10 May, to the Duke of Hamilton in Scotland.

On his appointment in 1939 Godfrey gratefully accepted Juan March's offer of services to Britain, another spin-off from the Thoroton Network.

Spanish Civil War and Hillgarth

Given Thoroton's continued presence in Spain at the outbreak of the Civil War and the importance of Alan Hillgarth, this section gives a brief description of relevant issues.

In 1931 the peseta dropped by 33% and dangerous political and financial forces were at work. King Alfonso was in exile and strikes, uprisings, assassinations, military plots and mayhem were everywhere.

During the run-up to the Spanish Civil War, Soviet agents were active in Spain and were directly involved in starting the war.

Soviet intelligence was under the control of General Ulansky who was also responsible for logistics. 920 Soviet military 'advisers' entered Spain along with hundreds of air force and military officers and enlisted men. Between September 1936 and March 1938, one hundred and ten shiploads of Russian military supplies left Odessa for Spain. It is certain that the existing BNI 'skeleton' Network would have monitored these ship movements and of the men and materials involved. Public knowledge of these activities only became evident in 1956, the source being the German Military Attaché's files in Ankara. Britain was also a supplier of armaments to the Reds (Soviet tanks were based on the British Vickers and US Christy designs) and thirty seven of the ships employed were flying the Red Ensign. Thus if British Intelligence was well informed much, if not all, of this information would have been kept under wraps. The Foreign Office would have welcomed confirmation of safe delivery in Spain and news of other countries' activities. March's shipping lines, Transmediterranea and the Mid Atlantic, had been funded during the Civil War by the Spanish Communist Party (PCE) as covers for the importation of arms. March financed the first arms shipments to the Balearic islands where many working class local people were murdered by Nationalist forces in Ibiza and Formentera, which had been abandoned, 439 prisoners being put to death and fifty five killed in an air raid on the beautiful island of Ibiza.

Thoroton's term of office as Commissioner of the Federation in Madrid had come to an end in 1923 but he was living in Spain up to the start of the Civil War and he had retained his contacts with Juan March whom, we also know, had links with Krupp and Sir Basil Zaharoff, who had become the international arms agent for Vickers. Perhaps some intelligence connected with these matters may have been amongst the papers destroyed by Thoroton before his death.

We have already noted Hillgarth's involvement with Churchill and March in the Spanish generals affair. In 1940 Churchill had given a sideways promotion to Sir Samuel Hoare by making him Ambassador to Spain although, in the event, this posting turned out to be of crucial importance in the war effort. Churchill knew Hoare as an appeaser and considered his pro-Nazi reputation might help to keep the peace with pro-German elements in Madrid. Hoare proved to be quite useful in this respect even though unknown to him he fell victim to the pro-British Baron Rüder von Etzdorf who was working with SOE and who had been given a diplomatic posting to Madrid. Etzdorf had obtained the detailed Vichy plan for the liquidation of France's 330,000 Jews which had enabled him to sow dissension in the divided Vichy police services and so facilitate the exfiltration of Jews. He had gone on to organise Jewish escape lines from Occupied Europe to Lisbon. Hoare, on the other hand, had encouraged Pierre Laval, when he was Prime Minister of France, in support of Italian Fascist forces in Africa and in various other pro-Axis ways.

Churchill appointed Hillgarth to the British Embassy in Madrid. He worked closely with Tom Burns, who was responsible for propaganda and pro-British PR as head of Information at the Embassy between 1940 and 1945. These contacts linked up with Juan March and, at a dinner party Burns asked his host how he had made his first million. "That", replied March, "is a question you do not ask a millionaire". Ernest Hemingway remarked, in 1940, "Juan March lifts his finger and Franco complies".

Hillgarth's role in the secret service had far reaching consequences. He played a role in securing the safe passage of HMS *Repulse* on her voyage to Barcelona in 1938, the *Repulse* then being under the command of Captain H Godfrey RN. This action was significant because Hillgarth negotiated a guarantee from the Nationalist forces not to attack the battle-cruiser when it entered Republican-held Barcelona to evacuate British personnel.

When Godfrey became DNI he appointed Hillgarth as Naval Attaché to the British Embassy in Madrid. In 1943 Hillgarth wrote a report on British espionage activities in Spain and continued his surveillance of Majorca, sending numerous Memoranda on the situation to the Foreign Office in London. He became, in effect, one of Churchill's top personal agents. About this time Churchill said of Hillgarth, "of whom I think very highly…is an extremely independent person" and, to Sir Samuel Hoare, "I am finding Hillgarth a great prop". Hillgarth's relationship with Juan March crops up again in the publication of Ben Mackintyre's *Operation Mincemeat* (2010)[7]. Mackintyre is not aware of the Thoroton link between March and Hillgarth but provides a forceful impression of major Spanish sympathies being much more on the side of the Axis in WW II than they were on the side of the Central Powers in WW I. In Franco's Spain this is understandable.

Later, Hillgarth served in the Eastern Theatre as Naval Intelligence Officer for the Orient. Retiring with a CMG he and his wife then went to live in Ireland where he maintained his contact with Juan March, collaborating with him over the Rio Tinto Company which Hillgarth represented in Ireland on behalf of March. He also became a Director of the Helvetia Finance Company, March's nominee business in London. Like Thoroton, he left no written memoires considering his information to be classified under the Official Secrets Act. He died, a rich man, in Ballinderry, Tipperary, on 28 February 1978.

The 'Skeleton Network'

There remains the speculation concerning the possible continuance of the Network in that it would underline the significance of his work in both war and peace in Spain.

It is an established fact that nations endeavour to maintain their intelligence networks in peacetime if on reduced budgets and against certain critics. Then there is the recognised importance of neutral countries in this situation and the ever present concern over submarine warfare, the hidden enemy. "The only thing that ever really frightened me during the war was the U-Boat peril" (Winston Churchill in 1940, writing in 1949). "The shadow of the U-Boat blockade already cast its chill upon us. All our plans depended on the defeat of this menace" (*The Second World War*, Book II

---

7.   Mackintyre's account is now subject to doubt following the investigation of the sinking of HMS Dasher in 1943.

Alone, Chapter XXX Ocean Peril). In the case of Spain, there was the desire of the Spanish government that the old Network should continue to function, in Spain's own interests. Similar continuity is reflected in such a service as the Radio Security Service (RSS), set up prior to 1939 by MI5 and the Post Office. This was used to locate unlicensed wireless transmissions and from whence they came. As M R D Foot remarks (in his 2008 autobiography *Memories of an SOE Historian*) "The service no doubt remains in being, and it is quite proper that it should remain under wraps", since it contributes to the safeguarding of the nation. He makes the same comment about the interception of enemy, and friendly, communications. Certainly, the Cold War period gave no encouragement for nations to eviscerate their spy structures[8].

The March family is also unlikely to have withdrawn from the scene. Given their now international role (membership of the Council for Foreign Relations is one example) it would seem probable that what we have termed 'the Network' now operates worldwide.

This is a period not too well covered in the history books. Andrew's *Secret Service* while featuring the country well in the World War I period, makes little reference to Spain in World War II only noting that "GC and CS (was) to master Italian ciphers 'all but completely'" during this period. Richard Deacon pinpoints Juan March as Britain's "chief contact" and, with his friendship with Sir Basil Zaharoff and Admiral Canaris, he was a very significant figure. "March wrote to a Naval Intelligence friend in Madrid" concerning Canaris' distrust of the Nazis and also of Zaharoff's claim to be "horrified at the idea that Germany may once again perpetrate another world war". The NID at Gibraltar at this time was under Don Gómez-Beare, later Naval Attaché in Madrid during Sir Samuel Hoare's ambassadorship. Gómez-Beare was close to March and, through him, well versed in Canaris' thinking. March also informed the NID that Canaris was considering working with the British Secret Service against Hitler. Canaris had said to March: "The NID of today is not so circumspect as that of Admiral Hall's day. It is run by amateurs, brilliant men no doubt, but often irresponsible and apt to talk. I have penetrated them and MI6, and I know. So if any German, however important or discreet, felt tempted to work with the British Secret Service, be sure I would find out about it. Now in that Secret Service there are conflicting minds and it could well happen that one section of the Secret Service would keep faith, but that the other would not hesitate to betray any such German either to me, or someone else in the Abwehr. And that might force me to take action I should not wish to take."

Deacon speculates on the possible interpretation of this "somewhat obscure advice"; Canaris was to continue to leak information to and from Spain, and through mysterious envoys to London, but the NID does not seem to have paid much attention

---

8. As exampled by BRIXMIS, British Commander-in-Chiefs' Mission to the Soviet Forces of Occupation in Germany, described as Britain's Most Daring Cold War Spy Mission, Tony Geraghty, Harpers Perennial, 1997. 2003 Statewatch News On Line states that "UK communications surveillance operations based on Gibraltar continue to this day".

to these reports. Earlier, Canaris had recalled his World War I experience and said he did not think German U-Boats would be able to re-fuel in Spain if the Spanish bases were in unsympathetic hands. Canaris' own direct contact with the British was to come to an end in a strange, secret meeting in June 1944 in a convent situated at 127 rue de la Santé in central Paris. This was the headquarters of *Jade Amicol* where he met with Arnould, a French secret agent Jesuit posing as a coal merchant. Canaris' efforts to work with the Allies terminated here when his proposals were rejected: "Finis Germani!", he declared and then left the convent. He was to be hanged by Hitler in Berlin in April 1945, as the Russians entered the city, for his part in the plot.

Circulating close to this shadowy world were the Duke and Duchess of Windsor, then dividing their time between Lisbon and Madrid. They were under close surveillance. It is reported that Wallis Simpson's unsavoury reputation as a Nazi spy, supporting the Duke's pro-Nazi sentiments and reporting back his 'pillow talk' to Berlin, only came to be revealed much later. Nazi ambitions in this quarter culminated with the plan to kidnap the Duke and Duchess while they were on a hunting trip near the Spanish frontier. Walter Schellenberg had been chosen to organise this and in Madrid he had "accomplices in the house where the Duke was staying. Servants at table were in my pay and reported to me all that was said". However, at the last moment, the British Secret Service got warning of the plot, the Duke cancelled the trip and guards were positioned around his villa outside Lisbon. We do not know the identity of any NID agents involved but this incident demonstrates that this so-called 'Skeleton Network' was capable of animation.

Chapter 14:
'Blinker' Hall and Thoroton from 1926

I n 1932 the letter Thoroton wrote to Hall is evidence of the significance of the Network in Spain. The NA document summarises the situation:

Britain's permanent secret service was founded in the twentieth century. It was then that spying started to lose its stigma as a dishonest and disreputable way of making a living and started to become to be seen as a legitimate way of collecting military intelligence.[1]

In March 1936 Hall spoke at the Naval College at Greenwich on "Intelligence in Wartime".[2] Addressing a large audience, including members of the Foreign Office and representatives of all three services, he gave out four guiding principles which are as true today as they were then: acquisition of information concerning the enemy; sifting this information for truth and falsehood; decisions regarding appropriate usage of this information, or the withholding thereof; and the need to cover one's tracks and prevent the enemy from finding out how such information was obtained. This provides the precise framework for the Thoroton and other networks.

In July 2007 we visited the Churchill Archives Centre at Cambridge University and were able to finally extract all that there was to find in the Hall Papers concerning the work of the NID and the role of Thoroton. On the latter, there was very little but what there was was instructive. They threw a bright light on the founding and development of Room 40 and upon a number of issues which bore upon Thoroton's work. In addition to the Hall Papers we were able to study the Clarke Papers and the CHAR Collection, the latter on microfiche, but found no trace of Thoroton therein.[3]

Hall's autobiography

Of special interest is the correspondence concerning Hall's autobiography and the remaining extant chapters which had been written. The two leading figures in this were Ralph Straus, who was actually working on the autobiography with him, and J B Pinker, his literary agent, the former living in Hyde Park Mansions, the latter writing from his office in the Strand. Only some five chapters were completed out of a target of thirty-five. These five are all that are to be found in the Churchill Centre. Much else never reached the official files.

1. *NA, Garcia Sanz, op cit.*
2. *Intelligence in Wartime, 'Blinker' Hall's autobiography original draft (unpublished) Churchill Archives Centre, ref Hall 2/1, see Annex C.*
3. *The Clarke Papers are those of William F Clarke (1883-1961) Intelligence Officer who was appointed by Hall to code-breaking in Room 40 in 1916 and in 1919 transferred to the Government Code & Cipher School (GCCS). CLKE 1 concerns 8-14 November 1919, GCCS. The CHAR Collection concerns 8-9 November 1919, GCCS. CHAR relates to the Chartwell Papers, ref CHAR 13 concerning the Admiralty 1911-1915.*

Ralph Straus was an erudite writer, the author of some eighteen books including the lives of John Baskerville and Robert Dodsley, 'poet, publisher and playright'. His *The Unspeakable Curll*, Chapman & Hall, London 1928 (limited to 535 copies) contains what he calls a 'Handlist' (or checklist) for 1706-1746, running to 111 pages. Hall was in excellent hands for his autobiography. By coincidence, Straus was known to Colonel Thoroton's son-in-law, C A Stonehill, but it is more likely that A E W Mason might have been the go-between.

Preliminary thinking on the biography appears to have started about 1926 when Tom Hohler wrote on 9 January to Hall from Santiago in Chile, confirming his role as the original source of the famous Zimmermann Telegram. This is of special interest since the Telegram was acquired by intercept on 17 January 1917 from the only cable remaining to Germany and which travelled a somewhat indeterminate route via West Africa and Brazil and/or Buenos Aires to Valparaiso. Hall wrote to Captain Guy Grant, the British Naval Attaché in Washington DC in May 1916: "From there I cannot make out where they are sent, whether via China or Russia through the connivance of a neutral legation or not?" Patrick Beesley seems to be the only historian to have picked up on Tom Hohler, Barbara Tuchman's 1959 The *Zimmerman Telegram* not mentioning him.

In his letter, Tom Hohler asks Hall if, in fact, anyone other than himself had been at the very initial and crucial stage of discovery. He concludes that he was the only one and was, in fact, acting alone at that time.

Valparaiso in Chile is only a little over one hundred kilometres to the north-west of Santiago where Hohler was living in 1926. He had been British Chargé d'Affaires in Mexico City in 1916. He had won the allegiance of two English brothers who were in the printing and Telegraph service there. Hohler had managed to save the printer's life when he had been unjustly found guilty of counterfeiting cartones, small, substitute cards used as currency in the inter-regnum between the various coups and revolutions. The actual forger was a man in his employ. He suffered the death penalty. To pay off this debt of honour the brothers had offered their unequivocal services to Hohler who asked, in turn, for copies of all cables despatched or received by the Swedish Chargé d'Affaires Cronholm and von Eckhardt, the German Minister in Mexico. Beesley states that Hohler had left Mexico for Washington at the end of 1916, having briefed his successor Edward Thurston on the system for obtaining copies of German and Swedish cables. Since Hall confirmed, in 1926, that Hohler was the individual responsible he was clearly endorsing his initiative in creating the procedure which he had bequeathed to Thurston who succeeded him the very same month that the Telegram was despatched. The final Zimmermann Telegram was despatched to Mexico on 19 January 1917.

Another figure emerges from the Hall Papers at this time, 1926. That year Franz Rintelen von Kleist, The Dark Invader, was in London and was invited by Hall to dinner accompanied by some others, one of whom was A E W Mason. Amongst their reminiscences were those concerning von Rintelen's period in the German Officers

Prison of Donnington Hall following his arrest by Hall. Von Rintelen, who had been a reserve Officer in the German Imperial Navy, had been responsible for sabotage in Mexico and then had been sent on to conduct sabotage and subversion in America. Von Rintelen's subsequent incarceration as prisoner 8891 in the American prisons, the Tombs in New York and the so-called "Grand Hotel" prison in Atlanta, Georgia compared unfavourably with his English experience.

Considerable work went into the autobiography over a period of eight years. The list of those who contributed includes such names as Dudley Pound, A S Benn, Dennis Larking, Hohler, Thoroton, J Crease, Drake and A E W Mason.

In spite of, or perhaps because of, the extensive work put in on the book when it came to be reviewed by the Admiralty for possible publication it was turned down (Ref Hall 1/5). The blow fell on 4 August 1933. Five reasons were given and three of them could be said to refer to Thoroton amongst others. These three were: first, it "referred to individuals by name"; second, it gave information on "funds in connection with officers working in foreign countries"; third, it revealed "naval methods of intelligence work in general". (In passing, it may be noted that Hall had offered the Turkish government £50,000 if they would remove the mines from the Dardanelles and a further large sum if they would seize and hand over a German warship in one of their ports. We do not know what sums of money were allocated to Thoroton.)

Five days after receiving this disappointing news Hall was writing to the Admiralty, accepting the decision. This was to cost him £855 "to clear the matter up" with Pinker and a further £250 to Straus for the work he had put in to date: over £1,000 out of Hall's pocket. Absolute secrecy had to be maintained on this cancellation and no reason for it could ever be given in public should any questions be asked. They greatly feared in particular the American press getting onto the story. One well-intentioned, but singularly inept proposal came from an MP who asked whether a question in the House might help Hall. Both Pinker and Straus expressed their appreciation of Hall's acceptance of the decision and the promptitude of his re-funding them and the other participants in serial rights. Ralph Straus himself proposed that a part-fictional, part-factual book be written in which Hall's identity would emerge mistily from the narrative, but this was never undertaken. The affair was finally wound up on 22 September 1933.

Amongst the extant chapters are Chapter 3 "A Private Censorship" Ref 3/2; Chapter 5 "The Cruise of the Sayonara" Ref 3/3; Chapter 6 "A Little Information for the Enemy Ref 3/4; Chapter 7 "Lord Fisher and Mr Churchill Ref 3/5; and "The Zimmermann Telegram" Ref 3/6. But, it is Chapter 2 "Intelligence in Wartime" Ref 2/1 which is most relevant.

Chapter 3 "A Private Censorship" describes how the work began and the risks Hall ran in developing it. It was essentially unofficial and concentrated on the censorship of private correspondence in Great Britain. A major slip, literally, a censor's slip of paper was found left inside an envelope at a time when censorship did not "officially" exist. This letter had been addressed to an MP who threatened to make an issue of it until he was quietly taken aside.

Then Hall describes how a "War Trade Intelligence Department" came into being. This proposal of his eventually found its way to the Prime Minister, Asquith. Captain Hall then found himself invited to put the idea to Asquith and at their meeting the Prime Minister asked "an unexpected question". This was, "How much will it cost?" Hall had not given any thought to this issue but replied, "About half a million pounds". Asquith made no comment. Shortly afterwards Hall was invited to No 10 Downing Street and found himself in a place he had never imagined entering. On being asked his business he was conducted to the Cabinet Room where the Cabinet was in heated argument over a number of issues. No one noticed him so he stood in the doorway. He espied an empty armchair in the middle of the table. Then Asquith entered and silence fell. Sitting in the hitherto vacant chair, Asquith spoke: "Well, gentlemen, we have Captain Hall here and I can see that you are all in agreement with his views. Good. Then we can take steps at once to form the new department". No one had spoken, Hall had not spoken. He did not even remember leaving the Room or passing out of No 10. All he knew, as he walked back to Admiralty, was that the War Trade Intelligence Department now existed.

Chapter 5, the cruise of the Sayonara, concerns Ireland and is not directly relevant to this history, nor is Chapter 7 on Lord Fisher and Mr Churchill, nor really the chapter on the Zimmerman Telegram although, because of its transmission linkages, it brushes Spain. The Germans were using a Madrid wireless station very actively on a daily basis for cipher messages on naval and diplomatic matters, their spy reports and intrigues in Morocco and on ships observed passing Algerciras. The reception given to their submarines off the Spanish coast was an important element and the arrival of a U-Boat in Cartegena was reported as having made a good impression on the Spanish there. It failed to make such a good impression on the German Chargé d'Affaires in Madrid as it was found not to have on board the replacement ciphers and propaganda material he had urgently been requesting. It was, moreover, the telegram, which had been transmitted via Holland and Spain, and handed in by the German Naval Attaché in Madrid which led eventually to Mata-Hari being shot at Vincennes. It would seem inevitable that the Network was involved in all these issues. As was reported by von Rintelen , "England had agents in their pay in these countries reporting on German wire messages".

Chapter 6, "A Little Information for the Enemy", concerns disinformation designed to mislead the enemy over a wide range of activities. This was a particular forte of British Intelligence and one which the Thoroton Network was involved with in Spain, as in the case of the extensive subsidies paid to Spanish newspapers. Hall summarised this aspect of disinformation under four headings: misleading the enemy to ensure his wrongful transfers of forces to combat imaginary threats (a device beautifully carried out in World War II by Operations FORTITUDE, TITANIC, TAXABLE and GLIMMER at the time of D-Day and by MINCEMEAT concerning the landings in Sicily); destabilisation of the enemy by eroding their civilians' confidence; subversion of neutral countries; warnings to 'friends' of the consequences for them if the enemy was to win. All this, it will be recalled, was the second of the five reasons later given by the Admiralty which prevented the publication of Hall's autobiography.

In 1932 another ex-NID agent, Guy Locock CMG, was working as Deputy Director of the Federation of British Industries (Federation) in London (Ref. 1/3). Although by this time Thoroton had retired from the Federation in Madrid, Guy Locock and Thoroton were very probably known to each other due to their mutual NID and Federation backgrounds as well as the fact that both were assisting Hall with his autobiography.

On 21 May 1933 Ralph Straus wrote from his home at 8e Hyde Park Mansions, London, to Hall and made reference at the end of his letter: "Here are the Thoroton chapters". Our hearts leapt up at this statement and we turned the page anxiously. Alas, no Thoroton material was to be found there, nor elsewhere in all the files we examined. On checking with the Archivist we asked whether the Hall literary estate might be holding any relevant pages. This she did not know but, as we would most likely need the permission of the Hall family to reproduce any extensive material, should we wish to do so, we could of course enquire also regarding "the Thoroton chapters". We already knew that some photographs, supplied by Thoroton to Hall, had perhaps not been returned as he had written a reminder to this effect.

On 21 July 2007 we wrote to the Literary Estate of Admiral Sir Reginald Hall explaining our research and giving details of our specific interests in Hall's autobiography. Amongst other details we referred to the missing "Thoroton chapters" returned by Straus on 21 May 1933 as we hoped they might be retained at home; "the 1918 notes I sent you", asked for by Thoroton on 12 March 1932; and the missing two photographs which Thoroton had asked to be returned on 21 November 1932. These showed the "marble columns" and "the crates" enclosing them, used as covers for an arms shipment.

The family replied, in the person of Hall's grandson, Timothy Stubbs, on 2 August, in a letter from which the following extract is taken:

"I am very happy that you should use any information you may glean from my grandfather's papers. I wish I could say that I had additional papers myself; sadly, this is not the case. I seem to remember that my mother (the Admiral's daughter Faith) told me that a great many of the Admiral's papers were destroyed upon the death of Ralph Straus".

Timothy Stubbs ended by wishing us "every success with your research on the life of your grandfather" and added, in a nice PS, "'Blinker' Hall was pretty frightening to a small boy!"

It was on 5 October 1932 that Thoroton accepted an invitation from Hall to lunch with him. In his letter Thoroton wrote:

"…I shall be very pleased to come & lunch with you on Saturday. I had seen in the Press and also heard privately that you were contemplating a book, and in view of the blither in 40 O.B. I really think it is time. I do not really think I kept any papers dealing with the subjects you mention but will see. As a matter of fact I kept very few papers my idea being only to keep those which I thought necessary to defend myself in case of an attack being made on me for some of my more questionable activities..."

This was the genesis of Thoroton's assistance with the autobiography for which he is credited as being amongst the most significant of Hall's contributors, even to the extent of his checking with Juan March in Spain over various incidents.

His reference to "the blither in 40.OB" is of interest. This refers to Hugh Cleland Hoy's book *40.OB or How We Won the War* which was published by Hutchinson, London. Cleland Hoy is identified as 'Private Secretary to DNI' for the period November 1916 to December 1917, a period of fourteen months out of the four years of the war. On his own admission he never entered Room 40. We are not in a position to assess "the blither" but several issues may be referred to here as they are all ones with which Thoroton would have been completely au fait.

Cleland Hoy refers to the British and French agents active in Morocco particularly in respect of the "spasmodic raids" in 1915 and 1916 undertaken by Abdel Malek who was in touch with Berlin and was "very highly paid by Germany" to foment revolt against the French. Increasing demands by Abdel Malek for arms, ammunition and money were met by Germany but doubt existed as to whether they actually got value for money. Secret Intelligence identified a German U-Boat delivery to the coast of Morocco and some discussion took place as to whether this should be frustrated by British or French forces. It was finally decided that as Morocco was under French administration it would be more appropriate if the French were to carry out the assignment. Accordingly when the U-Boat surfaced off Larache (El Araiche on the Atlantic coast between Asilah and Moulay Bouselham) it was sunk by bombs delivered by French aircraft.

Another incident concerns the vital matter of wolfram running. A Spanish ship had a rendezvous in Maderia to tranship wolfram to two first class German submarines. Ambushed by British naval forces one was captured and the wolfram transferred to the British ships and sent to England. The other submarine escaped.

According to Cleland Hoy, the NID uncovered and spiked a coup d'etat by alerting the King to the plot. King Alfonso invited its unsuspecting leader to the Palace and engaged him in pleasant conversation, finally revealing that if the plot was to materialise there would be dire consequencies for all involved since all the details of the plot were known as were the names of the protagonists. At this the coup d'etat collapsed. If this was not "blither" then it is certain that the uncovering of the plot was due to the Network.

Reference is also made to the Rio Tinto copper mines, control of which was wanted by the Germans who hoped to obtain this by fomenting revolution in Spain. However, as we know, from other sources, the mines were largely British owned and that Juan March was on the Board, but his position here was no guarantee that only Britain would benefit from the mines as he was a supplier to both sides of the conflict and his underlying impulse was always the profit motive. However, as we have seen, it was Britain rather than Germany that won his allegiance. Cleland Hoy also makes reference to a NID inspired disinformation scheme whereby it was put about that Germany was thinking of declaring war on Spain.

Hall Ref 2 /2 concerns Edward Bell, who was the American Ambassador to Great Britain. It gives his impressions of the men he met with while in London and as such provides a sort of bird's eye view on this galaxy of significant personalities involved in the intelligence game. Oliver: "don't understand him. He works 23 hours a day". He calls Sir Eric Geddes, an Honorary Vice-Admiral at the Admiralty in 1917 (and previously Director General of Military Railways in France and, before the war, a Director the North Eastern Railways) "probably the best man I met". Geddes' appointment had been a "great step forward" and he successfully challenged the old guard represented by Oliver. Jellicoe is described as "a lovable man – I'm very fond of him", but he was a man finally to be dismissed by Geddes. Admiral Sir Alexander Ludovic Duff, of the Anti-Submarine Division, was "very able". On 1 January 1917 Gibraltar warned Duff "Enemy submarines may be expected to pass through the Straits going east during the night of 1 to 6 January inclusive. Make every effort to intercept them". Hall he saw vividly: "no man could take his place…coldest blooded proposition that ever was. He'd cut a man's heart out and hand it back to him". Rear Admiral Herbert Hope, doyen of Naval Intelligence: "a wonderful man".

Thoroton writes to Churchill

We obtained a copy of the manuscript of the letter written by Thoroton to Winston Churchill on 10 May 1936. This consists of three pages on Villa Stella Maris headed paper and derives from Churchill's speech in the House of Commons on the additional Navy Vote and "particularly that part of it which dealt with the Command of the Fleet Air Arm". Thoroton's letter is concerned with the maladministration of such a Garrison as that of Gibraltar because of the division between military and naval commands. He writes that since Gibraltar exists "primarily if not entirely for maritime purposes" that the defence command is in military hands "gives rise to many difficulties and much duplication of work". This problem exists in "all naval bases". Thoroton considers this a "matter of considerable importance" and ends by expressing the hope he has "written enough to rouse your interest but not so much as to bore you".

It can be said that Thoroton's concern over the command structure at such locations as Gibraltar, and his support of Churchill's concepts in this regard, was fully vindicated in 1940. At that time Churchill complained that "...It is surprising that the violent impact of the air upon our control of the Mediterranean had not been more plainly foreseen by the British government before the war and by their expert advisers".

A relevant sidelight on this issue, and of the difficulties experienced by Hall with the conventional 'red tape' Navy, is seen again in the 2007 book by William Stevenson, *Spymistress – The Life of Vera Atkins, The Greatest Female Secret Agent of World War II*. Ian Fleming, appointed to NID's Room 39 by its new chief Rear Admiral John

Godfrey, "could convey to Churchill further troubling naval realities…that the Royal Navy clung to certain old traditions that failed to confront modern realities. A navy pilot is treated as a coxswain, his airplane just a version of the longboat. My navigator has command, and as the Observer. Commissioned observers cannot fly with non-commissioned pilots who, as petty officers, also cannot sit in at flight briefings in the wardroom". It might be said that Thoroton's letter of 1936, and Churchill's inability to challenge all shibboleths, were still relevant in 1939.

Chapter 15:
Indo-China, Morocco and China
from 1933

Correspondence between Marshal Lyautey and Thoroton demonstrates the depth and longstanding nature of their relationship. These letters make reference to Thoroton's wartime collaboration with the French in Morocco so are relevant to this history.

In the autumn of 1933 Marshal Lyautey wrote to Thoroton, at the Junior United Service Club in London, with introductions to three individuals in French Indo-China and Morocco. Lyautey wrote from Thorey where he was to die, a year later, at the age of eighty. The men involved are the Governor-General of Indo-China, Monsieur Pasquier; the Resident General of Morocco, General Ponsot; and the Superior Commandant of Troops in Morocco, General Hue. This shows that Thoroton was very active in 1933 planning, and undertaking in part, an extensive foreign tour. He was fifty eight years of age and this is five years, three months before his own death. Earlier in the year Thoroton had reported to Hall that he was suffering from his usual attack of gout and had a "cure" in Malta but was still walking with a stick so we can assume that by October he was much recovered.

Lyautey died on 27 July 1934. His last letter to Thoroton was written in October 1933, on black edged funeral paper, marking perhaps the recent death of the last of his fellow officers, General Durosay. This was not long before the time of his last letter to Fr Patrick Heidsieck who had been principally responsible for his return to the Faith. Also about this time Lyautey writes his last letter (dated 13 February 1933, from Paris) to Louise Baigneres whom he had first met in 1889 when she was twenty four. He was the love of her life whom he never married just as she never married: a tragic story.

In his 3 October letter Lyautey refers to Thoroton's "loyal and useful collaboration"; regrets that he knows no one in Nanking anymore; but is more than happy to make the other introductions.

Lyautey's letter to M. Pasquier in Indo-China says: "Colonel Thoroton was chief of Intelligence Services in Gibraltar and during the whole war he rendered me in Morocco the most serious services by his loyal collaboration. He was able to constantly obtain information on German intrigues notably in the Spanish zone, the most valuable intelligence, and which I would have been unable to procure by my own means. During this time he often came to Morocco to accompany me to Fez, to Marrakech and on the fronts so as to be able to understand the situation and to meet the personnel of my Intelligence Service with whom he was in constant contact."

As this is the only letter of introduction Thoroton kept it seems evident that he did not make a visit to Indo-China in 1933 or 1934. However, he did visit Morocco as we only have Lyautey's covering letter (dated 18 October 1933). Lyautey had already "advised them verbally of your arrival and assured them of the good memory I have of your collaboration".

By 1933, Sultan Youssef having died in 1927, Morocco was firmly in the hands of Si Hadj T'hami El Glaoui, Pasha of Marrakesh. Glaoui controlled enormous business interests, including four out of the five French newspapers in Morocco, and was a friend of Winston Churchill. Possibly Thoroton met Glaoui on this visit.

Turning to Spain, following his retirement from the Federation in 1924, his visits to his villa in Malaga in subsequent years would have ensured a continuation of contact with Spanish and other friends and collaborators. That China and Indo-China also occupied his mind in the 1930s is evidence of his on-going interest in events outside Europe.

Shanghai, the harbour, in a CJT postcard of 24 May 1906.

Chapter 16:
Last days and summing up

Little further need be said here regarding his last days in Malaga, Spain, and Canford Cliffs, Bournemouth.

By 1936 Spain was in a state of anarchy; Juan March had departed in February at the time of the victory of the Popular Front; Franco was about to be flown in by Douglas Jerrold; fighting broke out in Malaga on 17 July. The newspaper *HOY* reported that Thoroton had gone for a holiday in the Canary Islands.

The family group photograph at his villa Stella Maris shows one aspect of his last days. Another photograph shows him with Henryano Kerchaer, another wartime agent and witness to his will.

His last recorded departure from the Iberian pensinsula was on 22 June 1937 when he sailed on the Royal Rotterdam Lloyd *Sibajak* via Southampton for The Grove, Canford Cliffs.

We have Charles the Bold's will dated 6 April 1936. He died 17 January 1939 at the age of 64. Most of his estate went to his widow and to Evelyn Flora St Aubyn Stevenson, who is the woman referred to in the American secret service report to Hall.

The Grove passed out of family hands in the late 1940s, was demolished as was Stella Maris and so vanishes from history.

Charles the Bold emerges from the shadowy world of secret intelligence here for the first time in any degree of chiaroscuro. His personal character and abilities equipped him for the strange tasks he undertook and we have come to discover some of his achievements. That said, his full history remains "wrapt in mystery" still.

As has been demonstrated, the major part of Thoroton's work (the activities of the Network) remains still largely unknown. The Erri Berro episode shows how much is known about just one incident and it was certainly not the most significant achievement of the Network. The destruction by Thoroton of his private papers; the disappearance from the NA of the records of Contraband work, filed under his own name; the inaccuracies in several of the "accredited" histories referring to him personally; the continuing cover-up concerning Juan March (Thoroton's 'ace in the hole'); his correspondence with 'Blinker' Hall over Hall's autobiography which was destroyed on the death of Ralph Straus: these are all examples of his continuing "wrapt in mystery" status.

Thoroton can now be seen to have been responsible for creating the first modern Intelligence Service and one of the most active of the British spy organisations of the First World War, as Carolina Sanz explains in her book on the Straits of Gibraltar, relative to economics, politics and international relations in the First World War

This was an organisation which broke all the previous rules of intelligence and counter-intelligence and, with the sanction of the FO, took control not only of Military Intelligence in Spain but also all related FO activities and contacts with foreign Naval Attachés. The Network extended its reach beyond the primary targets of the secret service (already described) into commercial, social, financial and industrial and mining intelligence and, furthermore, into close co-operation with the Spanish Security Forces. It was certainly the first such Secret Service to operate in Spain, a neutral country so coveted by Churchill as constituting a primary intelligence ground. It became the first port of call for the Spanish government's need of intelligence inside its own country and went on living into the Second World War in spite of its official closing down in 1919[1]. Indeed, this is partly confirmed by M R D Foot in his *Memories* where he writes that, after Room 40's First World War activity "it then proved too useful to be dropped, and all three armed forces as well as the FO kept decipher teams going during the 1920s and 30s".

When Hall was questioned at the Dardanelles Commission in 1916 (ref TNA ADM 116/6437) on what qualities he looked for in a good agent, he replied: "If you can get an agent in a high position, you can generally get a cross-cut on him. One of the principal duties we have is to put together all the reports on a certain subject; and in fact the system really is this. You have an agent...you take all his reports for a month; you check them through, and if out of 20 statements he makes 18 are correct and two wrong you count him as a 90 per cent man".

What seems to shine through Thoroton particularly is his wholehearted integrity and reliability, combined with a flair or gift for winning over friends and companions in arms and in harnessing them to a great, and not without risk, cause. Was there a "band of brothers, brought together from very different backgrounds to fight the common enemy"? The accolades accorded him by his superiors; by his French allies in Morocco, notably the warm affection of Marshal Lyautey; his acceptance by the Sultan; his long retention of the essential services of Juan March; above all, perhaps, the close understanding and appreciation he enjoyed with his chief, Rear Admiral Hall (later Admiral Sir William Reginald Hall KCMG CB); all these qualities give us the colour of the man: 'the cut of the jib'. That there was also, along with his cool-headed judgement and discernment, a devil-may-care streak is shown in his risk taking with the beautiful Beatrice von Brunner with her love potions mixed with poison. Discreet, and silent as the Sphinx, Charles the Bold might be described as something of a five carat diamond in Room 40's galaxy, Churchill's "brilliant confederacy".

Sir William Stephenson was quoted, by Judge William H Webster, former Federation Director and next CIA Director, before the US Senate Intelligence Committee in April 1987: "Secrecy demands integrity. I can't put it better than that"[2]. Thoroton was no exception to the rule outlined by Wesley Wark, the University of Toronto historian who specialises in intelligence. Wark says, "There are very few

---

1. See Garcia Sanz, *op cit*, particularly her *Conclusions*.
2. For relevant statements, see also John F Kennedy, at the US Military Academy, West Point, June 1962, quoted, William Stevenson, *Spymistress*.

memoires or biographies of secret intelligence service folk. It's a world of secrecy and security" [3].

That the Spanish Government sought his retention in Spain on his retirement from the Royal Marines in 1919, and where he served as Commissioner to the Federation of British Industry in Madrid for five years, also argues for a keen business brain as well as for their appreciation of his secret intelligence services in their country's interests.

Some of the characteristics of Arthur Thruston may be applied to Thoroton. As was said of Thruston, he was a complex character, modest and even contemptuous of ambition, in the worldly sense of the word. Kind but strict, far-seeing, just: a simple but intellectual man, chivalrous and fearless. His society was a cheerful presence to his companions and, by his tact and sympathy, he won over men of different races and creeds. Much of this would seem to fit equally well with Thoroton.

Perhaps he is best summed up by the family motto which, being translated, is: 'God is our shield – the trumpet calls'.

Thoroton arms

3. www.trueintrepid.com

Annex A

CHRONOLOGY

Date	British events	Charles the Bold*
1875	Queen Victoria reigns	Charles Julian Thoroton born 9 August 1875
1885	General Gordon killed	1885-1890 Allhallows School, Honiton, Devon
1891	London-Paris cable laid	Rossall School, Fylde, Lancs. (scholarship)
1893	Rhodes extends British control in South Africa	Enters Royal Naval College as 2nd Lieut RM
1895	Jameson Raid in South Africa	Sits military & naval examinations Qualifies Military Law First sea tour, HMS Empress of India
1900	Relief of Mafeking, Boer War	Promoted Captain 3 November Marries Theodora Mayor Lives at 2 Church Path, Alverstoke
1901	Queen Victoria dies	Officer Commanding RM Ascension Island to 1904
1903	British explorers reach South Pole	Son Thomas born
1904	Entente Cordiale signed	HMS Black Prince Pacific Ocean
1905	Suffragettes' protests	Musketry qualification
1906	British Empire covers 1/5th of the world HMS Dreadnought launched	W/T course completed Daughter Katharine Phoebe Grace born
1910-11	King Edward VII dies Siege of Sydney Street	Promoted Major Home Fleet HMS Hogue Responsibility for Ascension Island Represents RMs, Delhi Durbar
1911-13	SS Titanic sinks Emigration reaches record levels	Chatham Division to Cormorant
1913-19	The Great War	Senior Naval Intelligence Officer Gibraltar Mediterranean Theatre and Contraband Control
1915		Promoted Temporary Lieutenant Colonel
1917		Awarded CMG
1919-23	Irish War of Independence, national strikes	Retires from RM Commissioner Federation Madrid
1924-39	Commonwealth replaces Empire. The Great Crash Churchill warns of weak defences Spanish Civil War World War II	Lives in Spain (Madrid & Malaga) and England (Bournemouth) 1932 Gib to Plymouth SS Malwa 1933, granddaughter Katharine Thoroton Stonehill born Travels in Morocco 1935 Gib to Plymouth SS Viceroy of India 1937 Lisbon to Southampton SS Sibajak Dies 17 January 1939
* Excludes Orders, Decorations, other than CMG		

Annex B

Analysis of PRO/National Archives files:

November 1995-2010

1. November 1995

The following files relating to Colonel Thoroton were available at the PRO, Kew, in November 1995.

   i.   Ref W41 (16) 20576 and Ref W41 b 1356/50701/110

   ii.   5 July 1915: Ref 89229.

FO has no knowledge of Colonel Thoroton's services nor his position in Morocco. Letter from Marshal Lyautey to Vice Admiral F E E Brock (SNO Gibraltar) dated 26 April 1915, from Fez: "The Admiralty ought to know (what Thoroton is achieving) in Morocco..." Sir Edward Grey (Foreign Secretary) adds in his own hand that he too wants to know.

   iii.   December 1915: Ref 328 F89,229-15/FO 372-691.

No files found.

   iv.   Ref 1150-243199 (398) 1917 Spain and Ref.1150-227496 (398) 1917 Spain

Both these files refer to smuggling (contraband) and Thoroton.

   v.   Ref 2150 1155/251 1918 & 166421/322/T 30 Sep. Italy

   vi.   Ref 322 164421/762 1918 Italy

   vii.   Ref FO 372-1137 & Ref 175 on.

   viii.   Ref W3 87734

   ix.   Ref 141 F156820-19

   x.   Ref 150 163285/f 947 – 19

   xi.   Ref 341 58304

   xii.   Ref 350 D F18/22901

   xiii.   Ref W41 f 156229

No 1916 files were found.

2. FO Index Files, March 2007

   i.   Ref W41 (16) 20576 and Ref W41 b 1356/50701/110

Both above files found in drawer N° 578.

On this visit the December 1915 file and none of the 1917 cards were to be found in spite of a search by a NA archivist.

3. FO Index Files, July 2008

   i.   ADM 223/758

   ii.   ADM 223/758

   iii.   ADM 231

   iv.   ADM 234

v. ADM 236

vi. FO 566/1220

No additional information obtained and no trace of the missing December 1915, 1916 and 1917 card files. NA archivist unable to elucidate this problem.

At time of writing (January 2010) Howard Davies, Standards Manager Information Policy & Services Directorate, TNA, 102 Petty France, London, SW1H 9AJ (www. opsi.gov.uk/ifts/index.htm) reports "unavailability" of the missing files and could give no further information on the subject. Some light on this problem has been shed by the BBC History magazine of October 2004 concerning a loophole in the forthcoming UK Freedom of Information Act (FOIA) of 1 January 2005. The headline of the article read "Legal loophole could spell doom for historic research". It went on to say "There is nothing to stop records being destroyed prior to a request". (Institute of Historical Research). Prior to enforcement of the Act information deemed to impinge on national security was destroyed or concealed. Katherine Gunderson, of the Campaign for Freedom of Information (CFI) wrote in the same issue of BBC History: "We are concerned that information could be destroyed in anticipation of the Act". Then Richard Smith, in the Office of the Deputy Prime Minister, disclosed that "initiatives are coming down to us to whither away our records" before the FOIA was enforced. Some scholars protested at the time that documents "dating back sixty years or more were 'weeded' during this period". A case of 'cherry-picking' perhaps in 1995 and 2007.

In 2010, Laundered Archives (of the British Secret Service during WW I) were described by Velazco, Navarro and Arcos in *La inteligencia como disciplina científica*, Ministry of Defence, Madrid.

In July 2011, an on-line check of latest releases from the NA gave "Contraband Spain & Portugal" FO 382/1960 (Code ref 1141/1136, files 151-1003, 1918) but no mention of Thoroton. "Contraband Missing documents 2011-Spain" again provides no relevant information.

Annex C

Intelligence in Wartime,

This is the original draft (Ref 2/1) of Chapter 2 of 'Blinker' Hall's unpublished autobiography from the Churchill Archives Centre in Churchill College, Cambridge.

The following eight and a half pages are part of the autobiography on which Thoroton collaborated and which was the subject of correspondence between them, also held in the Churchill Archives Centre. My correspondence arose from the Archivist referring me in July 2007 to the Literary Estate of Admiral Sir William Reginald Hall. Admiral Sir William Reginald Hall's grandson, Mr Timothy Stubbs, in a letter dated 2 August 2007, graciously gave me permission to quote from and reproduce relevant texts.

As has been seen, Thoroton collaborated closely with Hall over the writing of the autobiography. The significance of this chapter lies in the fact that here Hall gives the whole framework of his methods under which Thoroton and other Intelligence officers worked.

INTELLIGENCE IN WARTIME

Spy system no good for movements of ships as time lag

in getting information through is too long for effective

counter action to be taken.

All right for acquiring knowledge of enemys material and

resources; found to be quite effective for this vide

results at the end of the war... one submarine wrong only.

A very useful check on enemys materiel is through Insurance

Practically every private firm insures articles under

manufacture and these insurances are reinsured through other

insurance firms. This was the case with Germany where most

of the reinsurances were effected in Switzerland. Sent out

there a big man in Insurance world who lived there for some

months and throug whom, we secuted lists of all war

materiel reinsured; after s little pratice, we could

pretty well place what articles were being manufactured

. "This of course did not apply to Government yards where

no insurance was carried; we had to depend on agents for

this latter work and they did well as we had a full list

of all ships building.

Agents could also assist in giving information as to morale

behind the line and were of assistance in shewing where

to put the screw on in blockade.

Similarly, one used neutral counties largely for information.

HALL 2/1

In one neutral country, a lady.. English.. wa married to one
of the secretaries through whom all despatches and
telegrams to the head of the stare passed. By this means
we were able to read everything the Ambassadors in the
enemy country were saying to the head of their state
and it might be mentioned that it was through this source
that the first solid information of the coming collapse
was received.

Information such as this cannot be trusted to the post.
One had to devise means so that every time the copies were
ready, they were passed by hand to another agent who
brought them out of the country. The system lasted the
whole war from 1915 onwards.

In the late war, movements of ships of the enemy were
known through their use of wireless coupled with our
ability to read their cyphers. Both deciphering and
directional wireless were used to the full
Ciphers are of course a subject which does not come in
to this lecture but the methods of getting the original
cypher books may be of interest and possible use.

Naval cypher ex Magdeburg

Naval books and ciphers ex enemy destroyers sunk in action
and recovered by trawlers sent out for that purpose.

Zeppelins and their cyphers

Submarines and the same; corps pf divers .

In no case was a cypher bought or stolen; by doing

either of these, an astute enemy would be able to work

off dud information on you.

We plnated several cyphers on them with some success

Rotterdam and the cypher. *Guy Locock.*

Relieving pressure on the front by threatened invasion.

by false information.

Use of newspapers.

Daily Mail special editions; quote articles

Portions blacked out

Times and gold ship example; letters from german agent

sent in their code; result of this being Go wernor

of Bank of England wanted the gold.

Defence of convoys. Example; questionaires taken off

enemy agents in Norway; imperative for them to ascertain

how many subs we had working with our convoys.

raragraph in Times re sinking of sub.

Ex tract from intercepted witeless quoting the Times

Confirmed by papers fron sunk sub in Straits of Dover.

Zimmerman telegram; important that enemy should beleive

that Americans were responsible for interdeption. Articles

in American press praising work of American secret service

Diplomatic cyphers. How acquired. Pipe line to Absdan

raid; escape of Wasmuss; naval officer invalided; told me

story of attack on ehemys camp and how Wasmuss got away

in his pyjamas on horse back leaving his baggage.

Enquiries throug India Office as to where baggage was;

HALL 2/1

4.

Final discovery of baggage in cellars of India office;

search by Cozens Hardy and discovery of cyphers.

Imporatnce of never breaking line of enemy communication.

Once across it, let it run on. Far safer than breaking it

as then one has to find the new line and that is not so easy¦

Example of Chakravaty in America; we read all his letters

and let them go on. When America came in to tne war, they

without warning arrested Chak and we had great difficulty in

tracing the new line of communication.

Combined work of agents and wirelss intercepts; example

of Erri Berro and tungsten .

Importance of covering ones tracks when making use of

information in order to prevent enemy finding out how

information is being obtained.

Example of staff officer in Berlin and reward offerd

by Germans for his name.

Importance of patience in I.D. work. Very often valuable

information will come in which of itself would be of little

use at the time but which if kept till the proper moment

will have due effect.

Examples. I.. Publication of list of names of 180 submarine

c.os names as having been captured or sunk. This could have

been published very much earlier but would not have had

the effect it did as by keeping it, we published it at a

time when German morale was on the decline and it was

important to try and destry their confidence in the success

of their submarine campaign. Tis type of propagada is

HALL 2/1

invaluable as every family with a relative in a submarine knew it to be true.

Example 2 Boxes dropped by U35 in Cartagena harbour One sent to me ; contents being sugar with tubes of anthrax in each cube. Knowledge of this kept till it was time to undermine position of Ratibor in Spain. Herschell told the King of Spain about it with result that Ratibor left Spain.

Difficulties in handling information lie more in the direction of preventing use in suchAs way as to hazard the line of information. An example of this is A... H... when Foreign Secretary when dealing with the R...s He handed the S...t ambassador a copy of his own telegram. Result being entire change of system by the R...s and the destruction of the line of information.

Importance of orders being obeyed when hadling secret letters. Example. the capture of bag of mail from Constantinople when the messenger carrying it, disobeyed his orders and went by steamer to Brindisi ; steamer stopped on route, bag thrwon overboard unweighted; with result that names and addresses of agents became know and thw whole organisation destryed; never to be rebuilt as we had let them down.

Only basis on which an organisation can be built up and maintained is one of establishing confidence; one this has been shaken, the organisation will collapse Calassixc example of this is when our agents were

207

HALL 2/1

6

dealing with Talaat over passage of the straits to Constanti
nople. Could never eeestablish contact again nor would the
men acting for us try again as they too had been let down.
Better to pay too much than too little; pay even if you
cant get at the time what you want. Once the other side know
that you will carry out your word, there is always the
chance that in the end you will get what you want.
Necessity for close reading of information and
understanding what the natural deductions are.
Exnmple of Mowe and Bristol Mowe sends in by ship all
the captured masters; captain of cruiser interviews them
and send his report home by letter.
In report is statement that the last ship captured by Mowe
was one carrying 6000 tons of wesh coal. Mowe took her
in to mouth of Paran river; coaled from her to the extent o'
800 tons and then took her out and sank her.
Captain of Bristol did not see natural deduction to be
drawn from this; that ôf Mowe were going to continue her
cruise, she would have kept the coal ready for use. That
she sank the collieb after taking out what she wanted,
shewed that she was on her way home. In the result,
the extended patrols which were at once ordered out,
arrived ôn their patrol stations about 8 hours too late
and the Mowe got home safely. Had this information been
cabled, there should have been little doubt but that we
should have captured er sunk her.

HALL 21

Propaganda can be used for various purposes

I.. To deceive the enemy. (Falkland Islands)

in order to lead him to gake a certain course for

which you are prepared

or to try and relieve pressure from a position by

getting him to move for ces to resist a supposed movement

on your part.

2... To Undermine the morale of the enemy by attacking the

morale of the non fighting population

3.. To induce neutral nations to either keep quiet

ot give assistance where and when required. Very good rule

is if you dont help me, dont help him

4...To counter the war aims of the enemy by shewing

what would happen should they win. This had considerable

effect in America

The organisation of such propaganda falls naturally

under two heads

A.. Propaganda which must be carried out through agencies

in close touch with the highr command in order that H. Q.

should not find itself em barrassed by too zealous agents

B.. Civil porppganda which should be carried out under

the control of the Cabinet

None know better than the M.I how to run the former;

luckily for us, there was the closest and most cordial

relations between Mi and I D, all the war, so that we

were able to practically pool or resources and our brains.

8. HALL 2/1

Most foreign countries have the highest respect for our
leading newspapers and believe what they read in them
Particularly so in the case of the Times; one has to
be very careful though if intending to use the latter that
they shall in no way lose their prestige and whatever
information you ask them to publish, must be well within
the bounds of reason.

With the penny press of wide circulation one need not be
so careful; They are quite accustomed to eating their
words and digesting hte result. Here then, an intelligence
officer can have fairly free scope; if, as in the case of
one paper, they will publish special editions for export,
and have the relevant portion blakked out in the home
edition, it becomes easy to arrange that both editions
should be sent abroad; it would be difficult then for an
enemy to beldieve that the information was not correct.
Again, a useful method of propaganda was f und in the
St J....s club. Here met all the attaches and secreatries o
of neutral legations and embassies. One well known London
figure was employed in the I.D. much to many peoples
astonishment for this purpose alone. A good lunch with
the selected victim, a game of ecarte afterwards and the
tongue strings were loosed. Little by little the desired
information was passed on; the game stops. away g oes the
secretary hot foot to his chief; a long cable with the
valuable information passes over he wireds that night

HALL 2/1

9.

which cable, if the organisation is as it was in the war,

is fully understood by our own peeple; in practically

every case when this system was used, the information

reached the Germans in the neutral country. They like good

patriots at once passed it on by wireless to Berlin

and our listeners had the pleasure of passing up to me

that news that there was a leak somewhere and that such an

such information had reached the enemy.

Annex D

Thoroton correspondence with 'Blinker' Hall and Winston Churchill, 1932-1936.

Telephone
Canford Cliffs 88.

THE GROVE,
MARLBOROUGH ROAD,
CANFORD CLIFFS,
BOURNEMOUTH.

21. 11. 32.

My dear Admiral. Reverting to the Malaga arms smuggling, I have now heard from the original pirate who had the marble pillars "deported". and I enclose a photograph which may be of interest to you (please return). (1) Shows one of the marble pillars with the "marble" partially peeled off and (2) the crate in which each pillar was packed. My pirate says "The cavalry carbines were label, they were packed in artificial marble columns & blocks. I think there were 2500 and 20 rounds of ammunition for each in separate cases. For the Carbines 'ammunition' came from Spandau, that is to say the carbines had been captured from the French & then taken to Spandau workshops. The workshop foreman's checks were in the lead lined cases within the blocks. The B/L was to order & the shipper was some Swiss in Genoa who never existed."

What do you think of the surname of Compton Mackenzie? and what is really his particular crime having regard to what has been written with impunity by others? I suppose his case will make no difference to your plans? I hope you are flourishing - I just can't yet quite fit.

Yours sincerely,
C Thornton

Telephone
Canford Cliffs 35.

THE GROVE,
MARLBOROUGH ROAD,
CANFORD CLIFFS,
BOURNEMOUTH.

26. 11. 32

My dear Admiral. About ten days ago
I sent you some some typescript. As I didn't
register it, I am beginning to wonder if it might
not have got lost in transit. Would you be so
kind as to let me have a line saying whether
you got it or not?
The name of the ship which took the disgraced
rifles to Malaga was appears to have been
"Porto Pi" - but as far as I remember there was
no imputation against her.
I am enjoying an attack of gout - this season
of the year seems always to bring it..
Yours very truly
Thoroton

Telephone
Canford Cliffs 35.

THE GROVE,
MARLBOROUGH ROAD,
CANFORD CLIFFS,
BOURNEMOUTH.

12. 3. 33.

My dear Admiral. If you have finished with
the 1918 notes I sent you I should be grateful if
you would let me have them back, as I am having
a kind of "Pride's Purge" of documents consequent
on the building of a new study & general re-stows.
I hope your book progresses favourably, I am only
just recovering from the "cure" at Bath and still walk
with a stick.
Would you please note that my permanent address
is as above. Hill House is now empty and for sale
So if "you want to buy" a house there you are!
I haven't been able to get to Malaga this year but
had a good let for the villa there - so anyhow it is
not costing anything. I hear there are many [lights]
- Americans in S. Spain - but the Spaniards don't
Seem to like their Republic now they've got it!
Yours love.
Theodolin

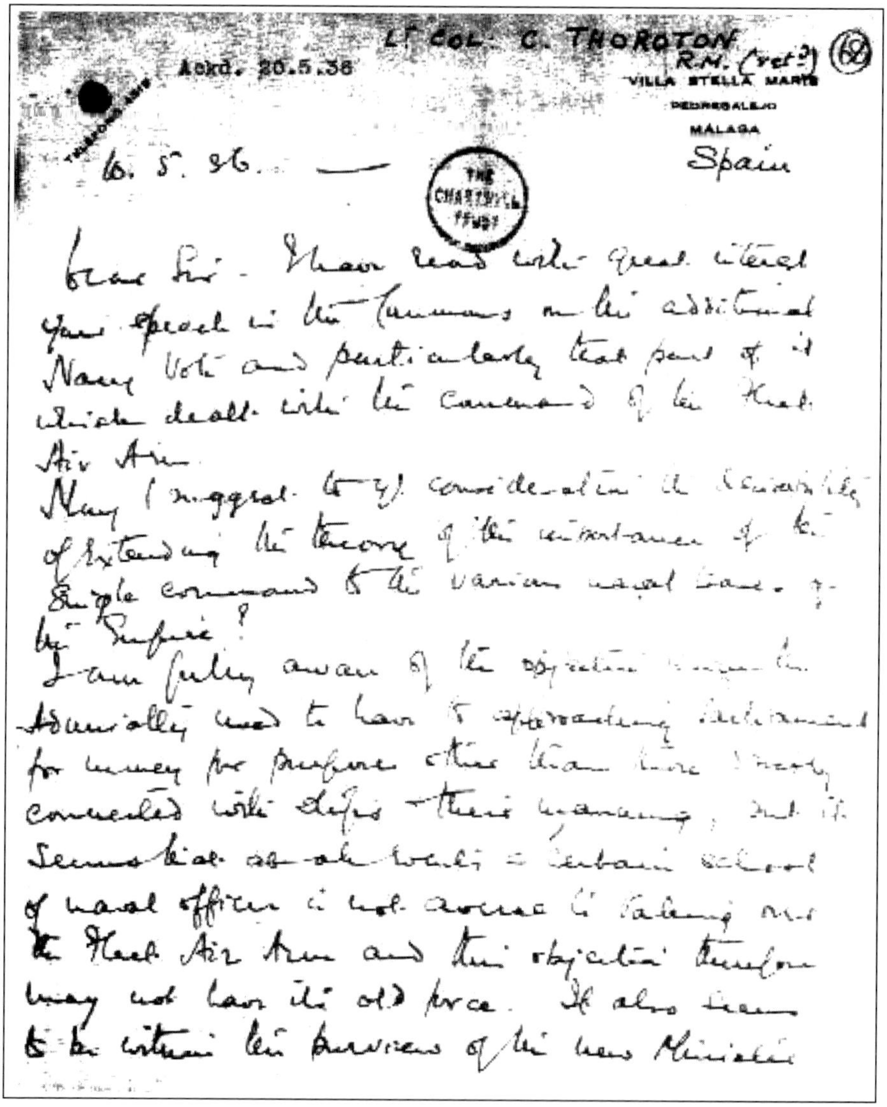

for coordinating defences ... to overcome such
a difficulty if it be treated actual
I was serving at Gibraltar as Naval ... senior
officer when war broke out in 1914 and the fact
that though Gibraltar exists primarily if not
entirely for maritime purposes (it has been
said "by the Navy and for the Navy") the Supreme
Command was in Military hands gave rise
to many difficulties & much duplication of
work. I believe the situation to be even more
Gilbertian today.
It does not seem to me to matter who provides
the troops at Gibraltar provided the C-in-C is a
Naval Officer and the staff entirely naval. At
present I believe you will find that a Naval
observer has to be stationed at the batteries, manned
by R.A. — I merely give this as an instance of
the Comic Opera situation.
I have written of Gibraltar as it seems it was,
but with suitable change under the same ...
by said of all "naval bases."
I apologise for troubling you with a letter,
but I think the matter of considerable
importance, and hope that you will think

it worth looking into.
I might perhaps to add that I have no
personal axe to grind in this matter, my
only desire being to correct what is undoubtedly
an anomalous situation.
As you are aware it would be possible to
enlarge almost ... on details but
I think I have said enough to rouse ... interest
but not so much as will bore you
Yours faithfully
Theodore

Annex E

German Analysis of British Secret Service, Informationsheft G.B., RSHA, Berlin, 1945

GERMAN ANALYSIS OF BRITISH SECRET SERVICE

In 1945, in the ruins of Berlin, Allied officers found a document in the RSHA Headquarters entitled INFORMATIONSHEFT G.B. (RSHA = Nazi Central Security Agency).

This is described as 'a general agent's guide book to Great Britain' and was the 100 page document prepared by Walter zu Christian on the basis of his 600 page report to Hitler. Amongst the many subjects covered one is of particular relevance here because it reveals German experience of the British Secret Service and pinpoints those individuals whom zu Christian (and, no doubt, Walter Schellenberg, his chief at Amt VI) considered to be at its very top, if hidden behind the scenes. The Report concludes that these were likely to be Lord Hankey (commissioned into the Royal Marine Artillery in 1895, recruited into NID in 1901, Intelligence Officer Mediterranean 1907-1908; in 1914 appointed by Lloyd George as Secretary of the War Cabinet) and Sir Robert Vansittart (Permanent Undersecretary of State at the Foreign Office).

Needless to say both these names appear in the 'Gestapo Arrest List for GB', Hankey at H31a, Vansittart at V6.

The German analysis of the British character is also instructive.

"The British character (which finds expression in the syntax of their language) and certain national peculiarities – unscrupulousness, self-possession, cool thinking and ruthless action – have contributed to their becoming the undeniable masters in this sphere". The "shapelessness and arbitrary" nature of the British Secret Intelligence Service (which is one key to its success) is then compared to that of the 'Free Masons' whose 'structure' it resembles. The British "shapelessness" is compared favourably with German rigidity and precision.

Annex F

Etappendienst of the German Imperial Navy in World War I

SECRET NAVAL SUPPLY SYSTEM. Article by Robert Derencin, www.uboat.net, 2005.

Translation, corrections and abbreviations by Philip Vickers, 2009.

Introduction: Strategic situation immediately before WWI.

From the last years of the 19th century until 1914 Germany was a strong and powerful European country. But, unlike other European countries such as the United Kingdom and France, Germany did not have numerous colonies around the world. She had some colonies and territories in Africa, the Far East and in the Pacific but they were small and hardly defendable in any possible war conflicts. The geographical position of Germany adversely affected the activities of the German Imperial Navy. Lastly, Germany had a strong merchant marine. In a possible war situation the merchant marine ships would be unable to return to Germany because of a possible naval blockade of the German coast. After some time, because of the short supply of fuel, water and food, the ships would have two options: to surrender or to scuttle. In such a situation none of these ships could serve as auxiliary cruisers.

For these reasons the German Imperial Navy established the Etappendienst (Secret Naval Supply System) in 1911. This service was part of German Naval Intelligence and its main mission was collecting information and supplying German auxiliary cruisers, merchant ships and last, but not least, submarines.

At the beginning of World War I almost all German colonies and territories were lost (except some in Africa). Some German merchant ships were able to return to Germany, some were interned in enemy countries (Great Britain, Australia, Canada and elsewhere, and some were interned in neutral countries. Submarine warfare became increasingly important to the German war effort and the Etappendienst became the crucial support of the U-Boats, collecting information (espionage) and supply.

Methods of work

The Etappendienst was planned on a long-term basis to work in enemy environments. Individuals who were selected for the service had to work under-cover. They had to be placed in the right positions geographically and in the right working environments. The best such places were harbours and ports all round the world. As ever, the biggest quantity of the world's traffic of people and cargoes was made by marine transport. In World War I navies and merchant fleets of involved and neutral countries transported huge numbers of people (soldiers) war materials and other cargoes. If an agent collected a lot of information he could become a suspect. Neutral countries tried to keep their neutrality and to maintain good relations with all sides of the warring nations. They tried to minimise the activities of foreign intelligence officers in their territories. Thus, their counter-intelligence officers endeavoured to keep a sharp look-out in their ports and harbours.

Shipping agencies, fishing companies and ports and harbour authorities around the world were the best places for German agents. Those selected had to be intelligent and to have enough expertise to work in those environments and to be able to collect and distribute correct information. They had to be able to organise supplies for German ships and submarines. They would sometimes be required to organise the movement of other German agents. Thus, the best candidates for such a service were naval officers with some specific characteristics. They had to endure long periods of inactivity in the pre-war period during which time they had to get to know the situation in their area and, sometimes, to establish their own espionage networks.

Once the war began they had to be able to keep their activities on such a level that they remained undetected. Collecting information was much more important than sabotage which could expose an agent more readily. They needed to know foreign languages. Finally, even though most agents were naval officers, they had to successfully blend in as civilians.

Communications during WWI.

Agents had to have good communication with their superiors in Germany. Without that no amount of information collection was of value. Few ways of communication were at their disposal. The could use the diplomatic post but this was difficult unless they were using the diplomatic post in a neutral country. They could use ordinary post but there was always the possibility that their messages would be detected by censorship in enemy countries. For this reason, invisible ink was employed. But, all these methods were too slow for actions which required immediate response.

On 5 August 1914 the British ship Telconia cut through the German transatlantic under-sea communication cables in the North Sea. As a result, Germany had to communicate abroad by cables which were under control by the Allies or by radio. German use of neutral countries' cables became important, notably those of Sweden. On 3 August 1914 the British Admiralty had prohibited the use of wireless telegraphy in ports and harbours of the United Kingdom and the Channel Islands. After entering any port, or after such an order given by any naval, military or customs service or police officer, wire antennae had to be lowered and disconnected from radio equipment for as long as the ship remained in British territorial waters.

The United States was neutral in the first part of the war. Even so, in 1914 the US Navy took control of some high-powered radio stations, some of which had been built or were owned by German radio companies; These stations were able to communicate with Germany but under US Navy control. On 6 April 1917 the US declared war on Germany and the US Navy took over 53 commercial radio stations of which they closed 28. Until the end of the war all radio traffic from the United States was under the control of the US Navy.

While it was impossible for any German agent to use radio transmissions in Great Britain in the United States they had two possibilities. They could use the normal diplomatic links of the German Embassy (diplomatic post, couriers and radio communication), or commercial radio traffic by means of shore based high powered radio stations. Ordinary commercial codes were permitted by the US Navy - numbers, names, types of cargo, geographical position, etc – but the messages could be written ambiguously and then coded and sent to Germany. After America entered the war such communications became impossible.

During the war the Allies established their own radio intelligence services for monitoring enemy radio traffic and for code breaking. The very successful work of Room 40 in this field is well known. The British established a chain of direction-finding stations. The French also had an excellent radio intelligence service in WWI but concentrated on German Army traffic rather than on naval traffic.

During the war the French service uncovered the location of one German espionage network in the port of Marseilles. German agents were sending information about Allied ships and convoy routes and times of departure from Marseilles. Then, the German Navy Command in Berlin sent the information and orders by the high-powered German Radio Station Nauen to German U-Boats operating in the Mediterranean. In the end the German agents were uncovered and captured. British and French worked together on monitoring German diplomatic messages from Madrid to Berlin and vice versa.

German wireless telegraphy

Some German agents may have had their own radio stations but radio equipment at that time was massive with long wire antennae. Also, a good power supply was needed and if an illegal station was placed near a port or harbour, or near a naval base, there was a strong possibility that any transmissions would be detected in the vicinity. Such transmissions could hamper naval or merchant marine stations' transmissions locally.

In the pre-war period the German company Telefunken constructed and maintained many high powered wireless telegraphy radio stations around the world. It maintained such stations in Argentina, Brazil and China (in Shanghai where it was even the owner); in Cuba, Mexico, Morocco (in Cueta), Norway, Peru, Portugal, Spain (three stations), Sweden and Uruguay. Some were government stations, some were public service stations. Many Telefunken engineers and technicians remained there and some were Etappendienst agents. Their transmissions would have reached Nauen from where the Germans communicated with their ships and submarines all around the world. The Nauen station still stands, located to the west of Berlin.

Activities of a German agent in Spain

Between 30 November 1915 and 20 October 1916 a young German naval officer was a member of the Etappendienst in Spain. His name, Wilhem Canaris.

He was a perfect candidate for the service, having naval and under-cover experience and fluency in several languages. He collected information, mainly in the port of Cartegena and on the Spanish Mediterranean coast, from supervisors and foremen. At least one German submarine was observed in Cartegena taking on fuel supplies. Canaris was never a member of the German Embassy in Madrid and he never held diplomatic immunity. On one occasion British agents learnt that Canaris was going to leave Spain and to return to Germany via France. His journey became complicated and he had to return to Spain where he was collected from Cartegena, along with two other agents, by the U-35 under the command of Kapitänleutnant Arnauld de la Periere, the ace of aces. Although the Allied Intelligence officers had intercepted the messages detailing the voyage they were unsuccessful in their efforts to catch him in Cartegena. The three agents first found shelter on an interned merchant ship, then left the ship and boarded a Spanish fishing vessel from which they climbed aboard the U-35 and so travelled to Germany.

The Etappendienst was reactivated by Canaris in 1927, bringing back into service old colleagues and friends from WWI and recruiting new agents around the world. The service "slept" until 10 August 1939 when it again went into action on the eve of war. It was probably the best German secret intelligence service in both world wars and it remained undetected by the Allies throughout World War I.

Annex G

Vice Admiral Brock to Admiralty, 1915

H.M. Dockyard, Gibraltar.

19th June, 1915.

N.78/37.

Sir,

I have the honour to submit herewith copy of letter dated 26th April, 1915, which I have received from General Lyautey, the French Resident General in Morocco, in which he states that H.M. the Sultan, Moulay Joussef, has expressed his desire to confer on Major Charles J. Thoroton, R.M.L.I., a Moorish decoration.

2. I beg to report that I sent Major Thoroton to visit General Lyautey at Rabat on duties in connection with our co-operation with the French Intelligence Centre in Morocco, and he was introduced to the Sultan by General Lyautey personally.

3. I submit that I consider it advisable as a matter of policy that permission be given for Major Thoroton to accept and wear this decoration, under Article 162 King's Regulations and Admiralty Instructions.

4. I am informing General Lyautey that I have submitted the matter for the consideration of the Admiralty, and beg to request that His Majesty's commands in the matter may be communicated to me.

I have the honour to be,

Sir,

Your obedient Servant,

(signed) E.W. Brock

VICE ADMIRAL

SENIOR NAVAL OFFICER.

etary of the Admiralty,

LONDON.

Annex H

The Order of St Michael and St George

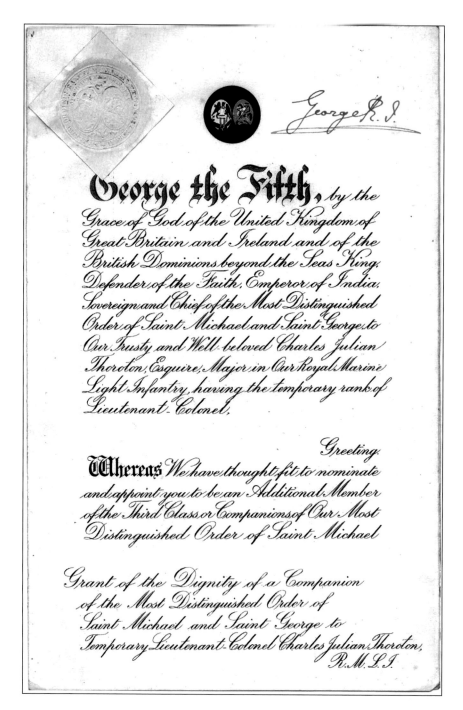

George R.I.

George the Fifth, by the Grace of God of the United Kingdom of Great Britain and Ireland and of the British Dominions beyond the Seas King, Defender of the Faith, Emperor of India, Sovereign and Chief of the Most Distinguished Order of Saint Michael and Saint George, to Our Trusty and Well-beloved Charles Julian Thoroton, Esquire, Major in Our Royal Marine Light Infantry, having the temporary rank of Lieutenant-Colonel,

Greeting.

Whereas We have thought fit to nominate and appoint you to be an Additional Member of the Third Class or Companions of Our Most Distinguished Order of Saint Michael

Grant of the Dignity of a Companion of the Most Distinguished Order of Saint Michael and Saint George to Temporary Lieutenant-Colonel Charles Julian Thoroton, R.M.L.I.

and Saint George;

We do by these presents grant unto you the Dignity of a Companion of Our said Most Distinguished Order, and We do hereby authorize you to have, hold, and enjoy the said Dignity as an Additional Member of the Third Class or Companions of Our said Most Distinguished Order, together with all and singular the privileges thereunto belonging or appertaining.

Given at Our Court at Saint James's under Our Sign Manual and the Seal of Our said Most Distinguished Order this Fourth day of June, One Thousand Nine Hundred and Seventeen, in the Eighth Year of Our Reign.

By the Sovereign's Command.

Grey.

Chancellor.

Sources and Acknowledgements

The origins of this investigation into the British Secret Services, and into the life of Colonel Thoroton RMLI, have been described in the Introduction. Information on this member of Churchill's "brilliant confederacy" was referred to by Patrick Beesley, in his Room 40 book, "as likely to endanger the security of the nation in the 1980s", and it has been seen this would seem to still apply to the 2000s today. In spite of this cover-up, we have been able to discover a remarkable number of original documents which lead to a far more complete understanding of the situation and, indeed, point to possible reasons for the security blanket of today. In this context the trail moves from the Mediterranean in World War I to the present day world of international intrigue.

Helping from the outset were, quite naturally, the Royal Marines themselves. Major Mark Bentinck (of the Royal Marines Historical Records at Gosport, now part of the Naval Historical Branch in Portsmouth) was to provide us with the first and vital break-through by introducing us to Lt Col Donald B Bittner USMCR of the Marine Corps Command and Staff College in Quantico, Virginia. Donald Bittner was, and is, a virtual walking encyclopaedia on the history of the Royal Marines and it was he who provided all the original and essential information which enabled us to take off in several different research directions. We enjoyed the hospitality of Donald and his wife Val at their home in Stafford, Virginia and participated in their life at Quantico.

As we had begun working from Thoroton's awards and decorations we made contact with the Central Chancery of the Orders of Knighthood at St James Palace in London, as has been explained already. We knew that the PRO, as it was then, now the National Archives (Kew), was to be our prime source and innumerable visits were made there over the period 1995 to 2008. So helpful has the staff been that it would be invidious to mark out so many individuals but their untiring efforts are fully acknowledged here.

We had hoped that the Globe & Laurel article entitled 'Charles the Bold – RM Secret Agent Extraordinary' of Jan/Feb 1998 might flush out more information but it was the wrong medium. The Royal Marines Archives provided the obituary of 1939 from the same RM journal. Both the Royal Marines Historical Society and the Royal Marines Museum deserve our thanks for their assistance. About this time we began building up a reference library of our own (see the Bibliography) and, in this, various family members contributed greatly: our son Simon Vickers (now head of the Book Department of Lyon & Turnbull in Edinburgh) found invaluable books; our daughter, Myfanwy Foster, combed local libraries in England; and Hugo Vickers helped with reference books and relevant Churchill material.

When it comes to acknowledging the contributions made by other authors I am deeply indebted to all those listed in the Bibliography. One in particular stands out significantly: I want to repeat here how grateful I am for the generosity of Judith Evans (as Rights Controller) for her permission to reproduce the Erri Berro story from her father's outstanding book, Room 40.

The work of three Spanish historians (Mercedes Cabrera, Maria Dolores Elizalde and Carolina Garcia Sanz) has brought to light a host of previously unresearched papers. A reading of Garcia Sanz's 2011 book provides a truly deep interpretation of the Thoroton Network, some aspects of which have been incorporated into this biography. Sanz describes Thoroton's activities before, during and after the war as being lost in "a halo of mystery". The traces are lost, she writes, in "eloquent silences" and the absence of primary sources. *Finding Thoroton* goes some way to retracing his activities but much remains unknown.

One of our earliest academic trips was to Cambridge, to the Churchill Archives at Churchill College. This produced a wealth of relevant documentation, the outstanding element being the Admiral Sir Reginald Hall Papers, supplemented by the Clarke Papers. The Churchill Archivists, Sophie Bridges and Caroline Herbert, were of the very greatest assistance. In correspondence with the Hall family we were delighted to be told, by Hall's grandson Timothy Stubbs, that we were free to reproduce at full length from the available fragments of Hall's autobiography, the autobiography which Thoroton had collaborated on during the drafting period. The book was never to be published but we have been able to quote from certain chapters here thanks to Timothy Stubbs, who was to confirm, with regret, that the missing chapters on, and from, Thoroton were no longer in existence. The photographs which Thoroton had sent to Hall were never returned and are now irretrievably lost.

It soon transpired that in addition to such academic research, other routes needed to be followed given the secrecy still surrounding Thoroton. The spread of his area of responsibilty (from the Iberian Peninsular, along the North African coast to Greece and out into the Atlantic to Ascension Island and the Canaries) all contributed to a maze-like route that we had to follow. As a result, unexpected sources would suddenly surface out of the blue.

Lord Thomas of Synnerton, the renowned authority on Spain, welcomed us at the House of Lords and offered every assistance possible. He also introduced us to Jimmy Burns, the younger son of Tom Burns who had been Secretary at the British Embassy in Madrid in liaison with Alan Hillgarth, Churchill's prime secret service link with Spain in World War II. M R D Foot was another valued helper.

A vital target of our research was Thoroton's number one agent Juan March Ordinas, "the last pirate of the Mediterranean". We tapped many sources in this field including the Collecion can Verga in Majorca, directed and run by Don Miguel Monjo, who provided us with hitherto unseen material. This linked with the Spanish TV company, Catalyuna TV, whose coverage of March was extensive, the two leading figures involved being Señora Mercedes Cabrera Calvo-Sotelo and Professor David Stafford. At that time Señora Cabrera was Head of the Complutense University of Madrid. She was the author of several books on Juan March. We met with her in

Madrid in the context of her academic research and spent a long time discussing our mutual subject and this yielded unique information.

Carolina Garcia Sanz' 418 page book *La Primera Guerra Mundial*, an impressive work, contains very extensive new information on BNI in Spain and the Thoroton Network. I have quoted freely from it. This original research gives Thoroton the greatest number of references (53 in all) ahead of the next man, the Conde de Romanones (44 references) and well ahead of Arthur Hardinge with 24 references.

I would like to have quoted more concerning Thoroton from this book but sufficient has been included to more than justify the subject and to emphasize the exceptional nature of the contribution made by Royal Marine elements inside BNI in the Western Mediterranean. All this has been supplemented by extensive correspondence with Carolina on our behalf and I am most grateful to her for her continuing interest in the story of Charles the Bold.

David Stafford proved of exceptional assistance and was generous enough with his time to read and comment on the first draft of this book. I have also quoted from several of David Stafford's books in the text.

Much information on Morocco has been provided by Charles Pelletier Doisy, whose family there was in close friendship with the Marquess of Bute, while his brother Jean has put his knowledge of naval affairs and submarine warfare at our disposal. For much of the Moroccan story we have relied on family archives and the correspondence with Marshal Lyautey. The Royal Palace Archives in Rabat, however, remained silent. The Cervantes Institute in Tangier provided help. In France, the office of the Legion d'honneur keeps no record of awards to foreigners and the Socialist bias of the Republic has pushed Lyautey into the background.

In the world of academe, the Pforzheimer Collection in the Beinicke Library of Yale University was invaluable. Already well known to us (many of its most illustrious books having been provided by Charles Archibald Stonehill, my wife's father) it was opened to us by Bob Barry Junior (Stonehill's present day successor). This was providential as the Collection is still largely unsorted and unclassified and stored in the basement. Our salvation came through Kevin Rupp, the Chief Librarian, who plunged into the interstices of the basement and came up with the very documents we had come to find, plus others. Steve Jones and the staff at the Beinicke were of the greatest assistance.

Still in America, the National Archives at College Park, Maryland came up with a unique American secret service report on Thoroton; Nicholas Scheetz, Manuscripts Librarian at Georgetown University, provided leads; and other enquiries were directed to David Khan. George Morton was a great help on our American travels. In the Caribbean, William Stevenson greatly helped us. We reached another valued helper Nigel West who was on voyage in the South Pacific, two welcome contributors".

Tracing Thoroton's agents was not at all easy. A E W Mason information surfaced in the Beinicke but his agents, A P Watt & Son, had no information for us. Elizabeth King at the Royal Academy of Arts at Burlington House made every effort to help us with Sir Gerald Kelly PRA but the family line had gone cold. Compton Mackenzie is very prolifically documented, Andro Linklater's Life covering much of his secret service work. Professor Keith Jeffrey of Queen's University, Belfast helped us over Professor Dixon's work while Dixon was cruising off the Spanish coast on Hall's behalf.

Warwick University's Modern Records Centre provided us with the history of Thoroton's work with the Federation in Spain, the first time any such information had become available. Lord St Leven brought us a shade closer to Thoroton's long-term friend, Mrs Flora St Aubyn Stevenson, the St Aubyn family being the long-time owners of St. Michael's Mount in Cornwall.

On the naval front, as well as those sources already noted, we were assisted from the beginning by Nicholas Soames, Minister of State for the Armed Forces. Bridget Spiers of the Ministry of Defence Whitehall Library; Mr S J Spear, Naval Secretary (Honours & Awards) at Whale Island; Bruce Purvis (Wiltshire County Library); Alan King (Portsmouth Central Library); Ian Mackenzie (Admiralty Library, Portsmouth) and Alan Ramsay all of whom were of individual assistance. Sir John Scarlet of SIS, wrote to tell us they held no record of Thoroton's work in their archives. ('C' still signs his name in the traditional green ink.)

Amongst the web sites contacted, Spero News and Catalyuna TV; Wikipedia, Answers and World War I Information all provided valuable data. The Juan March Foundation web site provided much on the present day programme of the March family. German Naval Intelligence in World Wars I and II, under the title *Etappendienst*, is well covered by Robert Derencin on www.uboat.net, which provides hitherto unknown information. Other media sources include: The London Gazette, Time magazine on Juan March, and the BBC, Who's Who, Kelly's, Debrett's and the DNB.

The Italian Embassy, London, and Prince Savoia of Italy in Savoy; the Swedish Royal Court; the German Military Archives in Berlin and Freiburg and the Spanish National Military Archives were also contacted. Our attempts to open the Russian bear enigma through the 'Memorial' Library in Moscow were unproductive.

Throughout the entire work the crucial key has been provided by my wife Katharine, Charles the Bold's granddaughter. I am especially indebted to Park Honan for his generous critical support and to David Stafford for his professional commentary, both of these being of inestimable value. Photographic aid has been furnished by Gerald Stonehill and by his son Christopher. Myles Thoroton-Hildyard's book, The Thorotons, has provided family background. Our own Thoroton Family Archives have supplied the personal story. I am also grateful to John Molloy-Vickers for his research. Friends who have helped include Hugh Smith for reference books and a helpful reading of the manuscript; Melissa Wolf for other books and for reading and commenting on the original draft. Edwin Lovegrove assisted with information on the de Haviland Rapide. Mercedes Druon and Anna Gude provided all our Spanish and Catalan translations. Colonel (RM) Dick and Rosemary Sidwell for their great help with background information. Also John Nicholson for his contributions. Alain Puypalat's assistance which enabled me to make a start on the electronic front. Ferdi McDermot helped with publishing advice. Andy Martin's initiation of the website www.secretintelligence.co.uk is gratefully acknowledged.

Early on Captain Derek Oakley MBE of the RMHS together with the valued comments of John Rawlinson, Honorary Secretary of the RMHS who made several invaluable contributions. Here I must add a heartfelt thank-you to Alfred Blaak whose computer expertise, literacy, knowledge of history and design capabilities have insured the final run-in to the tape. My special thanks go to my RM Editor Colonel Brian Carter OBE whose steadfastness combined with his exacting and essential understanding of the subject has enabled *Finding Thoroton* to see the light of day.

The remaining errors are my own but to this 'other confederacy' I can contribute much of my enjoyment in researching Charles the Bold.

The author has provided all the images in this book, all of which fall outside copyright time requirement except images from the Thoroton Family Archives (TFA) which holds the copyright of these images, and the Annex C images which should be accredited to Timothy Stubbs.

Bibliography

Adam-Smith, Janet, *John Buchan – A Biography,* Rupert Hart-Davis, London, 1965.

Andrew, Christopher, *Secret Service – The Making of the British Intelligenece Community,* Heinemann, London, 1985; *The Mitrokin Archive,* Allen Lane The Penguin Press, 2000; *The Defence of the Realm – The Authorised History of MI5,* Allen Lane, 2009.

Beesley, Patrick, *Room 40 – British Naval Intelligence 1914-1918,* Hamish Hamilton, London, 1982; *Very Special Intelligence,* London, 1997.

Beevor, Antony, *The Battle for Spain,* Phoenix, Orion Books, London, 2007.

Benavides, Manuel de, *El ultimo pirata del Mediterraneo,* Barcelona, 1934.

Bernados, George, *Essais et edits de combat,* La Bibliothèque de la Pleiade.

Brenan, Gerald, *South from Granada,* Penguin Classics, London, 2008.

Brissard, André, *Canaris, le petit Admiral de l'Espionage Allemand.* Librairie Académique, Perrin, Paris, 1970.

Buchan, John, *Greenmantle,* with Notes by Kate Macdonald, OUP, 1999; *The Power House,* House of Stratus, Thirsk, 2003.

Burke's Landed Gentry & Burke's Companionage, 1952 & 18th Edition, London.

Bywater, Hector & HC Ferraby, *Strange Intelligence – Memories of Naval Secret Service,* 1931.

Cabrera Calvo-Sotelo, Mercedes, *El Poder de los empresarios; Politica y economica en la Espana contemporanea* 1875-2008, Taurus, 2008; *Juan March,* 1880-1962, Marcel Pons Historia, Madrid, 2011.

Cave Brown, Anthony, *The Secret Life of Sir Stewart Menzies – Churchill's Spymaster,* Sphere Books, London, 1987.

Chambers, Richard, *The Last Englishman,* Faber & Faber, London, 2009.

Childers, Erskine, *The Riddle of the Sands - A Record of Secret Service,* with an Introduction by David Trotter and Notes by Anna Smith, Oxford World Classics, 1998.

Churchill, Randolph S, *Young Statesman 1901-1914,* Heinemann, London, 1967.

Churchill, Winston S, *The World Crisis 1911-1914,* The Easton Press, Conn USA, 1991; *The Second World War,* Cassell, London, 1948.

Comer Clarke, *If the Nazis Had Come,* Consul Books, London, 1962.

Coleby, John, *A Marine or Anything, (Royal Marine Spies of World War I era),* Royal Marines Historical Society, 1993.

Compton Mackenzie, *Aegean Memoires,* 1932 & 1940, Chatto & Windus; *Water on the Brain,* Cassell, 1933; *Greek Memoires,* Cassell 1939; Life and Times, *Octave 5,* Chatto & Windus, 1966.

Cuthbert, Alan, *The Man Who Never Was,* Paton Memorial Lecture, 2001.

Davis, Col Dr Jim, Dr Anna Johnson-Winegar, *The Anthrax Terror DOD's Number-One Biological Threat,* Aerospace Power Journal, Winter 2000.

Deacon, Richard, *A History of the British Secret Service*, Muller, London, 1969; *The Silent War- A History of Western Naval Intelligence*, David & Charles, Newton Abbot, 1978.

Dictionary of National Biography 1941-1950, OUP, 1953.

Diaz Nosty, Bernard, *La irresistible ascension de Juan March*, Sedmay, 1977.

Farago, Ladislas, *The Game of the Foxes*, Book Club Associates, London, 1972.

Ferguson, Niall, *Empire – How Britain Made the Modern World*, Penguin, 2004.

Ferrer Guasp, *Juan March, la cara oculta del poder,* Palma-Illes Balears, 2004.

Foot, M R D, *Memories of an SOE Historian*, Pen & Sword, 2008.

Fortesque, John, in Henry Williamson's *Tarka the Otter*, The Folio Society, London, 1995.

Foster, C S, *Nelson*, John Lane, The Bodley Head, 1929.

Fuller, J F C, *The Decisive Battles of the Western World*, Vol 3, Eyre & Spottiswood, London, 1963. c

Furlonge, Geoffrey, *The Lands of Barbary*, John Murray, London, 1966.

Garcia Sanz, Carolina, *Gibraltar and its Field: A Regional Study of the International Relations of Spain during World War I, including, Counterespionage, security, and international relations in Spain during World War I;'Hispania'*, Vol. LXVII, May-August 2007. (Institute of History); *La Primera Guerra Mundial en el Estrecho de Gibraltar*, SCIC, Biblioteca de Historia 73, Universidad de Sevilla, Madrid, 2011.

Gilmore, David, *The Transformation of Spain – from Franco to Constitutional Monarchy*, Quartet Books, 1985.

Goodwin, Doris Kearns, *No Ordinary Times*, Simon & Schuster, USA, 1995.

Grant, Robert M, *U-Boats Destroyed*, Putnam, 1964.

Gray, Edwyn, *The Killing Time – The German U-Boats 1914-1918*, Pan Books, 1975.

Green, Roger Lancelyn, *AEW Mason – The Adventure of a Storyteller*, Max Parrish, London, 1952.

Griffiths, Richard, *Marshal Pétain*, Constable, London, 1970 (privately annotated by Paul Maze, 1975).

Hall, Reginald, *Unpublished Autobiography*, Churchill Archives, Churchill College, Cambrige University.

Halpern, Paul G, *The Naval War in the Mediterranean 1914-1918*, Allen & Unwin, 1986.

Hanker, D S, *History of the Intelligence Corps*, 1965.

Harris, Lawrence, *With Mulai Hafid at Fez: Behind the Scenes in Morocco*, Smith & Elder, London, 1909.

Harris, Walter *Morocco That Was*, Eland, London, 2002.

Hastings, Selina, *Evelyn Waugh – A Biography*, Sinclair-Stevenson, London, 1994.

Hill, George, *Ma Vie d'Espion (I.K.8)*, Payot, Paris, 1933.

Hills, George, *Rock of Contention – A History of Gibraltar*, Hale, London 1974.

Hinsley & others, *British Intelligence in the Second World War*, HMSO, 1979.

Howe, Frederick, *The Confessions of a Monopolist*, Chicago Public Publishing, USA, 1906.

Hopkins, Peter, *The Great Game – The Struggle for Empire in Central Asia*, 1994.

Howson, Gerald, *Arms for Spain – The Untold Story of the Spanish Civil War*.

Hoy, Hugh Cleland, *40.OB or How We Won the War*, Hutchinson, London, 1935.

Hudson, Derek, *For Love of Painting*, Peter Davies, 1975.

James, William, *The Eyes of the Navy – A biographical study of Admiral Sir Reginald Hall*, Methuen, London, 1956.

Jeffrey, Keith, *MI6 – The History of the SIS*, Bloomsbury, 2010.

Jones, R V, *Most Secret War,* Coronet Books, Hodder & Stoughton, 1979.

Kennedy, Paul, *The Rise of Anglo-German Antagonism 1860-1914*, Random House, USA.

Knightley, Philip, *The Second Oldest Profession*, André Deutsch, London, 1986.

Lee, Laurie, *As I Walked Out One Midsummer Morning*, André Deutsch, London 1966.

Le Queux, William, *The Great War in England in 1897*, London, 1894 ; *The Great Invasion of 1910*, London, 1906.

Le Reverend, André, *Un Lyautey Inconnu – Correspondence et Journals inedits*, 1874-1934, *Librairie Academique*, Perrin, 1979.

Linklater, Andro, *Compton Mackenzie – A Life*, Chatto & Windus, London, 1987.

Lund, Paul, *The Secrets of Codes*, A & C Black, London, 2009.

Lyautey, Louis Hubert Gonzales, *La Role Sociale de l'Officier,* Revue des Deux Mondes, 1891.

Mackintyre, Ben *Operation Mincemeat*, Bloomsbury, 2010.

Mason, A E W, *The Winding Stair*, Pan Books, London, 1949; *The Four Corners of the World, 1916 & 1918*: including *The Silver Ship; One of Them; Peiffer; The Summons, 1917.*

Massot i Montaner, Josep, *El Consol Alan Hillgarth et les Isles Balears (1936-1939)*, L'Abadia de Montserrat, 1995.

Maughan, William Somerset, *Ashenden or the British Agent*, Heron Books, London, 1967.

Maxwell, Gavin, *Lords of the Atlas*, Pan, 1970.

Messimer, Dwight R, *World War I Verschollen U-Boat Losses*, Naval Institute Press, Annapolis, USA, 2002.

Miller, Geoffrey, *Straits Trilogy,* The Millstone, 1995-2011.

Mieg, Jean Louis, *Lyautey – Paroles d'Action*, Editions de la Port, Rabat, 1995.

Navy Lists 1914-1918.

The Naval Records Society Vol. 126, 1915-1918.

Niebel, Ingo, *Al Infierno o la Gloria. La Vida y Muerte del Cónsul y Espía Wilhelm Wakonigg en Bilbao 1900-1936*, Alberdania, Irun, 2009.

Nottingham University, Msc & Special Collections, THF/x/3/8/1/1-23

Occleshaw, Michael, *Armour Against Fate – British Military Intelligence in the First World War,*Columbus Books, London, 1989.

Pérez-Gruesco Elizalde, Dolores, *Les relations entre la Grande-Bretagne et l'Espagne pendant la Première Guerre mondiale par le biais des services de renseignements,* GMCC 226, IHHC Revue d'Histoire, France, 2007; *Los Servicios de Inteligencia británicos en España durante la I Guerra Mundial,* Revista de Historia Militar, vol.XLIX, 2005.

Powell, Charles, *Juan Carlos of Spain – Self-made Monarch,* 1996.

Preston, Paul, *Franco ,* Basic Books, 1994 and *A Concise History of the Spanish Civil War,* Fontana 1996.

Ramsay, David, *'Blinker' Hall, Spymaster,* Spellmount, The History Press, 2008.

Rankin, Nicholas, *Churchill's Wizards – The British Genius for Deception 1914-1945,* Faber 2008.

Rintelen, Franz von, *The Dark Invader - Wartime Reminisences of a German Naval Intelligence Officer,* Lovat Dickson, 1935.

Sagar-Fenton, Michael, *About St Michael's Mount,* Bossiney Books, Launceston, 1999.

Sayers & Kahn, *Sabotage – The Secret War Against America,* Harpers, 1942.

Schirmann, Léon, Mata-Hari, *Autopsie d'une Machination,* Editions Italiques, 2001.

Shipman, Pat, *Femme Fatale – A Biography of Mata Hari,* Weidenfeld & Nicholson, 2007.

Stafford, David, *Churchill and Secret Service,* Abacus, John Murray, 1997; *Roosevelt and Churchill – Men of Secrets,* Overlook Press, Woodstock, NY, 1999.

Stevenson, William *A Man Called Intrepid – The Secret War 1939-1945,* Macmillan, London, 1976; *Spymistress – The Life of Vera Atkins,* Arcade Publishing, NY, 2007.

Sutton, Anthony G, *Wall Street and the Bolshevik Revolution,* Arlington House, USA, 1974; Wall Street and the *Rise of Hitler,* Bloomfield Books, UK, 1976.

Thomas, Hugh, *The Spanish Civil War,* Harper & Row, NY, 1997.

Thompson, Julian, *From Sea Soldiers to a Special Force,* Sidgwick & Jackson, Pan Books, 2001.

Thoroton, Robert, *Antiquities of Nottinghamshire.*

Thoroton-Hildyard, Myles, *The Thorotons,* Flintham, Notts. 1990.

Thruston, AB, *African Incidents – Personal Experiences in Egypt and Inyaro,* John Murray, London, 1900.

Thomson, Basil, *The Scene Changes,* Doubleday, Doran & Co, NY, 1937.

Tuchman, Barbara *The Zimmerman Telegram,* Constable, London, 1959; *The Guns of August,* Ballantine Books, NY, 1994.

Turbergue, Jean-Pierre, Mata-Hari – *Le Dossier Secret du Conseil de Guerre,* Editions Italiques, 2001.

Vickers, Philip, *Charles the Bold – RM Secret Agent Extraordinary,* Globe & Laurel, Jan/Feb 1998.

Waagenaar, Sam, *Mata-Hari,* (adapted by Jacques Houbart), Fayard, 1965.

Walton, PS, *The British Army in 1890,* Victorian Military Society, Dorking, 1981.

Wheeler, Private, *The Letters of Private Wheeler 1809-1828,* Foreword by Liddell Hart, The Windrush Press, Gloucestershire, 1993.

West, Nigel, *C-C – HQ,* The Secret Wireless War 1900-1986, Widenfield & Nicholson, London, 1986; *Historical Dictionary of Naval Intelligence,* Scarecrow Press,

2010, *MI5*, Triad Grafton, 1987, *MI6*, Grafton, Collins, 1988, *The Secret Wireless War* Who's Who 1925.

Wingate, R, *Mahdism and the Egyptian Sudan*, MacMillan, London 1891.

Yardley, H, *Studies in Intelligence*, Vol. 27, N° 2, Summer 1983.

Abstracts

Intelligence in Wartime (Churchill Archives Centre); Thoroton correspondence with Hall and Churchill 1932-1936 (CAC); How the German Secret Service Operated (Ladislas Farago); German Analysis of British Secret Service (Informationsheft GB, RSHA, Berlin, 1945); Secret Naval Supply System of German Imperial Navy in World War I (2005, Robert Derecin, www.uboat.net); Vice Admiral Brock correspondence with the Secretary of the Admiralty (1915, CAC); Juan March correspondence concerning Thoroton (1924, Can Verga).

Research was also conducted in Rome at the Italian Ministry of Foreign Affairs Archives; at the Cervantes Institute, Madrid; National Maritime Museum; The Society for Nautical Research; the Royal Naval Museum; the Imperial War Museum and the CIA Library Archives, Langley, Virginia, USA.

Index

Back cover

Thoroton family medals. Apart from the five at top, all are CJT's: l. to r. Commander of the Crown of Italy; Companion of the Order of St Michael and St George; Commander, Moroccan Order of Ouissan Alaouite; Knight 1st Class Order of the Sword of Sweden; 1914-1918 Star; British War Medal, 1914-1918; Victory Medal 1918; King George V Coronation and Delhi Durbar 1910, Officer Legion d'honneur.